PERFORMANCE PSYCHOLOGY

Anyone who has ever competed in a sport, taken an exam, or appeared on stage understands the importance of performing at the right time. Those who excel in these conditions often develop ways to cope with the stress involved, but what cognitive and emotional strategies allow some people to thrive under pressure whilst others are inhibited by it?

In *Performance Psychology: Theory and Practice*, Stewart Cotterill examines not only how stressful situations can affect performance, but also the means by which we can reach our potential regardless. Featuring chapters on decision-making, emotion, resilience and mental toughness, cognition and perception, ageing and experience, confidence, and recovery, this is the definitive textbook in the field, mapping the core theoretical concepts but also offering practical guidance on how performance can be improved. Also including chapters on motor skills and nutrition, it is a complete and comprehensive overview of this growing field of study.

Including study questions and further reading in each chapter, *Performance Psychology: Theory and Practice* will appeal not only to students and researchers across applied psychology, but also coaches and performers looking for ways to realize their potential when it really matters.

Dr Stewart Cotterill is a consultant sport and performance psychologist, and a leadership and performance researcher at the University of Winchester, UK. He is a Registered Sport and Exercise Psychologist (HCPC), Chartered Psychologist, and BASES accredited Sport and Exercise Scientist. He has extensive applied experience in a wide range of sports at a national and international level. He is also author of *Team Psychology in Sports: Theory and Practice* (2013).

PERFORMANCE PSYCHOLOGY

Theory and Practice

Stewart Cotterill

Routledge
Taylor & Francis Group

LONDON AND NEW YORK

First published 2017
by Routledge
2 Park Square, Milton Park, Abingdon, Oxon OX14 4RN

and by Routledge
711 Third Avenue, New York, NY 10017

Routledge is an imprint of the Taylor & Francis Group, an informa business

British Library Cataloguing in Publication Data
A catalogue record for this book is available from the British Library

Library of Congress Cataloging in Publication Data
A catalog record for this book has been requested

ISBN: 978-1-138-83127-8 (hbk)
ISBN: 978-1-138-83129-2 (pbk)
ISBN: 978-1-315-73667-9 (ebk)

Typeset in Bembo
by Wearset Ltd, Boldon, Tyne and Wear

CONTENTS

ACKNOWLEDGEMENTS

I would like to thank everyone at Routledge for their support and hard work in bringing this project to fruition. I would also like to thank the many passionate and committed researchers and practitioners within the field of performance psychology upon whose shoulders this book is written.

I would like to thank Brian and Lilian for the chair in which much of the work took place, and to 'Team Cotterill' Karen, Isabelle, and William for just being you!

ABOUT THE AUTHOR

Dr Stewart Cotterill is a consultant sport and performance psychologist, and a leadership and performance researcher at the University of Winchester, UK. He is a Registered Sport and Exercise Psychologist (HCPC), Chartered Psychologist, and BASES accredited Sport and Exercise Scientist. Stewart has extensive applied experience in a wide range of sports at a national and international level. His current research interests include the psychology of performance, leadership in sport, factors determining team performance, and professional practice in sport and exercise psychology. He is also author of *Team Psychology in Sports: Theory and Practice* (2013).

PREFACE

The ability to perform, when it matters is a key characteristic of many performance domains of human endeavour. Anyone who has competed in sport, has appeared in front of an audience, performed on a stage, had a tight deadline to meet, or performed a task with little room for error will appreciate the impact that pressure can have on the ability to perform. Those individuals who are successful, and successful on a regular basis have developed strategies to cope with, and excel under this performance pressure.

Performance Psychology: Theory and Practice seeks to understand what performance psychology is and also explores what pressure is and the impact it can have upon performance. Crucially the book also explores the psychology of performance and seeks to understand how individual performers can maximize their potential by achieving positive performance outcomes on a consistent basis.

The book explores the theoretical underpinning of practical strategies that enable the performer to complete important tasks effectively when it counts. Building upon the author's experience and expertise both as an applied performance psychology consultant and as a researcher, *Performance Psychology: Theory and Practice* explores a range of factors that both influence and determine performance including: performing under pressure, decision-making, emotion, resilience, mental toughness, cognition and perception, ageing and experience, confidence nutrition, and recovery. The book also explores how to develop the ability to perform by considering the development of motor skills, key psychological skills, and also explores how to most effectively prepare for the demands of the performance environment.

This booked is aimed at individuals who are looking to enhance their theoretical and practical understanding of factors that both influence and determine performance. The book will further appeal to coaches, educators, and teachers involved in developing individuals who thrive under pressure, and also appeal to practitioners who are looking for theory, strategies, and techniques to use with individual performers.

Each chapter considers the key psychological theory and research that underpins contemporary understanding of the specified topic. The chapters also explore the practical implications of this knowledge and consider a relevant case study. *Performance Psychology: Theory and Practice* also provides expert advice on key psychological issues and mental skills pertinent to successful performance when it counts. Finally, the book also considers key questions that remain unanswered within the field of performance psychology and important future avenues for research.

1

INTRODUCTION

The notion of performance is a key aspect of many domains of human endeavour, and is increasingly recognized as a fundamental component of many related professions. This notion of performance – performing key skills effectively at the right time – is a characteristic of many domains including sport, medicine, acting, musical performance, the military, emergency services, air traffic control, and the performing arts. While there are significant differences between these domains regarding the skills required, the rewards for successful execution, and the consequences for failure, the underpinning psychology appears to be similar.

In looking to better understand the nature of the phenomenon across performance domains it is important to understand the nature of performance itself and the psychological factors that underpin performance. There is much theory and understanding that exists across a broad range of psychological disciplines that has not historically been drawn together to understand the nature of performance, and with that understanding how to maximize individual performance potential.

This chapter will seek to clarify what performance is, and clarify what is meant by the 'psychology of performance' and 'performance psychology'. The chapter will also touch on the notion of flow before presenting an overarching model of factors that determine performance.

Psychology of performance

What is performance?

Performance appears to be a fundamental part of the human experience, with Matthews, Davies, Westerman, and Stammers (2000) in their book on *Human Performance* suggesting that "Humans beings are born to perform" (p. 1).

Raab, Lobinger, Hoffman, Pizzera, and Laborde (2016) in their book on this topic described being interested in

> human performance in everyday life, often in relation to achieving specific goals such as winning a competition in sports, music or arts, improving stabilizing, or re-establishing performance when preparing for such events that are important and meaningful for a group or individual.
>
> *(p. 1)*

While there is significant interest in the notion of performance it has not historically been well defined. Much has been made of how to perform, but not what performance is. Using the context of sport as an example, performance has specifically been described by Thomas, French, and Humphries (1986) as "a complex product of cognitive knowledge about the current situation and past events, combined with a player's ability to produce the sport skill(s) required" (p. 259). This definition emphasizes two important components of decision-making: cognitive knowledge; and motor, response execution (Gutierrez Diaz del Campo, Gonzalez Villora, & Garcia Lopez, 2011).

Effective performance (under pressure) has been suggested to involve the consistent execution of complex motor skills in a flawless or near perfect manner (Singer, 2002). Effective performance has also been characterized by an optimal mindset that keeps the performer focused on the task at hand at the expense of other competing stimuli (Gould, Dieffenbach, & Moffett, 2002; Kao, Huang, & Hung, 2013; Krane & Williams, 2006). An associated term of relevance here is that of sport expertise. Sport expertise has been described as the ability to consistently demonstrate superior athletic performance (Janelle & Hillman, 2003; Starkes, 1993).

There is also a distinction between different aspects of performance. In some domains performance is about flawless (or near flawless) execution of complex motor skills to achieve specific targets or goals. In other performance domains the execution of the skills in themselves is the required outcome (e.g. musical or artistic performances).

Psychology of performance

The psychology of performance seeks to understand the cognitions and behaviours initiated by striving for competence or even excellence (Matthews et al., 2000). A range of psychological factors have been highlighted as influencing performance in the short-term and long-term. These include technical and tactical skills, information processing, memory, emotion, and cognition (Raab et al., 2016).

It has also been suggested that the general task of performance psychology relates to the description, explanation, prediction, and optimization of performance-orientated activities. Mitsch and Hackfort (2016) highlighted three specific issues of concern relating to performance psychology: (1) the psychological fundamentals of performance-orientated activities in various action domains; (2) psychological transfer effects of performance-orientated activities in regard to personality development, self-esteem, time management, stress control, communication skills, etc.; (3) optimization of the capability to achieve demanding mental tasks. Put simply, the psychology of performance is about understanding the psychological factors that both influence and determine performance.

Performance psychology

During the last 15 years, and due in part to an increasing appetite from performance domains outside of sport, we have witnessed the emergence of the professional field of performance psychology. Despite being a developing field, performance psychology is beginning to have an increased appreciation within the scientific literature (Barker, Neil, & Fletcher, 2016). A range of definitions of performance psychology have been suggested including this definition suggested by Hays (2012, p. 25), "performance psychology refers to the mental components of superior performance, in situations and performance domains where excellence is a central element". Understanding the psychology of performance though goes beyond just the mental components and should also consider the importance of the interaction between the individual and the environment in which they perform. Performance psychology focuses on the psychology of human performance in domains such as sport, the performing arts, surgery, firefighting, law enforcement, military operations, business, and music. Presently, evidence-based practice in performance psychology focuses on performance excellence and/or restoration and well-being in individual performers and groups (Cremandes et al., 2014). One associated term is that of flow. Swann, Keegan, Piggott, and Crust (2012) highlighted the importance of flow states which have been consistently linked to the notion of peak performance, for elite performers under pressure. A perspective supported by Broomhead et al. (2012) who highlighted the impact that a positive mindset can have upon musical performance.

Flow

Csikszentmihalyi (1990) used the collective term 'flow' to group the characteristics of peak psychological performance states. Flow was specifically defined by Csikszentmihalyi (1975) as "an optimal and positive psychological state attained through deep concentration on the task in hand and involving total absorption". Flow experiences tend to be harmonious for the individual and involve a sense of everything coming together, or clicking into place, even in challenging situations. Based on these feelings the performer is often left feeling that something special has just occurred and those experiences can be highly valued and positive (Csikszentmihalyi, 2002; Jackson & Csikszentmihalyi, 1999). Csikszentmihalyi (2002) outlined nine dimensions that are proposed to combine and interact to make up these flow experiences. These dimensions have subsequently been divided into flow conditions and flow characteristics (Csikszentmihalyi, 2000). Flow conditions are prerequisites for flow to occur, and include: challenge-skills balance (e.g. situations that are challenging to the individual, but in which they are still able to meet the challenge by extending beyond their normal capabilities in order to accomplish the task); clear goals inherent in the activity for the individual to strive towards; and unambiguous feedback to either inform the athlete that they are progressing towards these goals, or tells them how to adjust in order to do so. Flow characteristics describe what the individual experiences during flow, including: concentration on the task at hand (e.g. complete focus with no extraneous or distracting thoughts); action-awareness merging (e.g. total absorption, or feeling at one with the activity); loss of self-consciousness (e.g. decreased awareness of self and social evaluation), while a sense of control over the performance or outcome of the activity can also be experienced, as can a transformation of time (e.g. the perception of time either speeding up or slowing down). The combination of these dimensions led to flow being characterized as an autotelic experience, a term Csikszentmihalyi (1975) used to describe these experiences as being enjoyable and intrinsically rewarding. Flow states have been associated with increased well-being (Haworth, 1993), enhanced self-concept (Jackson, Thomas, Marsh, & Smethurst, 2001), positive subjective experience (Csikszentmihalyi, 2002), and (crucially) performance (Jackson & Roberts, 1992). Gould, Eklund, and Jackson (1992, p. 362) in their report on Olympic Wrestlers also concluded that these optimal performance states

> have a characteristic that is referred to variously as concentration, the ability to focus, a special state of involvement, the zone, flow state, ideal performance state, awareness and/or absorption in the task in hand. In this state of mind, the athlete is totally absorbed in task-relevant concerns.

Flow is particularly relevant for elite performers who apply their skills at the highest levels, under the most intense pressure, and with the greatest rewards at stake. At these levels even minor improvements could have significant impacts on performance outcomes (Swann et al., 2012). Furthermore, Catley and Duda (1997) reported that skill level is significantly correlated with the experience of flow, while Engeser and Rheinberg (2008) also suggest "it is likely that individuals with higher ability have higher flow values" (p. 161). As a result, coaches, performers, and psychologists have been committed over the past 25 years to developing systematic and consistent strategies to allow the performers or teams to achieve this peak performance state.

Model of performance psychology

While many authors discuss the psychology of performance, and performance more broadly, this is often from a very specific perspective. This means that the 'bigger picture' perspective is often lost. This book seeks to present a coherent overview of a range of related factors that all both influence and determine human performance.

Presented in Figure 1.1 are a range of empirically supported factors that to varying degrees determine the degree of success that is achieved. Specific components of the model include: the performer (and their individual characteristics), the quality of preparation for performance, environmental factors, state factors, cognition, confidence, coping strategies, and the architecture of the human body and neural processes.

The remaining chapters of this book will systematically explore each of these factors in detail. Chapter 2 introduces key aspects of the human 'machine', focusing on human performance. The chapter specifically explores the nervous system, nutrition for cognition and performance, and also the importance of sleep and recovery. Chapter 3 considers cognition and cognitive processes. It specifically explores cognition, creativity, problem solving, and perception. The fourth chapter focuses on the psychological construct of pressure. It explores sources of pressure, response of the individual, and relevant coping strategies. Chapter 5 considers the decision-making process and key influencing factors. Chapter 6 focuses on the role of emotion in determining performance. The seventh chapter explores the importance of resilience to performance under pressure. The chapter also explores associated constructs including mental toughness, hardiness, and grit. The eighth chapter focuses on the impact ageing can have on performance ability, considering the mediating role that accumulated experience can have on performance levels. Chapter 9 focuses on the importance of confidence in influencing performance, and crucially how to increase confidence beliefs. The tenth chapter explores the use of psychophysiology to understand performance, but also to look

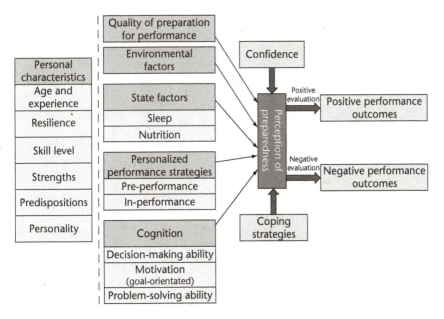

FIGURE 1.1 Determinants of performance model

at how psychophysiological indicators can be used to enhance performance. The eleventh chapter explores how to develop effective motor skills, which are seen as one of the key foundations for effective performance. Chapter 12 considers some of the key psychological skills that can be both developed and utilized to enhance performance under pressure. Chapter 13 considers how performers can most effectively practice and prepare for the performance environment. The final chapter considers what the future directions for research might be relating to performance. Also, the key questions that need to be addressed in terms of applied practice and performance.

Study questions

1. How would you describe the concept of performance psychology?
2. To what extent do you feel experiences of flow are important to achieving successful performance outcomes?

Further reading

Matthews, G., Davies, D. R., Westerman, S. J., & Stammers, R. B. (2000). *Human performance: Cognition, stress and individual differences*. Hove: Psychology Press.
    An important 'broader' psychology text that seeks to provide a coherent overview of human performance and the underpinning psychological factors.
Raab, M., Lobinger, B., Hoffmann, S., Pizzera, A., & Laborde, S. (2016). *Performance psychology: Perception, action, cognition, and emotion*. London: Academic Press.
    A very interesting contemporary text that explores performance psychology specifically from the perspective of perception, action, cognition, and emotion.

2

HUMAN PERFORMANCE

Introduction

Many authors have considered the effect that a wide range of psychological constructs and functions can have upon human performance. However, what has been considered less frequently in the performance literature are those factors that underpin the operation of the brain and the central nervous system.

There are limitations to human performance that are imposed by the architecture of the human body. At a fundamental level this includes the design of the system, its organization, and the structure of basic components such as neurons. There are also limitations based upon the fuelling and regeneration/recovery of the human performance system. In terms of nutrition there is also a reason why the body requires a range of specific vitamins and minerals to perform effectively. There is also variability in performance based on when meals are taken, and what those meals are composed of. Also, hydration has been highlighted as a key factor influencing cognition and performance. The recovery and adaptation of the mind and body is also important if the aim is to maximize performance.

This chapter will explore each of these factors in turn considering the structural limitations that exist in the nervous system, the impact that nutritional intake can have on cognitive functioning, and also the importance of effective rest and recovery.

The nervous system

Structure

The human nervous system is made up of two main parts – the central nervous system (CNS) and the peripheral nervous system (PNS). The CNS is divided into two key components: the spinal cord and the brain, while the peripheral nervous system consists of the nerves that extend to all the other organs in the body. The

PNS can be further subdivided into the autonomic nervous system and the somatic nervous system. The peripheral nervous system includes a large system of nerves that are linked to the brain and spinal cord. It comprises sensory receptors, that process changes in internal and external stimuli and communicate that information to the CNS.

The spinal cord is connected to a section of the brain called the brain stem and runs through the spinal canal. Nerve roots exit the spinal cord to both sides of the body, with the spinal cord carrying signals (messages) back and forth between the brain and the peripheral nerves. The spinal cord serves as the connection between the brain and brain stem to all of the major nerves in the body. Spinal nerves originate from the spinal cord and control the functions of the rest of the body. Impulses are sent from receptors through the spinal cord to the brain, where they are processed and synthesized into instructions for the rest of the body. These data are then sent back through the spinal cord to muscles and glands for motor output.

The adult human brain roughly weighs between 1,200 and 1,500 g and contains about one trillion cells. The brain is located in the cranial cavity and consists of the cerebrum and cerebellum, and houses the nerve centres responsible for coordinating sensory and motor systems in the body. The cerebrum, or the top portion of the brain, is the location of higher-level thought-related brain activity. It comprises of two similar (in terms of structures) hemispheres, each controlling the opposite side of the body. Each of these hemispheres is further divided into four separate lobes: frontal, parietal, occipital, and temporal.

Frontal lobe: controls specialized motor control, learning, planning, and speech. The frontal lobe contains most of the dopamine-sensitive neurons in the cerebral cortex. The dopamine system is associated with reward, attention, short-term memory tasks, planning, and motivation.

Parietal lobe: integrates sensory information among various modalities, including spatial sense and navigation. The two specific functions of this area relate to somatic sensations and perception, and the integration of sensory input from somatic and visual regions.

Occipital lobe: includes the primary visual cortex and visual association areas. The majority of the functioning of this area is devoted to the processing of visual information.

Temporal lobe: integral to auditory perception, receptive components of language, visual memory, declarative (factual) memory, and emotion. Patients with right temporal lobe lesions commonly lose the ability to interpret non-verbal auditory stimuli (e.g. music). Left temporal lobe lesions interfere greatly with the recognition, memory, and formation of language.

The cerebellum is located underneath the rear part of the cerebrum, and controls balance and fine motor movements. Its main function is maintaining coordination throughout the body.

The brain stem, which connects to the underside of the brain, consists of the midbrain, pons, and medulla. The midbrain is found in between the hindbrain and the forebrain. It regulates motor function and allows motor and sensory information to pass from the brain to the rest of the body. The pons houses the control centres for respiration and inhibitory functions. The medulla also helps regulate respiration, as well as cardiovascular and digestive functioning.

Neurons

The basic unit of the nervous system is the neuron. Synapses form between the neurons, allowing them to communicate to other neurons or other systems in the body. The general flow of information in the system is that the peripheral nervous system (PNS) takes in information through sensory neurons, then sends it to the central nervous system (CNS) to be processed. Each neuron in this system generally has four morphological regions, each with its own specific function:

1. The cell body
2. Dendrites
3. Axon
4. The terminal end bouton

The nervous system is not just composed of neurons though, the nervous system has another group of cells that is 9–10 times more numerous than neurons. This group of cells is known as glia or sometimes neuroglia. These cells surround the neurons providing them with support and insulation, and help to form myelin (important in the process of neural communication).

Functioning

To generate complicated patterns of behaviour, the human nervous system has developed an amazing ability to process information. Neurons can receive and deliver signals at over 100 synapses and can combine and process synaptic inputs, both linearly and non-linearly, to implement a rich repertoire of operations that process information (Koch, 1999). Neurons can also establish and change their connections and vary their signalling properties according to a variety of rules. Due to the fact that many of these changes are driven by spatial and temporal patterns of neural signals, neuronal networks can adapt to circumstances, self-assemble, auto-calibrate, and store information by changing their properties according to experience (Laughlin & Sejnowski, 2003).

Human psychological performance is ultimately limited by this underpinning architecture of the brain and the nervous system. The transmission of the messages from neuron to neuron within this complex system is ultimately limited by how fast electrical impulses can be conducted along the trillions of axons that link each neuron to the dendrytes of the next neuron. Another limiting factor for neural communication and information processing is the energy consumption needs of active cells. The human nervous system consumes metabolic energy continuously and at relatively high rates per gram of matter, comparable to the metabolic demands of the heart (Ames, 2000). As a result, powering the brain is a major drain on the human system's energy budget. In humans this proportion is 20% of all energy used for adults and 60% for infants (Hofman, 1983). This relatively high metabolic activity is pretty consistent regardless of whether we are completely passive and resting as well as when we are active (Raichle & Gusnard, 2002). A range of factors have been suggested to influence the processing efficiency of the neural system, including nutrition and sleep/recovery.

Nutrition

Nutrients and the brain

Nutrients are chemicals that are required by the body and brain to function and develop. Specifically the body needs both macro (carbohydrates, proteins, and fats) and micro (vitamins, minerals, and trace elements) nutrients to function effectively. Deficiencies in micronutrients in particular have been suggested to significantly impact upon cognitive performance. The body also requires a significant daily intake of water to function effectively.

Macronutrients

Glucose, amino acids, and fatty acids are the simple forms of carbohydrates (CHO), protein, and fat, respectively. Macronutrients are so called because the body requires them in significantly large (relatively) amounts.

Carbohydrates: CHO foods are digested and metabolized to produce glucose. Dietary CHOs have different effects on the amount and rapidity of glucose production. Monosaccharides (e.g. glucose and fructose) and disaccharides (e.g. sucrose and maltose) are rapidly absorbed from the small intestine. They produce a rapid glycemic response and provide a ready source of energy. Oligosaccharides (e.g. maltodextrins) and polysaccharides (e.g. starch, the major CHO in the human diet) have different rates of digestion and glycemic responses. Evidence from positron emission tomography (PET) scans suggests that increased neural activity (e.g. the learning of a complex visuospatial motor task and verbal working memory) is associated with increased use of glucose by the brain.

Proteins: These amino acids play a crucial role in the development and maintenance of the human body. Specific roles include building, maintaining, and repairing body tissue. Protein is particularly important to people who are physically active due to the constant need to repair damaged muscle tissue. Protein also has other roles in the body including the building of all the enzymes and hormones in the body, which also perform vital functions. In addition, proteins are used to aid the immune system.

Fats: Fatty acids are also an essential part of the diet. They provide energy, absorb some specific nutrients, and maintain core body temperature. Some types of vitamins rely on fatty acids for absorption and storage. Vitamins A, D, E, and K, called fat-soluble vitamins, cannot function without adequate daily fatty acid intake. Fatty acids can be divided into four general categories: saturated, monosaturated, polyunsaturated, and trans fats (White, 2009). Essential fatty acids such as omega-3 have been shown to serve important cellular functions.

Water

The human body is composed of anything between 55 and 75% water (depending upon body size). The body also requires between one and seven litres of water a day to function normally. This demand is increased significantly when undertaking significant exercise, and varies depending upon environmental temperature and humidity. Failure to consume sufficient quantities of water can result in dehydration. Dehydration has been described as "a complex condition resulting in a reduction in total body water. This can be due primarily to a water deficit (water loss dehydration) or both a salt and water deficit (salt loss dehydration)" (Thomas et al., 2008). Research in psychology has shown that a decrease in body weight of 2% (mild dehydration) or more can result in a fall in physical, visuomotor, psychomotor, and mental performance (Szinnai et al., 2005). Even a decrease in body weight due to dehydration of 1% has been linked to reduced concentration, a less effective memory, increased feelings of tiredness, and increased feelings of tension and anxiety (Ganio et al., 2011).

Micronutrients

As Table 2.1 demonstrates, micronutrients are directly or indirectly involved in a number of important cognitive processes that are also dependent on energy production in brain cells, the blood supply (fuel) to the brain, the release and absorption of neurotransmitters (chemicals that are released in the brain that allow the brain cells to communicate). This in turn underpins communications within the human nervous system.

As briefly mentioned previously the brain is highly metabolically active and as a result requires a constant supply of glucose to meet its energy needs. The 'burning' of this fuel in the brain requires several vitamins, including thiamin, riboflavin, niacin, and pantothenic acid. Certain minerals, such as magnesium, iron, and manganese, are also needed to complete the burning of glucose to produce energy.

A key requirement of good cognitive performance is the presence of a good delivery system (blood supply) for the required fuel, oxygen, macronutrients, and micronutrients. A good nutritional intake can help to maintain optimal blood supply to the brain and lower the risk of stroke (results from impaired blood supply to the brain), and enhance cognitive, and ultimately physical, performance. A range of proteins and vitamins (e.g. B and C) are needed to produce and maintain the communication that takes place in the brain (neurotransmitters). Any deficiencies here limit the brain's ability to communicate effectively within itself and other parts

TABLE 2.1 Micronutrients and cognitive functioning

Vitamins	Impact
Vitamin B1 – Thiamin	Insufficient intake impacts upon normal cognitive functioning.
Vitamin B3 – Niacin	Deficiencies can result in headaches, fatigue, depression, poor concentration, and delusions/hallucinations.
Vitamin B6	Required for some specific brain communication functions. Deficiencies can result in irritability, depression, confusion, and seizures.
Vitamin B12	Deficiencies can result in neurological problems including numbness, tingling, concentration problems, and memory loss.
Vitamin C	Helps maintain balance (reduces metal ions in the brain), also linked to brain communication.
Pantothenic acid	Deficiencies can result in headaches, fatigue, insomnia, and numbness.
Vitamin D	Important for normal development and function, deficiencies impact upon cognitive performance.
Vitamin E	Helps to keep brain cell membranes healthy, deficiencies can impact upon balance and coordination, and eye damage.
Minerals	*Impact*
Calcium	Regulates brain communication.
Sulphur	Important to cell health, deficiencies have been linked to depression.
Iron	Required for brain cell development and communication.
Potassium	Crucial for neural communication.
Phosphorus	Important for the healthy functioning of the brain.
Magnesium	Required for over 300 normal metabolic reactions, deficiencies can result in muscle spasms and muscle tremors.
Sodium	Essential for nerve communication.
Trace elements	*Impact*
Chromium	Important for brain function, supplementation has been linked to increased brain activity in older people.
Cobalt	Important for the conductivity of nerve cells.
Zinc	Helps to maintain cellular structure and regulation. Also has a role in brain communication – deficiencies impair mental and neurologic function.
Selenium	An important antioxidant in the brain.
Iodine	Crucial for normal development and the development of the central nervous system.
Fluoride	High levels can damage the brain.
Manganese	Influences communication between brain cells.
Boron	Deficiencies can reduce cognitive performance.

of the body. Micronutrients also impact upon the quality of the connections between cells in the brain. Let's use an internet analogy. Optimal cognitive performance is like using fibre optic cable broadband, whereas micronutrient deficiencies can leave the nervous system performing more like a telephone-line dial-up internet connection (which is much slower and less reliable, with intermittent performance).

Nutrition and cognitive performance

Nutrition essentially delivers four main classes of functional compounds that may affect brain functioning after absorption (Schmitt, 2010). Food provides energy for the brain (essentially glucose); building blocks (e.g. lipids and amino acids); micronutrients for enzymatic and endocrine processes (e.g. iron, zinc, B vitamins, iodine); and is a source of bio- or psychoactive molecules that can exert a multitude of brain-relevant actions (Gomez-Pinilla, 2008; Le Coutre & Schmitt, 2008). In addition, the organoleptic properties of food – such as taste, smell, and texture – may influence cognition and mood more directly (Le Coutre & Schmitt, 2008; Schmitt & LeCoutre, 2009).

The primary source of energy for the human brain is glucose, and as a result the functioning of the brain is dependent on this energy source (Amiel, 1994; Hoyland, Lawton, & Dye, 2008). An inadequate supply of glucose can result in a significant reduction in mental function (Amiel, Archibald, Chusney, & Glae, 1991). The brain self-regulates the uptake of glucose in order to meet metabolic demands, providing a highly controlled environment that has a very high threshold for physiological disruption. The view that the food consumed can reliably influence cognitive performance has received increased attention and empirical support (Dye, Lluch, & Blundell, 2000). It is possible that as well as the reduction of cognitive impairment, nutritional intake could be utilized to enhance performance to levels over and above normal functioning.

Previous psychological research has explored an array of food components and their impact upon cognitive performance, including the effects of the major food components (macronutrients) on performance (e.g. Benton & Owens, 1993); the role of micronutrients on cognitive performance, including herbal supplements (e.g. Kennedy & Scholey, 2000); and stimulants such as caffeine (e.g. Smith et al., 1999). Studies have also evaluated foods and food components in diverse populations, including the young and elderly (Kaplan, Greenwood, Winocur, & Wolever, 2001), and patient populations including type 1 and type 2 diabetics (Deary, 1998). Research has also shown that the relationships between nutrition and behaviour are often complex. Breakfast studies suggest that the absence of breakfast consumption can lead to impaired cognitive performance on tests of reaction time (RT) and short-term memory (e.g. Smith et al., 1994). This effect is most profound in studies of the elderly (e.g. Kaplan et al., 2001), and studies focused on school populations suggest that breakfast omission may detrimentally affect children's cognitive performance (e.g. Grantham-McGregor, Chang, & Walker, 1998; Murphy et al., 1998).

The potential effects of carbohydrates on performance have been widely reported, and glucose in particular has been implicated in the moderation of memory performance (for a review see Messier, 2004).

A quite consistent finding in the literature has been a drop in performance after the midday meal, known as the 'post-lunch dip' (Folkard & Monk, 1985; Owens et al. 2000; Smith & Kendrick, 1992). It appears that performance on tasks requiring sustained attention are more likely than briefer tasks of selective attention to be attenuated by lunch (Christie & McBrearty, 1979; Smith & Miles, 1986b). However, it remains unclear to what extent the 'post-lunch dip' actually depends on eating lunch (Folkard & Monk, 1985); an underlying rhythm in performance also seems likely to contribute, since vigilance (attention) has been reported to be worse in the early afternoon than late morning, in subjects not eating lunch (Smith & Miles, 1986a).

There is also a body of evidence suggesting that manipulations of blood glucose levels result in alterations in cognitive processing efficiency (Gibson & Green, 2002).

The nature of the effect that macronutrients have on mental performance seems to be dependent on the time of ingestion during the day. This is particularly true of CHO. For instance, Lloyd, Green, and Rogers (1994) failed to find differences in objective performance after breakfasts with low-, medium-, or high-CHO content but did find that the high CHO breakfast improved mood by reducing fatigue and restlessness. In contrast, high-CHO lunches produced greater impairment of performance on attention and reaction-time tasks than do standard high-fat meals (Simonson, Brozek, & Keys, 1948), high-protein meals (Spring, Maller, Wurtman, Digman, & Gozolino, 1983), or no lunch at all (Smith & Miles, 1986a, 1986b). Lloyd et al. (1994) also reported feelings of drowsiness, confusion, and uncertainty increased after low- and high-fat lunches but not after a medium-fat lunch. There was also a post-lunch improvement in reaction time after the medium-fat but not low- or high-fat lunches. All of which suggests that what you eat and when you eat it can impact upon cognitive functioning, and by association performance.

Nutritional supplements, cognitive performance, and health

In support of Dye et al.'s (2000) view that nutrition could be used to enhance performance there is increasing evidence that supports the positive impact that some specific nutritional supplements can have upon cognitive performance. However, it is important to note that the supporting evidence for the benefits of supplementation relate to highlighted deficiencies in the diet. As yet there is currently little real conclusive evidence that suggests that consuming more than the daily requirements of micronutrients will have a positive effect on mental performance. Indeed, for some vitamins and minerals excessively high consumption is associated with a range of negative side effects. As well as performance-related issues associated with deficiencies in the diet there are also general mental health and well-being implications. Deficiencies in select micronutrients, mainly certain B vitamins, have been linked

TABLE 2.2 Potential side effects of consuming large quantities of specific vitamins and minerals

Vitamin/mineral	Side effects
Vitamin A	Can lead to serious liver problems and a yellowing of the skin.
Vitamin B6	Brain cell damage reduced sensory and motor performance.
Vitamin C	Can lead to the formation of kidney stones.
Vitamin D	Dizziness, loss of appetite, diarrhoea, calcium build-up in the kidneys.
Zinc	Excessive consumption can cause bleeding in the stomach and severe abdominal pain.
Iron	Debilitating fatigue, headaches, rapid weight loss, and possible heart defects.
Calcium	Formation of kidney stones.
Potassium	Very high levels can result in heart irregularities, or in extreme cases heart attacks.

to depression and a number of other mental health issues. As a result, micronutrient supplementation, especially in individuals with overt or marginal deficiencies, could possibly improve overall mood state and psychological well-being. This is important as good robust mental health is normally a prerequisite for good psychological performance and performance under pressure.

Impact of too much supplementation

Increasingly there is evidence suggesting a potential problem associated with consuming too much of specific micronutrients. This issue is becoming increasingly prevalent due to the significant expansion of nutritional products that are 'fortified'. The most obvious example from many diets is that of breakfast cereals. Typical cereals such as corn flakes are fortified with vitamins D, thiamin (B1), riboflavin (B2), niacin, vitamin B6, folic acid, vitamin B12, iron, and sodium. Also, many sports drinks can be fortified. For example Red Bull includes sodium, niacin, pantothenic acid, vitamin B6, and vitamin B12. This in itself is not a problem, but many other protein supplements, energy drinks, and dietary aids are fortified as well (see Table 2.2 for further details of overconsumption).

Sleep

One night of sleep deprivation in humans diminishes waking regional brain activity predominantly in a bilateral prefrontal-posterior parietal-thalamic network mediating alertness, attention and higher-order cognitive processes. The cortical association findings are complementary to studies of slow wave and REM sleep demonstrating deactivation of these same cortical regions, with the implication that the need for recuperation during sleep may be greater in these areas relative to other brain regions. Brain activity, alertness, and cognitive performance impairments following one night of sleep deprivation suggest that the neurobehavioural function of sleep in humans is to restore and sustain normal waking brain activity and behaviour. These findings substantiate the biological necessity of sleep to normal brain functioning and are particularly powerful in underscoring the importance of adequate sleep for workplace productivity, public safety, and personal well-being.

Sleep has been identified as an important performance factor as it is one of the most important contributors to recovery (Cotterill, 2012). The recovery provided by restorative sleep has been suggested to be important for successful training and performance (Tuomilehto et al., 2016). This 'recovery' can help the performer adjust to, and cope with, the physical, neurological, immunological, and emotional stressors that the individual would have experienced during the day (Morin et al., 2006). Indeed just one night of sleep deprivation reduces cognitive activity, alertness, and cognitive performance (Thomas et al., 2000). Sleep has been described as a reversible behavioural state of perceptual disengagement from and unresponsiveness to the environment (Carskadon & Dement, 2011). Within sleep two specific states have been described: rapid eye movement (REM) and non-REM (NREM). NREM sleep is further divided into four stages (1–4) that equate to a 'depth of sleep' continuum. REM sleep has been linked to an activated brain in a movable body (Carskadon & Dement, 2011).

Griffin and Tyrell (2004) reported that poor sleeping patterns and insufficient rest is associated with individuals who suffer from high levels of anxiety and depression. Griffin and Tyrell further highlighted a link between excessive dreaming, poor sleeping patterns, and depression. Evidence suggests that when performers are stressed they spend more time in dream sleep and not enough time in slow-wave sleep where physical regeneration and recovery mainly takes place (Vandekerckhove & Cluydts, 2010). The reason why dreaming can be unhelpful to recovery is that the brain is in a similar state to when it is awake. Essentially, dreaming can be hard work. Dreams are real to your brain, and as such can be hormonally and emotionally draining, resulting in feelings of fatigue in the morning. Often little consideration is given to achieving optimal sleep in order to facilitate optimal performance (Cotterill, 2012). Humans are generally habitual creatures. As such, performers have preferred environments and routines that enable them to gain the maximum amount of quality sleep. Changes to these routines can impact on the quality and duration of sleep, and as a result significantly impact upon physical, psychological, and emotional recovery (Samuels, 2008). Performers who travel and stay in hotels need to consider the impacts upon their ability to recover effectively in these changing environments. Changes to the normal sleeping environment can have a negative impact upon the quality and duration of sleep (Savis, 1994). Sleeping on a harder or softer mattress with more or less ambient noise can all impact upon sleep (Bader & Engdal, 2000). This will, in turn, impact upon the amount of stressors the performer can cope with in subsequent days. Travelling to different time zones, which might upset the body clock can be problematic, as can different environmental conditions such as heat and humidity (Okamoto-Mizuno, Tsuzuki, & Mizuno, 2005).

Enhancing quality and duration of sleep

The inability to get to sleep is often classified in the literature as insomnia, which was defined by Roth (2007) as "the presence of an individual's report of difficulty with sleep" (p. S7). The literature relating to techniques that can be used to treat insomnia and other sleep-related issues suggests six different models of intervention that can be adopted: stimulus control therapy, sleep restriction therapy, relaxation training, cognitive therapy, sleep hygiene education, and cognitive-behaviour therapy (Morin et al., 2006). Hauri (1991) suggested the following six steps to enhancing sleep hygiene:

1. *Curtail time in bed* – only be in bed for the time you are sleeping.
2. *Never try to sleep* – engage in activities such as reading, watching television, or listening to radio discussions for as long as possible.
3. *Eliminate the bedroom clock* – time pressure is not conducive to sleep.
4. *Exercise in late afternoon/early evening* – linked to producing a core body temperature drop (conducive for sleep) 4–6 hours later.
5. *Avoid caffeine, alcohol, and nicotine prior to bed.*
6. *Regularize bedtime.*

Cotterill and Moran (2016) in their case study of a professional cricketer adapted Hauri's steps to focus on the following five steps:

1. To never try to sleep, specifically look to read.
2. To only use the bed for sleep (and to use the chairs provided in the hotel rooms for other activities such as watching television).
3. Eliminate the bedroom clock. Setting an alarm but not having the time displayed or easily accessible.
4. To remove caffeine and alcohol consumption prior to going to bed.
5. To engage in some light exercise where possible in late afternoon/early evening.

Summary

Optimal cognitive functioning is an aspiration of all performers across domains. The ability to think clearly and to make key decisions is an important requirement for performance. However, something that is often overlooked is an understanding of the factors that influence the brain's ability to function effectively. Outside of the hardware limitations that exist, nutrition, hydration, and recovery are key considerations in preparing the brain to perform optimally.

Study questions

1. To what extent do you think poor nutritional intake can impact upon cognitive performance?

2. Recognizing that rest and recovery are important for performance, what steps can be taken to maximize sleep duration and quality?
3. What impact do you think the increasing 'supplement' culture in sport could have upon cognitive performance?

Further reading

Dye, L., Lluch, A., & Blundell, J. E. (2000). Macronutrients and mental performance. *Nutrition, 16*, 1021–1034.

This article provides a good overview of many of the key links between nutrition and mental performance.

Samuels, C. (2008). Sleep, recovery, and performance: The new frontier in high-performance athletics. *Neurologic Clinics, 26*, 169–180.

A well-written overview of the importance of rest and recovery for performance, with a particular focus on the importance of good quality sleep.

3
COGNITION, PERCEPTION, AND ACTION

Introduction

To understand performance there is a need to understand the psychological processes that are constrained by the systems architecture, and underpin performance-focused behaviours. Cognition, perception, and memory have all been suggested to be key factors influencing performance (Raab, 2016). Indeed, these key influencing factors (including cognition and perception) have been highlighted as fundamental building blocks upon which performance is built. Understanding how the performer receives, interprets, and responds to information in the performance domain is important if the ultimate aim is to enable the individual to harness and exploit the information available within this performance environment.

This chapter will seek to clarify what cognition is, and define key cognitive 'skills' and functions including: attention, memory, problem solving, and creativity. The chapter will also clarify the nature of perception and its links to cognition and action, and how this determines the way in which the performer interacts with their environment.

Cognition

The term cognition is used in many different ways by both practitioners and researchers. At a broad level cognition refers to the higher order functions of the brain. It usually is considered to be a combination of skills including: attention, learning, memory, language, praxis (skilled motor behaviours); and so-called executive functions, such as decision-making, goal setting, planning, problem solving, and creativity. Most of the clinical literature on cognitive enhancement concerns the development of approaches to improve either attention or memory. This is because in daily life, individuals frequently complain that their memory is inadequate or that they cannot pay attention in certain cognitively demanding situations (Whitehouse, Juengst, Mehlman & Murray, 2012). Cognition is also seen as a faculty that enables us to solve problems, to be creative, and to use language in a range of forms (Goldstein, 2015). From a performance perspective the notion of cognition is important as key factors such as attention, memory, decision-making, problem solving, and creativity ultimately underpin effective performance under pressure.

Meta-cognition

Generally speaking meta-cognition can be viewed from the perspective of "higher order cognition about cognition" (Veenman, Van Hout-Wolters, & Afflerbach, 2006, p. 5). Meta-cognition was described by Flavell (1979) as an individuals' insight into and control over their own mental processes. More recent conceptualizations of meta-cognition have suggested a tripartite model of knowledge, control, and monitoring components (MacIntyre, Igou, Campbell, Moran, & Matthews, 2014).

Within the meta-cognition literature there is a distinction drawn between meta-cognitive knowledge and meta cognitive skills. Meta-cognitive knowledge refers to a person's declarative knowledge about the interactions between performer, task, and strategy characteristics (Flavell, 1979). Meta-cognitive skills refer to a performer's procedural knowledge for regulating their problem-solving and learning activities (Veenman, 2005).

Attention

Generally speaking attention refers to "a concentration of mental effort" (Matlin, 2002, p. 51), or "the concentration of mental effort on sensory or mental events" (Solso, 1998, p. 130). Attention is generally seen to be composed of four major dimensions: concentration, mental time-sharing ability, vigilance, and a skill in selective perception.

Concentration: Refers to a person's ability to exert deliberate mental effort on what is most important in a given situation.

A skill in selective perception: The ability to zoom in on task-relevant information whilst ignoring potential distractions (discriminating relevant stimuli from irrelevant stimuli.

Mental time-sharing ability: A person learns, as a result of extensive practise, to perform two or more concurrent actions equally well.

Vigilance: A person's ability to orientate attention and respond to randomly occurring relevant stimuli over an extended period of time (De Weerd, 2003).

Individuals vary in their ability to distribute visual attention spatially (e.g. Ahmed & de Fockert, 2012), to divide attention (e.g. Colflesh & Conway, 2007), and to shift the focus of attention (e.g. Heitz & Engle, 2007). People also vary in their ability to apply attention selectively (e.g. Bleckley, Durso, Crutchfield, Engle, &

Khanna, 2003), and to apply executive control to attentive processing (Conway, Cowan, & Bunting, 2001). A primary theme in attention research is that there is too much information in our environment for everything to be processed and, as a consequence, the processing of information needs to be selective (Chun et al., 2011). As a result, understanding human attentional processes is very heavily linked to understanding the relevant memory systems, processing performance, and ultimately processing capacity (load). One of the classic findings in memory research is that performing a secondary task during encoding reliably and often robustly impairs encoding success – a 'dual task' cost that is usually much weaker or absent during retrieval (Baddeley, Lewis, Eldridge, & Thomson, 1984; Craik, Govoni, Naveh-Benjamin, & Anderson, 1996). These observations show that encoding is particularly resource demanding whereas retrieval may be relatively automatic (Kuhl & Chun, 2014). Load theory has been suggested as a way to understand the capacity implications for the human system.

The central tenet of load theory (Lavie, 2010) is that perceptual processing can only become selective when the limits of perceptual capacity are reached. If a task imposes sufficient demands to exceed capacity, task-irrelevant items are not processed and can therefore be successfully ignored (in other words, early selection of relevant cues can occur). By contrast, if a task imposes only low perceptual demands, the remaining capacity is automatically allocated to the processing of task-irrelevant items, which may then cause distraction (reflecting late selection).

Memory

Memory, is not as the name suggests a unitary construct. Instead, memory can be conceptualized in many different ways, with each division of memory defined by its own distinctive characteristics (Bauer, 2013). There are close links between memory and other important aspects of cognition including attention and perception (Kuhl & Chun, 2014). There are also very close links between learning and memory (Eysenck, 2004).

It is now generally agreed in the literature that there are multiple memory systems (Jeneson & Squire, 2012). The key factors that determine whether working memory is sufficient to support performance, or whether performance must also depend on long-term memory, are the amount of information that can be held in mind and how amenable this information is to active rehearsal. If the capacity of working memory is exceeded, or if material cannot be effectively maintained by rehearsal (as can be the case for non-verbal material), performance must depend at least in part on long-term memory, even at short retention intervals (Jeneson & Squire, 2012).

In standard theories of memory (Atkinson & Shiffrin, 1968) information can be stored in long-term memory (LTM) only after it has been stored in short-term memory (STM), and even then, storage in LTM is a probabilistic event. Working memory can be described as a system of processes and stores used to maintain information during processing (Engle, Tuholski, Laughlin, & Conway, 1999), and working memory capacity is often measured with dual task paradigms such as the Daneman and Carpenter (1980) reading span task. There is now significant evidence to suggest that working memory capacity contributes to proficiency in a wide range of cognitive tasks (Hambrick & Engle, 2002).

Working memory is assumed to be a temporary storage system under attentional control that underpins our capacity for complex thought (Baddeley, 2007). Baddeley and Hitch (1974) suggested a working memory model that was composed of three specific components: the central executive (attentional control system), phonological loop, and the visuospatial sketchpad. All three systems have a limited capacity, but the nature of their limitations differs between them. There is also significant evidence that working memory functions are disrupted by emotional experiences including anger, elation, and anxiety (Baddeley, 2007). Recent research has established a link between working memory capacity and fluid intelligence (Hambrick & Engle, 2002), which is commonly defined as "the ability to solve novel problems and adapt to new situations" (Cattell, 1943). For example, using structural equation modelling, Kyllonen and Christal (1990) observed near-perfect correlations between working memory capacity and fluid intelligence.

Long-term memory refers to what can be recalled from the past when the information to be learned no longer occupies the current stream of thought, either because immediate memory capacity was exceeded or because attention was diverted from the memoranda. For example, Schacter and Tulving (1994) distinguished between procedural, perception representation, semantic, primary and episodic memory. A more modern approach to the idea of multiple memory systems comes from Cohen and Squire (1980) and Eichenbaum, Otto, and Cohen (1992). This view distinguishes between declarative and procedural memory and ties each to different brain systems. Declarative memory is seen as dependent upon the hippocampal system and related structures, whereas procedural memory is seen as dependent upon on-line tuning and modification of a variety of cortical and subcortical processors. Declarative knowledge relates to 'knowing that', and procedural knowledge refers to 'knowing how'.

It has generally been observed that memory performance increases after an individual practices on memory tasks involving specific types of materials and that an individual's familiarity with a given type of material is related to the amount of material recalled (Ericsson, 1985). Increases in memory performance are not in themselves inconsistent with the notion that the capacity of the human memory system is invariant, and these increases in performance have traditionally been accounted for in terms of chunking (Miller, 1956). Consistent with chunking theory Chase and Simon (1973) proposed that expert memory performance could be accounted for solely in terms of STM, where chunks were temporarily kept or activated. Recent research on memory performance shows that with practice and the acquisition of memory skills, performers can improve their recall performance on specific memory tasks with a particular type of stimulus material by between 100 and 1,000% (Ericsson & Kintsch, 1995). Performers' virtually perfect reproduction of presented information, especially in the digit-span task, suggests that after practice individuals are able to use LTM for reliable storage even at relatively fast presentation rates. This improvement is due to increased ability to store information in LTM and to the association of presented information with retrieval cues that allow reliable retrieval from LTM at the time of recall (Ericsson & Kintsch, 1995).

Problem solving

Problem solving refers to cognitive processing directed at achieving a goal when the problem solver does not initially know a solution method. This definition consists of four major elements:

> *Cognitive* – Problem solving occurs within the problem solver's cognitive system and can only be inferred indirectly from the problem solver's behaviour (including biological changes, introspections, and actions during problem solving).
> *Process* – Problem solving involves mental computations in which some operation is applied to a mental representation, sometimes resulting in the creation of a new mental representation.
> *Directed* – Problem solving is aimed at achieving a specific goal.
> *Personal* – Problem solving depends on the existing knowledge of the problem solver so that what is a problem for one problem solver may not be a problem for someone who already knows a solution method.
>
> *(Mayer, 1992; Mayer & Wittrock, 2006)*

Problem solving consists of two phases: creating the problem space and generating solutions to the problem (Newell & Simon, 1972).

A problem exists when a performer has a goal but does not yet know how to achieve it. Problems can be classified as routine or non-routine, and also as well defined or ill defined. The major cognitive processes in problem solving include: representing, planning, executing, and monitoring. In order to complete this process different kinds of knowledge are required: facts, concepts, procedures, strategies, and beliefs (Mayer, 1992).

Creativity

Creative solutions are central facets of many performance domains including business, performing arts, and sport. Managers must find new solutions for industrial productions; designers must develop creative solutions in industrial or web design to secure crucial competitive advantages; and performers in dynamic sports must make decisions in specific contexts that are unexpected and as a result are harder for their opponents to read (Memmert, Huttermann, & Orliczek, 2013). Creativity has also been suggested to be one of several key ingredients that characterize the movement from ability to competency to expertise to eminence (Olszewski-Kubilius, Subotnik, & Worrell, 2015).

Creativity can broadly be described as requiring originality and effectiveness (Runco & Jaeger, 2012). Guilford (1956) conceptualized creativity as the ability to generate different responses to a task as a consequence of divergent thinking, rather than finding a single predetermined solution, which requires convergent thinking. Guilford distinguished between divergent and convergent thinking in his structure of intellect model, emphasizing divergent thinking as a critical creative process. Divergent thinking is an inductive, ideational process that involves generating a broad range of solutions or ideas to a given stimulus (Guilford, 1967; Runco, 2007). This type of thinking is often contrasted with convergent thinking, a deductive process that involves systematically applying rules to arrive at a single, correct solution (Brophy, 1998; Guilford, 1967).

The process of being creative has been characterized as consisting of four phases (Lubart, 2001): the preparation phase; incubation phase; illumination phase; and verification phase. Kaufman and Beghetto (2009) further distinguished between four different levels of creativity: *Big-C*, the kind found in Darwin and others of that level; *Little-C*, or everyday creativity; *Mini-C*, or the kind found in the learning process; and *Pro-C*, the kind represented in the progression from Little-C to Big-C. Creativity is also strongly associated with both defocused attention and cognitive disinhibition, or what researchers technically refer to as reduced latent inhibition (Carson, Peterson, & Higgins, 2003; Kéri, 2011). Highly creative performers tend to notice stimuli that they know are irrelevant, which enables them to "think outside the box" and to take advantage of fortuitous events that they might otherwise ignore (Simonton, 2012).

Torrance (1966) emphasized three key properties of creative thought/behaviour: fluency, flexibility, and originality. *Fluency* is described as a generation of a large number of alternate solutions to a problem; *flexibility* is viewed as the generation of a variety of classes of solutions; and *originality* refers to the atypicality of solutions to the problem. Atypicality may be described with respect to one's own dynamic action landscape or to the socio-cultural landscape in a performance domain (Torrance, 1966).

Creativity has been suggested to be a habit (Sternberg, 2006; Tharp, 2005). Behind all innovations one finds creativity, so innovations arise from a habit. Like any habit, creativity can either be encouraged or discouraged. The main things that promote the formation of creative habits are (a) opportunities to engage in it, (b) encouragement when performers avail themselves of these opportunities, and (c) rewards when performers respond to such encouragement and think and behave creatively. If the opportunities, encouragement, or rewards are removed, creative tendencies will diminish. In this respect, creativity is no different from any other habit, good or bad (Sternberg, 2012).

Creativity ultimately requires the ability to combine seemingly unrelated ideas in new and original ways. Hence, researchers have tried to identify the cognitive capacities and inclinations that allow this to happen. These attributes may be loosely collected together as defining a creative cognitive style that transcends any particular domain (Reisberg, 2013). Specifically: creativity correlates positively with divergent thinking or the ability to come up with many alternative responses (Guilford, 1967). Ultimately research suggests that creativity is positively associated with the capacity to generate many and unusual associations (Rothenberg, 1983); tends to increase with the tendency to lapse into defocused attention (Carson, Peterson, & Higgins, 2005); is positively linked with openness to experience (Carson et al., 2005); and at the highest levels is likely to be associated with elevated scores on psychoticism or schizotypy (Batey & Furnham, 2008).

Perception

Perception involves detecting and interpreting changes in various forms of energy flowing through the environment such as light rays, sound waves, and neural activation (Bruce, Green, & Georgeson, 1996). The environmental, changes which can be perceived from these energy flows over space and time, are used to support the goal-directed actions of performers (Williams, Davids, & Williams, 1999). As a result, it can be suggested that changes in the nature of the environment can directly influence the behaviour of the performer.

Perception is generally seen as part of the information processing system (Raab, 2016). From a traditional information processing perspective it is seen as a complex phenomenon that is viewed as a source of information for higher order processes. The general view within information processing approaches to perception and action sees a linear process where perception leads to cognition, which leads to action (Lobinger, 2016).

There is also an ecological view of perception presented by Gibson (1986) in which perception is conceptualized as perceiving a stimulus directly. From a performance perspective perception has been cited as an important factor influencing the processing of both visual and auditory information (Raab, 2016). This information along with information from the body and memory are then used to underpin action, described by Magill (2011) as intentional movements that serve a specific goal. This link between perception and action is of critical importance across various performance domains. While the human system perceives all sensory information the dominant source of information is the visual system. There are two major approaches, which seek to rationalize the link between visual perception and action, indirect and direct perception. Indirect perception theorists (Bruner, 1957; Gregory, 1980; Neisser, 1967) argue that perception involves the formation of an internal representation suggesting that memory, in the form of stored knowledge of the world, is of central importance to perception (Eysenck, 2001). The indirect perception theorists further suggest that there is a need to understand the interrelationships of perceptual processing at different cognitive levels. Direct perception deals with visual perception by emphasizing optical flow patterns.

Gibson (1986) suggested that the optical array specified at the eye contains abundant information over space and time that allows the performer to directly and unambiguously perceive the layout and properties of events within the environment. In essence indirect perception emphasizes top-down processes where meaning is added by the organism, whilst direct perception emphasizes bottom-up processes with sensory sources of information already carrying meaning. The relative importance and salience of top-down and bottom-up processes depend on a range of factors. Eysenck (2001) suggested that visual perception may largely be determined by bottom-up processes when the viewing conditions are good, but involves top-down processes as the viewing conditions deteriorate because of very brief presentation times or lack of stimulus clarity. Indeed in the development of these two conceptual approaches to perception Gibson focused on visual perception under optimal viewing conditions, whereas constructivist theorists (Bruner, 1957; Gregory, 1980; Neisser, 1967) often used suboptimal viewing conditions. Eysenck (2001) further suggested that these two approaches instead of providing alternative views of visual perception actually look at different aspects. Indirect theorists have focused on perception for recognition, whereas direct theorists have emphasized perception for action (Milner & Goodale, 1998). As a result, it's this direct, ecological approach to visual perception that appears to better explain the link between perception and action. The accuracy and relevance of the information received from the experimental environment could ultimately result in a different set of responding actions.

Visual perception relates to the ability of the brain to interpret the visual information (visible light) captured by the eyes from the surrounding environment. The brain's ability to make sense of this information relates to both the environmental information and internal representations and previous experience (memory). The visual system has been shown to possess the capability to predict forthcoming events and fill the gaps in sensory data by adding information that has not yet been perceived but is nonetheless likely to occur (Didierjean & Marmèche, 2005; Hubbard, 2005). This anticipatory process may also be moderated by the observer's expectations, personal experience, and knowledge base. For example, studies have shown that knowledge of friction or gravity, or an understanding of the object's conceptual context or specific features, can affect the mental representation of the object's trajectory (Hubbard, 1995; Vinson & Reed, 2002).

Perceptual-cognitive skills

Perceptual-cognitive skill refers to the ability to identify and acquire environmental information for integration with existing knowledge such that appropriate responses can be selected and executed (Marteniuk, 1976). Knowing where and when to look is crucial for successful performance, yet the visual display is vast and often saturated with information both relevant and irrelevant to the task. Performers must be able to identify the most information-rich areas of the display, direct their attention appropriately, and extract meaning from these areas efficiently and effectively (Williams et al., 1999). Building on this information experts are able to generate accurate options of potential outcomes in specific situations based on the refined use of situational probabilities (McRobert, Ward, Eccles, & Williams, 2011). It is proposed that perceptual-cognitive skills combine to produce two specific judgements: anticipation and decision-making (Broadbent, Causer, Williams, & Ford, 2015), which then determine the course of action adopted and its ultimate success.

Summary

Cognition in its broader sense is an important determinant of successful performance. Understanding the mechanisms of attention and memory can help to maximize learning, development, and performance. Problem-solving ability and creativity can ultimately enhance performance in dynamic environments where new and innovative solutions are required to both novel and reoccurring problems.

Understanding the mechanisms that underpin the links between perception and action is also important to help to maximize preparation for, and performance in the 'real' performance domain.

Study questions

1. How important is the concept of creativity for performance across a range of performance domains?
2. To what extent do you feel cognitive skills such as attention are innate, or do you believe they can be enhanced with practice? Why?
3. What factors impact upon the individual performer's ability to effectively perceive the environment around them during performance?

Further reading

Broadbent, D. P., Causer, J., Williams, A. M., & Ford, P. R. (2015). Perceptual-cognitive skills training and its transfer to expert performance in the field: Future research directions. *European Journal of Sport Science, 15*, 322–331.

This article offers an interesting insight into the development of perceptual-cognitive skills for performance. It reviews a broad range of literature offering some key recommendations for practice.

Kuhl, B. A.; & Chun, M. (2014). Memory and attention. In A. C. Nobre & S. Kastner (Eds.) *The Oxford handbook of attention*. Oxford: Oxford University Press.

A good overview of the memory and attention systems. Crucially the chapter also explores the inter-relation between memory and attention and the implications for human functioning.

4

UNDERSTANDING PRESSURE

Introduction

Effective performance under pressure is normally characterized by the consistent execution of complex motor skills in a flawless or near perfect manner (Singer, 2002). These performances are also characterized by an optimal mindset that keeps the performer focused on the task at hand at the expense of other competing stimuli (Cotterill, Sanders, & Collins, 2010; Gould et al., 2002; Kao et al., 2013; Krane & Williams, 2006; Williams & Krane, 1993).

Optimizing motor performance under challenging circumstances is critical for many, including athletes, coaches, musicians, workers, and surgeons. As a result, much attention has been devoted to the understanding of pressure-induced performance decrements (e.g. Baumeister, 1984; Eysenck & Calvo, 1992; Masters & Maxwell, 2008). The ability to perform under extreme pressure is a quality sought in many performance domains, whether in the military, law enforcement, emergency medicine, aviation, the performing arts, or sport (Vickers & Lewinski, 2012). A number of studies have highlighted the problem of performers performing poorly under pressure (Baumeister, 1984; Beilock & Carr, 2001; Gucciardi & Dimmock, 2008; Lewis & Linder, 1997; Mesagno & Mullane-Grant, 2010; Mesagno, Harvey, & Janelle, 2011; Oudejans, Kuijpers, Kooijman, & Bakker, 2011; Oudejans & Pijpers, 2010; Wilson, Wood, & Vine, 2009). This chapter will focus on understanding what pressure is and how it manifests. The chapter will also explore how performers respond to pressure, and consider strategies that can be adopted to maximize performance under pressure.

Choking

Choking (under pressure) has been highlighted as having particularly damaging effects on performance, including: under-achievement, diminished enjoyment, reduced well-being, and a less positive self-identity (Hill, Hanton, Matthews, & Fleming, 2011). This choking response is seen particularly in relation to elevated experiences of anxiety and arousal.

Choking has been defined as "a critical deterioration in skill execution leading to substandard performance that is caused by an elevation in anxiety levels under perceived pressure at a time when successful outcome is normally attainable by the athlete" (Mesagno & Mullane-Grant, 2010, p. 343). A further definition has been offered by Mesagno and Hill (2013) who defined choking as "an acute and considerable decrease in skill execution and performance when self-expected standards are normally achievable, which is the result of increased anxiety under perceived pressure" (p. 272). Choking can be distinguished from general 'underperformance' based upon a number of factors: (1) the magnitude of the performance decrement (e.g. Baumeister, 1984; Hill, Hanton, Fleming, & Matthews, 2009); (2) a negative cognitive appraisal of anxiety (or debilitative anxiety; Gucciardi, Longbottom, Jackson, & Dimmock, 2010); (3) a perceived lack of control (Otten, 2009); and (4) self-presentational concerns through experiencing an emotionally painful event (Mesagno et al., 2011; Vealey, Low, Pierce, & Quinones-Paredes, 2014). Choking is also the result of striving to achieve success, rather than caused directly by physiological factors such as injury or fatigue (Mesagno & Hill, 2013). Choking under pressure has been suggested to be a specific response where the individual performs more poorly than expected given their skill level, in response to a high-pressure situation (based on Beilock & Gray, 2007).

Why choking occurs?

There are a number of ways choking under pressure is thought to occur. First, that the performer can be distracted from important aspects of the task and associated skill execution. Specifically by being distracted by anxiety-related thoughts such as self-doubt, fear of failure, and negative evaluation (Gucciardi et al., 2010; Mesagno, Harvey, & Janelle, 2012). Pressure can be particularly impactful in this way if the performer is not prepared for it, which can result in increased experiences of anxiety and a corresponding increase in task-irrelevant thoughts (Vealey et al., 2014). Pressure is also thought to cause performers who can't cope to focus too much on the execution of their well-learnt skills. This focus on 'how' to execute the skill, referred to as 'explicit monitoring', serves to disrupt the smooth and automatic execution of the skills (Beilock & Carr, 2001).

Two major sets of theories have been advanced to explain this phenomenon. In the explicit monitoring hypothesis it is argued that pressure induces performers to attempt to consciously monitor and control movements that normally are executed without conscious control (Baumeister, 1997). This process disrupts natural skill execution that otherwise would be automatically run, and tasks that do not require online attentional control are sensitive to these disruptions (e.g. Beilock, Carr, MacMahon, & Starkes, 2002). Another set of theories is represented by the distraction hypothesis. According to this view, pressure induces worry that consumes working memory resources that otherwise would be used to focus on the task, and performance suffers as a result. Studies have shown that tasks that rely on working memory are particularly susceptible to this type of performance failure (e.g. Beilock, Kulp, Holt, & Carr, 2004). Some of the research reported to support the explicit monitoring hypothesis has revealed that performers who choke often spend longer preparing and/or moving while performing, which is thought to reflect the additional information processing involved in explicitly monitoring one's performance.

Defining psychological pressure

Performance pressure has been described as an aspect of the situation, consisting of the importance of doing well on a particular occasion (Baumeister, 1984). Individuals feel this performance pressure based on the extent that they care deeply about the outcome of their performance and perceive that this performance is instrumental for goal attainment. Performance pressure in itself though is not necessarily a bad thing as it has also been highlighted to increase the performer's motivation to achieve his or her desired goal (Wallace, Baumeister, & Vohs, 2005).

A wide range of 'stressors' have been identified in the sport and performance psychology literature that are seen as potential contributors to perceptions of performance pressure (e.g. Giacobbi, Foore, & Weinberg, 2004; Noblet & Gifford, 2002). These stressors might influence both the well-being (DiBartolo & Shaffer, 2002) and performance (Humphrey, Yow, & Bowden, 2000) of performers. A number of specific sources of stress have been identified in the literature and several appear to be common across performance domains. This suggests that there could be a core group of stressors experienced by all performers (Noblet & Gifford, 2002). These common stressors include pressure to perform at a high standard, worries about performing poorly, and difficulties balancing performance and non-performance commitments (McKay, Niven, Lavallee, & White, 2008). Despite these commonalities, there is also evidence that certain stressors are unique to different performance environments. A range of sources of performance pressure have been cited in the literature including audience support. The notion that supportive audiences induce perceptions of pressure was suggested by Baumeister and Steinhilber (1984), whose archival research on baseball World Series and basketball championship series revealed that home teams tended to lose the decisive game of the championship series, in sharp contrast to their winning records in most other games (Wallace et al., 2005). Supporting evidence for this phenomenon has been found in other contexts including: golf (Wright & Jackson, 1991) and ice hockey (Wright & Voyer, 1995). The most direct evidence of supportive audiences harming performance was presented by Butler and Baumeister (1998), who systematically manipulated audience support in laboratory experiments and found that participants performed less well when performing for supportive versus unsupportive audiences.

Negative responses to pressure

The main negative response to pressure highlighted in the literature relates to experiences of anxiety. Researchers have shown that high-anxiety conditions negatively affect performance, including anticipation judgements and their underlying visual search behaviours, regardless of skill level (Alder, Ford, Causer, & Williams, 2016).

With two specific aspects outlined in the literature: cognitive anxiety (or worry), and somatic anxiety (physiological responses) (Martens, Burton et al., 1990). Performers who experience cognitive anxiety experience negative expectations about themselves, the situation at hand, and the potential consequences (Martens, Burton et al., 1990). Performers who experience high levels of cognitive anxiety are concerned about their ability to perform and fearful of the consequences of not performing well. Somatic anxiety is the physiological responses that result from the perception of the cognitive component of anxiety (Morris, Davis, & Hutchings, 1981). Examples of physiological arousal responses include: a rapid heart rate, shortness of breath, clammy hands, butterflies in the stomach, and tense muscles. Of those two components, cognitive anxiety has been shown to have the greater effect on performance (Hardy & Fazey, 1987; Martens, Burton et al., 1990). While Martens, Burton et al. suggested that a high level of pre-competitive cognitive anxiety is detrimental to performance, Hardy and colleagues (e.g. Hardy & Fazey, 1987; Hardy, Parfitt, & Pates, 1994), in their catastrophe model of performance, have argued that a high level of pre-competitive cognitive anxiety becomes a detriment only when physical arousal becomes too high. It is important though to remember that not all responses to pressure are psychological and physiological. Pressure also elicits effects on the kinematics of movement of the performer (Cooke, Kavussanu, McIntyre, Boardley, & Ring, 2011).

Coping

The ability to cope with stress is an important attribute for performers to have (Nicholls, Polman, Morley, & Taylor, 2009). Lazarus and Folkman (1984) defined coping as "constantly changing cognitive and behavioural efforts to manage specific external and/or internal demands that are appraised as taxing or exceeding the resources of the person" (p. 141). There appears to be an important distinction between problem-focused and emotion-focused coping (Endler & Parker, 1989; Lazarus & Folkman, 1984). Problem-focused coping refers to cognitive and behavioural efforts used to change the problem causing the distress. These strategies may include problem solving, and increasing effort. Emotion-focused coping, on the other hand, involves strategies used to regulate emotional arousal and distress. Strategies in this dimension may include behavioural withdrawal, wishful thinking, denial, and venting of emotion. Aldwin (1994) conceptualized coping as a function of the person and the environment. For example, the use of coping strategies may be influenced by personality characteristics, such as emotionality (Bolger, 1990) or by environmental demands (Mattlin, Wethington, & Kessler, 1990).

Some coping theorists have suggested that coping and emotional experience are related (Folkman & Lazarus, 1988; Lazarus, 1991). When a person experiences a stressful situation, specific coping processes can be associated with changes in on-going emotions. The relationship between emotion and coping has been described as bidirectional, with each affecting the other (Folkman & Lazarus, 1988). Initial appraisal (e.g. threat, harm, challenge) generates emotions that in turn influence coping processes. Coping then can modify a troubled person environment relationship, leading to a different emotional state.

Coping resources

Coping resources "comprise a wide variety of behaviours and social networks that aid the individual in dealing with the problems, joys, disappointments, and stresses of life" (Williams, 2001, p. 774). Sleep patterns, fitness levels, nutrition, and time management are all examples of general coping behaviours or lifestyle management that reflect internal resources (Raedeke & Smith, 2004) that help performers to deal with stress. The perception of receiving strong social support is an external resource that can help performers to deal with the demands of both practice and performance. Social support generally consists of the presence of other who the performer can rely on and who they know value and care for them (Williams, 2001). Previous research with elite sports performers provides support for Lazarus's (1999) view, that coping changes over time (e.g. Nicholls, Holt, Polman, & Bloomfield, 2006; Nicholls, Holt, Polman, & James, 2005). While the importance of coping strategies and resources is acknowledged, there is still to date, limited research that has sought to explore the nature of these performance-specific strategies, the impact they have, and crucially how best to develop their implementation by the performer.

Social support

Researchers across a range of psychology domains have highlighted that social support has a potentially stress-buffering effect (Cohen & Wills, 1985; Raedeke & Smith, 2004). There is evidence that social support also moderates the stress–illness relationship (e.g. Sarason, Sarason, Potter, & Antoni, 1985). The importance of social support for coping with performance stressors has been noted previously (Gould, Guinan, Greenleaf, Medbery, & Peterson, 1999; Holt & Hogg, 2002; Rees, Hardy, & Freeman, 2007), and the potential stress-buffering effect has been pointed out (Rees & Hardy, 2004). Coach/mentor social support has been found to relate to the performer's satisfaction with their performance experiences (Weiss & Friedrichs, 1986), and it has been related to important outcomes and the ability to adapt to new challenges (e.g. Petrie & Stoever, 1997; Weiss & Friedrichs, 1986). Rosenfeld and Richman (1997) described social support to be behaviours perceived by the recipient to enhance well-being. Social support is a multidimensional construct and may be divided into different types. Cutrona and Russell (1990) argued for five dimensions while Rees and Hardy (2004) argued for four. However,

Schaefer, Coyne, and Lazarus (1982) distinguish between three different functions of social support: emotional support, tangible support, and informational support. The essence of emotional support is to feel loved and cared for, which is achieved through reliance and confidence in other individuals. Tangible support involves more direct aid through loans, gifts, and transportation. Informational support is the provision of information or advice and provision of feedback.

Strategies to cope with pressure

Emotional regulation

A range of strategies have been suggested to help to regulate emotional experiences including cognitive reappraisal and distraction.

Cognitive reappraisal, which involves reinterpreting the emotion-invoking stimulus in a way that alters its emotional impact (Gross, 2002) is one form of emotional regulation. Individuals are instructed to think about the positive aspects of what they are experiencing (Shiota & Levenson, 2009). Reappraisal has been used to successfully regulate a wide range of negative emotions (Gross, 2002) and importantly, has been shown to be effective in reducing emotional arousal (Hofmann, Heering, Sawyer, & Asnaani, 2009).

Distraction refers to engaging in other neutral thoughts (Nolen-Hoeksema, 1991), or taking thoughts or memories in mind that are unrelated to the experienced emotional state (Watts, 2007). The use of distraction has been linked to decreased self-reported arousal when viewing emotional images (Thiruchselvam, Blechert, Sheppes, Rydstrom, & Gross, 2011) and is associated with lower physiological arousal including blood pressure and heart rate arising from emotional arousal (Gerin, Davidson, Christenfeld, Goyal, & Schwartz, 2006). In addition, Terry (2004) suggested the use of music as a pre-competition routine to regulate mood, arousal, and concentration. Pates, Karageorghis, Fryer, and Maynard (2003) showed that listening to music before performing netball shooting enhanced accuracy and also triggered positive emotions and cognitions. When using distraction in relation to choking, Mesagno, Marchant, and Morris (2009) also reported preliminary evidence that listening to music through headphones improved performance under pressure.

Avoidance coping

As discussed by Anshel, Kim, Kim, Chang, and Eom (2001), avoidance coping is an effective response to stress when performers need to distract themselves from a stressful situation. Some previous research has shown that high trait anxious performers tend to use avoidance coping (e.g. denial and wishful thinking) significantly more than low trait anxious performers (see e.g. Giacobbi & Weinberg, 2000). Furthermore, Anshel et al. (2001) suggested that avoidance coping may be appropriate when stressful encounters are beyond the individual's control or in response to something that occurred in the past. Krohne and Hindel (1988) also reported that table tennis players regularly used avoidance coping strategies during competition. This could be because rapid open-skilled tasks, such as table tennis, demand that the performers avoid attending to stressful encounters during performance since this would be a distraction from the task at hand.

Pre-performance routines

A particular approach that has been extensively reported as positively impacting upon performance is the use of preparation/pre-performance routines (Cotterill, 2011). These routines have been specifically characterized by Moran (1996) as "a sequence of task-relevant thoughts and actions which an athlete engages in systematically prior to his or her performance of a specific sports skill" (p. 177). Indeed, a number of studies in sport in particular have highlighted the positive impact that these preparatory routines can have on performance (Cotterill, 2011; Czech, Ploszay, & Burke, 2004; Douglas & Fox, 2002; Hazell, Cotterill, & Hill, 2014; Lonsdale & Tam, 2008; Mesagno & Mullane-Grant, 2010; Shaw, 2002). The use of routines to enhance performance is not just confined to sport research, other performance domains such as the performing arts (Čačković, Barić, & Vlašić, 2010; Clowes & Knowles, 2013; Vergeer & Hanrahan, 1998) and business (Burke, 2010) have also reported positive effects after adopting this approach. The existing body of literature relating to routines advocates a number of potential ways in which these routines can aid performance. These include: providing an attentional focus and reducing distraction (Boutcher, 1992; Cotterill et al., 2010; Czech et al., 2004; Hazell et al., 2014); acting as a trigger for habitual behaviours (Boutcher & Crews, 1987; Moran, 1996); diverting attention from task-irrelevant thoughts (Gould & Udry, 1994; Maynard, 1998); enhancing the recall of required physiological and psychological states (Marlow, Bull, Heath, & Shambrook, 1998); preventing performers focusing on the mechanics of the skill (Beilock & Carr, 2001; Mesagno & Mullane-Grant, 2010; Masters, Poolton, Maxwell, & Raab, 2008); reduce anxiety (Hill et al., 2011) and allow performers to evaluate the performance conditions and calibrate the required responses (Schack, 1997).

Of central importance when attempting to implement or develop pre-performance routines is to focus on the specific needs of the individual performer (Cotterill, 2011). An important, possibly crucial, component of this process is to understand the existing behaviours of the performer. Unless the performer is a novice regarding their stage of skill development they will already have ingrained pre-performance behaviours. The challenge then to the sport psychology consultant is whether to accept that these behaviours exist and try to work with them, or alternatively to try to impose a new set of behaviours which might be more beneficial to performance. Lidor and Singer (2000) suggested that if a new routine is to be developed the earlier this takes place in the skill learning process the better.

Cotterill (2011) in reporting the experience of developing pre-performance routines (PPRs) in professional cricket suggested a six-step approach: (1) understanding the task requirements; (2) video performance; (3) clarifying the meaning of existing behaviours; (4) develop a function and a focus for each behavioural component; (5) construct the new routine and (6) practice using the new routine.

There is increasingly literature on the use of pre-performance routines to cope with pressure and to enhance performance. However, there is currently little literature reported on how these routines developed, and whether they are stable over time. A greater focus on the design, implementation, and successful use of routines in ecologically valid environments is required to enhance the use of routines in the future to enhance performance.

Pressure acclimatization training

Acclimatizing refers to the performer adapting or becoming accustomed to increased pressure (anxiety inducing), by training with additional mild anxiety (Oudejans & Pijpers, 2010). Supporters of acclimatization training (e.g. Beilock & Carr, 2001; Lewis & Linder, 1997; Nieuwenhuys & Oudejans, 2011; Reeves, Tenebaum, & Lidor, 2007) believe that, if a performer can practice in a manner that helps them become accustomed to the pressure in competition, performance may improve in high pressure situations. Lewis and Linder (1997) conducted an initial acclimatization study that compared golf putting performance. Oudejans and Pijpers (2010) examined whether training could prevent choking in elite basketball players. They reported that the 'trained' group performed better post intervention compared with the control group. Similar positive results have also been reported in police officer shooting performance under pressure (Nieuwenhuys & Oudejans, 2011). However, there are also studies that have found no positive effect following acclimatization training such as Beseler, Mesagno, Young, and Harvey (2016), who applied an intervention programme to Australian Rules football set shot goal kicking.

Pressure acclimatization training offers the potential to better prepare performers for competition. However, more research is required that explores using this technique in a more diverse range of performance domains.

Positive priming

Priming has been suggested as another way to enhance performance under pressure. Priming can be described as "the influence a stimulus has on subsequent performance of the processing system" (Baddeley, 1997, p. 352). Ashford and Jackson (2010) specifically explored the use of priming working with skilled hockey players. The study reported that performance improved when comparing low- to high-pressure scenarios. Crucially they also reported that the priming condition outperformed the control and skills-only conditions.

Summary

Being able to not just cope but to excel under pressure is the aim for all performers across a diverse range of domains. Understanding what pressure is, and the mechanism through which it can have an effect are important. Crucially though the ability to develop techniques and strategies to enable the performer to maximize their performance outcomes is the logical next step to eradicate performance levels dropping and ultimately removing the potential for the performer to choke under pressure.

Study questions

1. To what extent do you feel choking (under pressure) exists within team sports?
2. What strategies could be used to help performers to cope with the pressure of the performance environment?
3. What factors do you think impact upon the effectiveness of pressure acclimatization training for performance?

Further reading

Cooke, A., Kavussanu, M., McIntyre, D., Boardley, I. D., & Ring, C. (2011). Effects of competitive pressure on expert performance: Underlying psychological, physiological, and kinematic mechanisms. *Psychophysiology, 48*, 1146–1156.

This article offers an interesting overview of the mechanics of how pressure impacts on performance. This impact is explored from multiple perspectives including kinematic, physiological, and psychological.

Mesagno, C., & Hill, D. M. (2013). Definition of choking in sport: Reconceptualization and debate. *International Journal of Sport Psychology, 44*, 267–277.

A useful starting point in looking to understand the concept of choking. The article explores current understanding and offers a more refined view of what choking is.

5

DECISION-MAKING UNDER PRESSURE

Introduction

Across performance domains, successful outcomes do not solely rely on proficient movement control; an effective decision on the required motor response is also required (Poolton, Masters, & Maxwell, 2006). In sport, a good decision maker is one who shows superior capabilities to "read the play" and select the most appropriate option under the pressure of game play (Baker, Coté, & Abernety, 2003, p. 15).

Effective performance is about making the right decisions at the right time and then committing to those courses of action. Often a key-determining factor of success is whether the performer can make the right decision at the right time. Part of this process relates to how the performer makes decisions (are they decisive), also past experience is important (has the individual had to make these decisions before), finally the knowledge the performer has is also important (what evidence does the performer have to support their decisions). Each of these different types of decisions takes different amounts of time and effort. The speed at which a performer can modify their decision based upon changing environmental stimuli is also an important factor in dynamic performance settings. With an understanding of how effective decisions are made, what factors impact upon these decisions, and how to make decisions under pressure, the performer can seek to further enhance their performance.

Using the context of sport as an example, performance has specifically been defined as "a complex product of cognitive knowledge about the current situation and past events, combined with a player's ability to produce the sport skill(s) required" (Thomas et al., 1986, p. 259). This definition emphasizes two important components of decision-making: cognitive knowledge; and motor, response execution (Gutierrez Diaz del Campo et al., 2011).

Due to time constraints, in some performance domains individuals are required to process both a decision and a movement in quick succession (Bard, Fleury, &

Goulet, 1994; Poolton et al., 2006). Performance can occur at the limits of human performance. Across a range of performance domains, there is evidence of a significant relationship between performer skill level and anticipation ability (McRobert & Taylor, 2005; Penrose & Roach, 1995; Renshaw & Fairweather, 2000). In these circumstances individuals often report that their motor reactions evolve from a given situation without any consciously controlled decision-making (Kibele, 2006). This type of decision-making has been labelled as 'intuitive' (see Gilovich, Griffin, & Kahneman, 2002, for a review).

This chapter will seek to explore what decision-making is. After providing clarity on the concept the chapter will explore the theoretical underpinning and explanations for the decision-making process and consider the environmental factors that both influence and determine decision-making under pressure.

What is decision-making?

In general terms decision-making (DM) can be viewed as the process of committing to a particular course of action. More specific definitions of DM have been suggested in the academic literature including "the selection of one option from a set of two or more options" (Klein, Calderwood, & Clinton-Cirocco, 1986, p. 186) and "a set of evaluative and inferential processes that people have at their disposal and can draw on in the process of making decisions" (Koehler & Harvey, 2004, p. xv). DM in this context is seen as a process that exists between the perceptual and executional aspects of performance. Effective DM requires the integration of perceptual information with knowledge that has been accumulated via previous experiences (Masters et al., 2008).

A distinction is often drawn between consciously and non-consciously controlled DM. Frequently, non-consciously controlled DM has been labelled as 'intuitive' (Gilovich et al., 2002). This concept of intuitive DM has been explored in a range of social work, performance, and business settings (Hogarth, 2001), and more recently in sport (Raab, 2003). Intuition in this context is defined as "an involuntary, difficult to articulate, affect-laden recognition or judgement that is based on prior learning and experiences and is formed without deliberate or conscious rational choice" (Raab & Laborde, 2011, p. 89). Or specifically in psychology is viewed as the judgements that appear in consciousness quickly, relying on no deep knowledge of reasons for that judgement, and is strong enough to act on (Gigerenzer, 2007). In performance settings, intuition is a way that some performers can find effective tactical solutions without considering all of the possible solutions and comparing them (Gréhaigne & Wallian, 2007). Intuitive decisions are thought to be reactive, effortless, speedy, non-consciously controlled, triggered automatically, and highly sensitive to action contexts (Kibele, 2006). However, there is currently a lack of consensus in the literature regarding how intuitive decisions occur. Some authors argue that intuitive decisions are the result of an awareness of some phenomenological internal and discriminative physiological state that evolves from non-conscious stimulus (Perrig & Wippich, 1995). While other authors assume that these physiological states may be induced rather than preceded by intuitive decisions (Hogarth, 2001). However, regardless of the underpinning mechanism, these intuitive decisions are crucial within performance settings.

Another important aspect of DM in some performance domains is the tactical and strategy choices that are made. These choices are underpinned by strategic and tactical knowledge. Gréhaigne, Godbout, and Bouthier (1999) clarified the two as follows: strategic knowledge reflects the competence to plan ahead and therefore influence decisions within a situation, whereas tactical knowledge is the situation-specific information accumulated through past experience that guides the DM about the selection of movements and their execution.

Another crucial perspective of DM for performance is that perception and decisions of action are strongly interwoven (Gréhaigne & Wallian, 2007). As such perception forms an important aspect of the DM process. With the perception of environmental information specific to the individual performance setting it is important that individuals improve their capacity to discriminate between informative and irrelevant cues (Pinder, Renshaw, & Davids, 2009).

Finally, Johnson (2006) suggested that a key feature of DM is that it is naturalistic, meaning that it is made by agents with a degree of task familiarity in the environment where they naturally encounter the decision. There also needs to be recognition that the majority of decisions in performance settings are dynamic and take place in real time, that is that individuals have to make decisions while in motion/performing. The implication of this is that real understanding of DM for performance can only be gained by understanding the real performance environment and associated constraints.

Theoretical models of decision-making

Within the psychology literature there are a number of consistent approaches that have been adopted that seek to explain the processes through which individuals make decisions. In particular, Classic Decision Making theory (CDM), Naturalistic Decision Making theories (NDM), and Ecological approaches to understanding DM have been particularly prominent (Cotterill & Discombe, 2016).

Classical DM theories view DM as a structured formulaic and highly cognitive process. This approach focuses on the accuracy of the decisions made and assumes that, in all DM settings, the correct decision outcomes can be identified through a process of rational analysis (Mascarenhas & Smith, 2011). The process of making an effective decision includes a clear identification of the problem, the generation of a range of possible solutions, critical evaluation of these options, and selection of a preferred solution (Beach & Lipshitz, 1993). There is a lot of support for this perspective in laboratory settings, usually when the speed of the decision is not important. However, applying this approach to understanding decisions made in time-pressured, complex, and dynamic situations across performance domains (e.g. sport, business, medicine) has been far more difficult (Balagué, Hristovski, & Vazquez, 2008; Beach & Lipshitz, 1993). Indeed, Montgomery, Lipshitz, and

Brehmer (2005) took this view a step further by suggesting that the CDM is not able to provide an explanation for decisions made involving "ill structured problems, uncertain dynamic environments, shifting, ill-defined or competing goals, action/feedback loops, time stress, high stakes, multiple players, organizational goals, and norms" (p. 2). A further criticism of this approach is that it fails to consider the expertise of the decision maker in the process (Mascarenhas & Smith, 2011). But while this approach might not adequately explain the process through which decisions are made during performance it can explain those decisions that are made when there is less time pressure (e.g. strategic decisions prior to the start of the performance).

Recent research has suggested that when performers seek to make decisions under pressure they are governed by goal driven heuristics which lead them to select the first solution that they think will be successful (Johnson & Raab, 2003; Payne, Bettman, & Johnson, 1993). Klein (1997) reported that experts across a number of domains (military, aviation, fire service, space exploration) make effective decisions, in their specific context, without lengthy consideration of all the options available to them. Building upon this view, Naturalistic Decision Making (NDM) has emerged as a framework through which greater understanding of the processes that expert decision makers engage in under time-pressured conditions can be achieved. There are a large number of different NDM models and theories that have been suggested (see Klein, 2008, for a review), however all of these NDM theories share some common principles. First, decisions are made by holistic evaluation of potential courses of action (Lipshitz, Klein, Orasanu, & Salas, 2001). Second, decisions are recognition based in that the decision maker relies on recognition of the situation and pattern matching courses of action rather than comparing alternatives (Klein & Calderwood, 1991). Third, decision makers adopt a satisfying criterion rather than search for an optimal solution (Klein & Calderwood, 1991), searching for a workable rather than optimal solution. More recent NDMs have also suggested that there is a combination of intuition and analysis in the making of decisions (Klein, 2008). Indeed, this NDM approach suggests that both intuition and analysis are important as a purely intuitive strategy relying solely on pattern matching generates flawed options and a purely deliberative and analytical strategy would be too slow. As a result, Klein (2008) suggested that the real process must be a combination of the two. In this approach the workload of the decision maker, task/situation familiarity, and level of experience appear to be crucial (Flin, Slaven, & Stewart, 1996; Klein, 1992; McMenamin, 1992). Recent evidence though has suggested that this NDM approach appears to be most applicable in explaining situations where time pressure and poorly defined goals dominate. These conditions are not necessarily true for performance, and as such this approach might not provide a full picture of DM in performance settings.

More recently ecological perspectives have been adopted in an attempt to understand DM for performance (Araújo, Davids, Bennett, Button, & Chapman, 2004; Araújo, Davids, & Serpa, 2005). This ecological approach stresses the lawful relations (e.g. relations based in the natural sciences) between any individual and the environment in which he or she functions (Turvey & Shaw, 1999; Turvey, Shaw, Reed, & Mace, 1981). Ecological psychology assumes a performer-environment, in which both components combine to form a whole ecosystem. Under this synergy, biology and physics come together with psychology to define a science at a new ecological scale (Turvey & Shaw, 1999). The ecological approach has predominantly developed using a Gibsonian approach, but other perspectives exist including those suggested by Brunswick, Barker, and Brofenner (Araújo et al., 2005). In this ecological approach, decisions are no longer just the result of internal cognitive processes but are self-organizing processes that emerge as a consequence of the individual's non-linear interaction with their environment. The perception and the action are viewed like an irreducible cycle (Araújo, Davids, & Hristovski, 2006). Specifically, that it is not necessary to follow a mental process to produce the required decisions; instead decisions emerge spontaneously out of the non-linear interaction of the elements under influence of personal, task, and environmental constraints that form each specific context (Araújo et al., 2004). The effectiveness of decisions are, therefore, clearly constrained by the level of attunement of each performer to the relevant information and the respective calibration of his/her movements to that information (Jacobs & Michaels, 2002). However, if this is true, the process through which the performer perceives the environment and identifies the correct energy flows is of paramount importance (see Jacobs & Michaels, 2002, for a review). Recent research has explored the applicability of this ecological approach in a range of performance-focus settings (Araújo et al., 2006; Hristovski, Davids, & Araújo, 2006).

Performers encounter may opportunities for action during performance. Due to the fast-paced nature of many performance domains these opportunities materialize and disappear in an instant. Also, throughout the duration of time in the performance domain the right course of action can change as the individual's action capabilities or the environment conditions change (Fajen, Riley, & Turvey, 2008). Fajen et al. further argue that the only explanation for this has to be a theory of direct perception (Gibson, 1986). Fajen and colleagues also argue that while there are a significant number of indirect perception theories that dominate they are only really successful in explaining failures in perception rather than successes. However, it might be that each of these three main approaches to understanding DM in sport (CDM, NDM, Ecological) actually focus on different types of decisions in the performance domain, so in a sense all explain some of the processes involved. As a result, a unifying theory of DM might offer a more complete explanation.

Factors influencing decision-making in the performance domain

The environment

There are a range of factors that impact upon DM ability and the appropriateness of a relevant course of action. Of these factors the environment has been highlighted as being particularly impactful, with numerous authors having argued that environmental characteristics exert a significant influence on the DM process

(Cotterill, 2014; Elbanna & Child, 2007). Often the specific 'context' in which the decision is made is highlighted as being crucial in understanding DM behaviour. The term 'context' refers to the characteristics of decision makers, decision-specific characteristics, and the features of the external environment (Elbanna & Child, 2007). One particular contextual factor with specific importance is the time pressure associated with making the decision.

Time pressures

There are several performance professions where decisions need to be taken rapidly, often within seconds. One such example of this would be Air Traffic Control (Joslyn & Hunt, 1998). Often these decisions need to take place in real time in response to changing environmental stimuli. This 'time pressure' is a significant factor in performance settings that can impact upon DM. Time pressure reduces a decision maker's flexibility by hampering their ability to generate alternative hypotheses and hypothesis-testing strategies (Macquet, 2009). Research in medical DM has also found that time pressure decreases the generation of diagnostic hypotheses (Dougherty & Hunter, 2003). Indeed, research in this area has reported that time pressure reduces hypothesis generation, as medical staff do not then have enough time to consider alternative hypotheses stored in their long-term memory (Alison et al., 2013). In less time-constrained environments the more time an individual has available to generate alternatives, the more alternatives they will be able to retrieve, as they are less cognitively constrained. To cope with the cognitive constraints associated with time pressure, it has been suggested that individuals may use heuristic processing (i.e. mental shortcuts to reduce information processing and cognitive load). Indeed, Croskerry (2002) reported that time-pressured doctors used representative heuristics when diagnosing patients, this in turn caused them to ignore important alternative symptoms.

Reviews of time pressure have identified a number of ways in which decision-making changes when time is limited including: a reduction in the quality of decision-making, more conservative options are encouraged; and a reduction in the propensity to take risks (Maule, Hockey, & Bdzola, 2000). Time pressure also results in a broader change in affective state (Maule et al., 2000). The resulting increase in stress levels can be a bit of a double-edged sword as both improved performance and performance degradation have been associated with increased stress.

Much of the research exploring decision-making under time pressure has reported a speed-accuracy trade-off (Young, Goodie, Hall, & Wu, 2012). This has been reported across performance domains including driving simulations (Hu & Stern, 1999), surgery (Zakay, 1985), and in military attack simulations (Ahituv, Igbaria, & Sella, 1998).

Nature of the task constraints

Another key factor influencing DM for performance is the nature of the DM context itself. Whether it is an individual decision (such as a tennis player), or a team decision (such as a military unit) the specific context will also impact upon the DM process. A number of professions have recognized the impact that the team element can have upon effective DM. Examples include aviation, the military, and medicine (Burke, Salas, Wilson-Donnelly, & Priest, 2004). As a result, seeking to develop DM at the team rather than the individual level is an important consideration in these performance environments. Finally, other factors highlighted as impacting upon DM in performance environments include the degree of ambiguity and risk present at the time that the relevant decision is taken (Lipshitz & Strauss, 1997). Shared mental models refer to an organized understanding of knowledge that is shared by a team. This sharing of knowledge is seen to enhance the accuracy of team member expectations of each other's needs (Banks & Millward, 2007). Cooke, Salas, Cannon-Bowers, and Stout (2000) suggested three different types of knowledge that can exist in mental models: declarative knowledge, procedural knowledge, and strategic knowledge. Declarative knowledge is seen as the facts, figures, rules, and concepts that exist relating to the task. An example of declarative knowledge could be the maximum number of players allowed to start for a team. Procedural knowledge refers to the steps, sequences, and actions that are needed to perform the task. In a sporting context this 'how' knowledge could relate to the process of scoring a goal in ice hockey. Finally, strategic knowledge is the overriding task strategies and knowledge of when to apply them. Relating back to the ice hockey example, this would refer to the different ways to achieve the scoring of a goal. For teams to effectively develop a shared mental model of the key elements of the task environment, changes in the knowledge of the individual team members occur.

Domain-specific knowledge

There has been limited research exploring the influence of domain-specific knowledge on decision-making in sports (Schläppi-Lienhard & Hossner, 2015). In NDM studies it has been shown how professional decision makers from different fields (fire fighting, nuclear power, aviation, military, medicine, paramedics) use their experience when making decisions (Schläppi-Lienhard & Hossner, 2015). Additionally skilled racquet sport athletes use their task-specific knowledge to estimate the likelihood of certain events in situational contexts (Alain & Proteau, 1977).

To date there is very little research that has specifically sought to assess the impact of domain-specific knowledge on decision-making performance (Schläppi-Lienhard & Hossner, 2015). One study that has explored domain-specific knowledge is that conducted by Schläppi-Lienhard and Hossner (2015) exploring decision-making in expert beach volleyball players. The study found that beach volleyball players reported similar gaze patterns that may be generalized as reception-set-approach-body direction-position in relation to the ball-shoulder-elbow-arm-wrist/hand-ball. This suggests an optimal gaze pattern in beach volleyball defence (Schläppi-Lienhard & Hossner, 2015). If this is true it would suggest you could then seek to 'train' optimal gaze behaviour strategies instead of waiting for them to organically emerge through engagement with the performance environment.

Implications for performance

Building upon the key points emerging from the existing body of knowledge a number of authors have suggested that developmental plans that explicitly target improvements in DM ability may be more beneficial than seeking to enhance DM simply by the accumulation of experience (Cotterill, 2014; Discombe & Cotterill, 2015; Mascarenhas & Smith, 2011). Also, as highlighted by McMorris (1998) playing 'real' or modified versions of games that prioritize DM in the performance environment might be beneficial. One such approach is 'Battlezone' training (Vickery, Dascombe, & Duffield, 2014), where small-sided games have been suggested as a way to develop decision-making, technical ability, and metabolic conditioning (Dellal et al., 2008).

Cotterill (2014) in seeking to present a coherent approach to the development of decision-making ability in the sport of cricket, highlighted three specific points at which interventions/training could take place: (1) Conscious cognitive (developing an understanding of past experience, tactical awareness, and the individual players' predispositions and tendencies; (2) Perception-action coupling (perceiving relevant cues and information); and (3) Abort and reset (responding to rapid changes in the environment). For further details see Figure 5.1.

This approach recognizes the fact that there are different aspects of DM in sport, and as a result a range of approaches might need to be adopted depending upon the

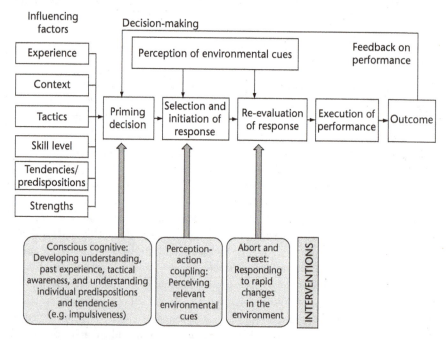

FIGURE 5.1 An integrated model for decision-making in cricket

Source: adapted from Cotterill, 2014.

demands of the sport. Crucially though, the task needs to be kept as ecologically valid as possible. For example, Davids, Renshaw, and Glazier (2005) highlighted the view that the removal of key information sources could impact upon transfer to the performance environment.

The use of video training has also been highlighted as an important way to develop exposure to relevant perceptual cues and knowledge about opposition athletes and their tactics (Araújo et al., 2005). This in turn can help in the explicit development of DM ability. In support of this approach, Baker et al. (2003) reported that players felt video training, organized training, and watching games on television helped them to develop their perceptual skills and that competition, video training, and organized training helped them to develop their DM skills, in essence using video as a substitute for direct experience. This approach is further supported by studies in a range of sports including squash (Abernethy, Wood, & Parks, 1999), table tennis (Raab, Masters, & Maxwell, 2005), and Australian rules football (Lorains, Ball, & MacMahon, 2013). Interestingly, Lorains et al. (2013) also reported that those athletes trained in above real time (video played faster than normal speed) improved performance earlier in the training intervention compared to those trained in normal speed (Lorains et al., 2013). This in particular offers significant potential for the future.

In line with research on stress exposure training (Driskell & Johnston, 1998), it has been suggested that 'time pressure exposure training' may be useful in policing and other performance domains (Joslyn & Hunt, 1998). Stress exposure training is designed to provide the decision maker with knowledge of the stress environment in order to identify and avoid performance errors. Time pressure exposure training could include information regarding the effect of time pressure on hypothesis generation and action prioritization. In addition, it could assist decision makers with behavioural and cognitive coping mechanisms to overcome any potentially maladaptive effects. Supporting this point, Salo and Allwood (2011), in their study on individual differences in police decision-making, concluded that training programmes should be attuned to individual needs to overcome barriers such as stress and burnout. This suggests that an awareness of individual differences in reacting to time pressure could be included in training.

Coaches could create exercises for the optimization of their athletes' gaze strategies. Also, athletes could be trained to focus on specific visual cues based on known opponent specifics simulated by the coach. Furthermore athletes could be provided with more tactical knowledge regarding certain situations and their probability of success in order to pre-specify superior reactions in advance of the upcoming rally (Schläppi-Lienhard & Hossner, 2015).

Summary

Making effective decisions is crucial for effective performance. As a result, an understanding of the processes underpinning the generation of these decisions is crucial to researchers and applied practitioners alike. There is an increasing body of literature that seeks to understand DM from a number of perspectives including classical DM, naturalistic, ecological, and intuitive approaches to decision-making. But, while each of these perspectives is useful a more integrated approach is required to really contextualize DM in performance domains.

Study questions

1. To what extent do ecological approaches to decision-making help to better understand the constraints that impact upon decision-making in sport?
2. In what ways could video-based training be used to enhance performer decision-making ability?
3. In what ways do time pressures impact upon the process of decision-making?

Further reading

Bar-Eli, M., Plessner, H., & Raab, M. (2011). *Judgement, decision-making and success in sport.* Oxford: Wiley.

This book provides an advanced consideration of current understanding and theoretical underpinning of decision-making in sporting contexts.

Hardman, D. (2009). *Judgment and decision making: Psychological perspectives.* Chichester: John Wiley & Sons.

This book provides a clear, concise, and up-to-date overview of the research in judgement and decision-making.

Vartanian, O., & Madel, D. R. (Eds.) (2011). *Neuroscience of decision making (Contemporary Topics in Cognitive Neuroscience).* Hove: Psychology Press.

This book presents individual chapters on a wide range of decision-making-focused topics from a neuroscience perspective.

6

THE ROLE OF EMOTION IN PERFORMANCE

Introduction

Performance can be a very emotional experience. Success can result in feelings of happiness and joy whilst failure can often result in disappointment, anger, and frustration. Many performance environments have been highlighted as having the potential to elicit intense emotional reactions in performers (Coombes, Janelle, & Duley, 2005). These emotional responses are generally characterized as a cognitive appraisal in response to an event that triggers a response (Frederickson, 2001).

Understanding emotions in relation to performance is important as these emotions have been suggested to influence attention, perception, motivation, motor control, and crucially performance (Uphill, Groom, & Jones, 2014). This chapter will seek to outline the nature of emotions and the emotional response. It will consider the relationship between emotion, cognition, and decision-making, and explore methods of emotional regulation. Finally, the chapter will explore challenge and threat state as a way to better understand emotional responses and the associated performance implications.

Defining emotion

There are three related, but distinct concepts that need to be considered when defining emotion: affect, emotion, and mood (Cotterill, 2012). Affect is often used at a general level to describe good and bad experiences (Vallerand & Blanchard, 2000). In general terms Lazarus (1999) proposed that emotion is a response to the meaning we attach to our interactions with the environment. Different emotional experiences influence our interactions with the environment in different ways. Emotions are seen as a short-term defuse state that emerges in response to a specific trigger.

Lazarus (2000) specifically defined emotions as a "phenomenon that is an organized psychophysiological reaction to on-going relationships with the environment, most often, but not always interpersonal or social" (p. 230). A second definition suggested by Fredrickson (2001) offers greater detail regarding the experience of emotion suggesting there is a consensus that an emotion is a cognitively appraised response to an event, either conscious or unconscious, which "triggers a cascade of response tendencies manifest across loosely coupled component systems, such as subjective experience, facial expression, cognitive processing and physiological changes" (p. 218).

Moods are described to be low-intensity diffuse feeling states that usually do not have a clear antecedent (Forgas, 1992), and are more enduring (Jones, 2012). They can be characterized as being relatively unstable short-term intra-individual changes (Tellegen, 1985). Lazarus (1991) defined moods as a "transient reaction to specific encounters with the environment, one that comes and goes depending on particular conditions" (p. 47). Emotions and moods differ in a number of specific ways. First the duration of both is highlighted as being different. Emotions are generally shorter (often lasting for seconds or minutes), whereas moods are longer (lasting in the region of hours or days). The onset of emotions is generally accepted to be much quicker with a much greater intensity. The antecedents for emotions are more specific and result in distinctive facial signals and physiological responses. Moods are less specific and do not necessarily result in easily identifiable responses. Moods can be important in their own right as it has been suggested that mood can be a predictor of performance outcomes (Beedie, Terry, & Lane, 2000).

Types of emotions

One of the main approaches to understanding emotions suggests that there are a discrete number of basic emotions that underlie our emotional experiences. Reeve (2005) in reviewing work on emotions highlighted between two and ten different types of emotions identified in the emotion-focused literature. Lazarus (2000) in his cognitive-motivational-relational theory (CMRT) of emotion identified 15 discrete emotions and also provided an insight into their potential functions and possible effects (an overview is presented in Table 6.1). In CMRT, emotions occur when events are appraised as having either a positive or negative significance for well-being (relational meaning) in relation to goals. Emotion is part of a changing person–environment relationship, and three components central to this process are motivation, appraisal, and coping. These combine and form core relational themes for each emotion that describes the transaction between the individual and environment.

A number of authors have identified a similar number of primary emotions. Lazarus (2000) highlighted the following as primary emotions: anger, anxiety, shame, guilt, hope, relief, happiness, and pride. These primary emotions were very similar to the seven emotions identified by Vallerand's (1983) review of emotions in sport (happiness, surprise, fear, anger, sadness, disgust/contempt, and interest).

TABLE 6.1 Emotions and their core relational themes

Emotion	Theme
Anger	A demeaning offence against me and mine
Anxiety	Facing uncertain, existential threat
Fright	An immediate, concrete, and overwhelming physical danger
Guilt	Having transgressed a moral imperative
Shame	Failing to live up to an ego-ideal
Sadness	Having experienced an irrevocable loss
Envy	Wanting what someone else has and feeling deprived of it but justified in having it
Jealousy	Resenting a third party for the loss or threat to another's affection or favour
Happiness	Making reasonable progress toward the realization of a goal
Pride	Enhancement of one's ego identity by taking credit for a valued object or achievement. Either one's own or that of someone or a group with whom one identifies
Relief	A distressing goal-incongruent condition that has changed for the better or gone away
Hope	Fearing the worst but yearning for better, and believing the improvement is possible
Love	Desiring or participating in affection, usually but not necessarily reciprocated
Gratitude	Appreciation for an altruistic gift that provides personal benefit
Compassion	Moved by another's suffering and wanting to help

Source: adapted from Lazarus (2000).

Despite differing views regarding the number of primary emotions in the literature there does appear to be five emotions that seem to represent a broad consensus among basic emotion researchers. These 'big five' emotions include anger, fear, sadness, disgust, and happiness. A range of cross-cultural studies conducted by Ekman (1999) appear to support the existence of these primary emotions within different countries and cultures. However, further work in this area suggests different languages and cultures do seem to differ in the number and categorization of their emotional terms. Also, the range of situations that trigger emotions vary across cultures. The fact that similar verbal labels are used across widely differing languages and cultures has also been used as evidence to support the existence of a discrete set of basic emotions. Scherer and Wallbott (1994) compared verbal labels for emotions in 37 countries and were able to translate the English terms for the seven emotions studied (anger, fear, sadness, joy, disgust, shame, and guilt) into each of the other languages.

There has historically been a tendency in the performance psychology literature to focus on negative emotion. Indeed, in the sport psychology literature there has been a significant focus on anxiety and anger, and a particular focus on anxiety in musical performance literature. Positive psychology however points to the equal prevalence and importance of positive emotions. Fredrickson (2005) described positive emotions as markers of optimal functioning and argues that cultivating positive emotions is a way to foster psychological growth. Fredrickson further suggested that positive emotions broaden the individual's thought-action repertoire and build enduring resources. This is at odds with a focus on negative emotions that reduce choices to fight or flight. This suggests that the performer should actively seek to encourage and promote positive emotional experiences and not just focus on the reduction of negative experiences.

Characteristics of the emotional response

Emotions are generally characterized by three specific responses:

1. Changes in behaviour;
2. Bodily responses (physiological);
3. Subjective experiences (feelings).

The majority of behavioural changes that occur when an emotional episode is taking place are well known and easily identifiable. For example, when someone is happy they laugh, when they are angry they shout, and when they are sad they become quiet and withdrawn. Facial expressions in particular characterize individual responses to specific emotional episodes. Behaviour and facial expressions communicate emotional feelings well, and as such can be manipulated to convey certain desired emotional responses (Cotterill, 2012).

Bodily responses to emotions are relatively automatic and have developed as an evolutionary response. Examples of bodily/physiological reactions include sweating when anxious and heart rate increasing when excited. Many of the body's responses are controlled by the autonomic nervous system (ANS). This system is composed of a network of nerve fibres that transmit signals to various organs, muscles, and glands. The ANS can be further divided into two sections: the sympathetic and parasympathetic nervous systems. The sympathetic nervous system specifically produces effects associated with arousal. These include the secretion of the hormone adrenalin that initiates and enhances sympathetic activity leading to changes such as accelerating heart rate, vasoconstriction (a constriction of blood vessels), increased respiration rate and depth, and reduced gastro-intestinal activity. The parasympathetic system tends to be in control during rest and usually has the opposite effects on the body to the sympathetic nervous system. Further details of both systems are provided in Table 6.2.

The feeling component of emotion is linked to self-awareness and consciousness. It is at this point that an interpretation of a positive or negative response to a stimulus takes place. The performer's appraisal of the event, not the event itself, determines their emotional responses (Roseman, Spindel, & Jose, 1990). Performers who are less prone to appraising a situation negatively are less likely to experience negative emotions. Similarly, performers who are more skilled at managing their emotions following appraisal of an event should experience fewer harmful effects of negative emotions than individuals who are less skilled at managing emotions (Hartel, Gough, & Hartel, 2008).

TABLE 6.2 Physiological changes governed by the autonomic nervous system

Parasympathetic	Sympathetic
• Constricts pupils	• Dilates pupils
• Stimulates salivation	• Inhibits salivation
• Inhibits heart	• Relaxes bronchi
• Constricts bronchi	• Accelerates heart
• Stimulates digestive activity	• Inhibits digestive activity
• Stimulates gallbladder	• Stimulates glucose release by liver
• Contracts bladder	• Secretion of epinephrine and norepinephrine from kidney
• Relaxes rectum	• Relaxed bladder
	• Contracts rectum

Parkinson (1994) suggested that emotional experience depends upon four separate factors: (1) appraisal of some external stimulus (generally seen as the most important factor, and highlighted by Lazarus, 1991); (2) reactions of the body (e.g. physiological arousal); (3) facial expressions (e.g. Strack, Martin, & Stepper, 1988); (4) action tendencies (e.g. preparing to advance in a threatening way when angry). Each of these factors was developed from earlier work on emotions including Lazarus (1991) for appraisal; James-Lange theory (Eysenck, 2004) for bodily reactions; Strack et al. (1988) for facial expressions; and Frijda, Kuipers, and ter Schure (1989) for action tendencies. Crucially it is important to note that these four factors are not seen as independent of each other.

Vallerand and Blanchard (2000) observed that emotions can determine action tendencies by leading a performer either towards, or away, from an object. They highlighted a link between the emotional episode and an overt behavioural response. For example, in soccer a player who loses the ball will either try harder to get the ball back, or will try and stay away from the ball to avoid making further errors. As a result, understanding how the individual reacts to an emotional episode is crucial to understand the impacts that emotions will have on performance.

Emotion and performance

There is a substantial body of research in psychology that has explored the impact that a discrete number of emotions can have on performance. In particular, anxiety and its relationship to performance has received a significant amount of attention (see Woodman & Hardy, 2001, for a review). Enhanced effort though might not be the desired response to an emotional episode as it can lead to a worse performance of motor skills (Masters & Maxwell, 2008). This in turn can result in disrupted cognitive and decision-making processes, and potentially result in a severe performance decrement such as choking (see Chapter 3).

Emotion and cognition

Positive and negative emotions appear to serve complementary cognitive functions. Negative emotions are most beneficial and adaptive in situations requiring immediate action, whereas the benefits of positive emotions – and the broader process of creative thinking – emerge over time (Fredrickson & Losada, 2005). Also, attention is influenced by emotion. Broadly, positive emotions broaden attention whereas negative emotions narrow attention (Fredrickson, 2001). Not only do positive emotions, such as amusement and contentment, encourage a broader focus of attention, they also manifest more creative thinking and approaches to problem solving (Fredrickson & Branigan, 2005). Arousal is proposed to narrow attention (Easterbrook, 1959), but the effect of high arousal emotions like anxiety on attention is not always so clear cut. This is supported by research showing that rather than simply narrowing their attentional field, anxious gymnasts (Moran, Byrne, & McGlade, 2002) and footballers (Wilson, Wood, & Vine, 2009) fixate their vision on threatening cues in the environment.

Emotion and decision-making

It is well established that emotion plays a key role in human social and economic decision-making (Heilman, Crişan, Houser, Miclea, & Miu, 2010). Lerner and Tiedens (2006) specifically explored the impact of anger on both judgement and decision-making. They suggested that the impact came not only from the valence/arousal component of the emotion but also from appraisal tendencies associated with that emotion. Building on this notion, Lerner and Tiedens developed an Appraisal-Tendency Framework (ATF) that suggests a specific emotion, such as anger, is associated with cognitive appraisals (e.g. someone else being responsible for the event causing the emotion, a sense of certainty about what happened, and a sense of ability to control the situation). These appraisals, in turn, have consequences for informational (affect as information), motivational (affect as motivator), and processing functions (affect as a spotlight). Lerner and Tiedens (2006) further highlighted that anger has specific impacts on outcome effects (e.g. anger leads to increased risk-taking and optimism) and process effects (e.g. anger-selective processing of information). They also suggested contrary to the generally held view the interesting idea that anger may in fact be a positive emotion, especially in the sense of motivating future behaviour. While the event causing anger may be negative, the effects on subsequent experience (feelings of increased energy and control) and thus behaviour may lead to the conclusion that anger (sometimes) can be a positive emotion, and have a functional utility.

This 'functional utility' of emotions is demonstrated across a range of studies where the degree to which the experience of an emotion is liked or disliked does not depend entirely on whether it is positive or negative but also on an appraisal of the situation in which it is experienced.

These is also evidence that suggests that performers can anticipate the emotional impact of potential future decisions using processes that involve the amygdala as well as the ventromedial prefrontal cortex (De Martino, Kumaran, Seymour, & Dolan, 2006; Weller, Levin, Shiv, & Bechara, 2007). This type of anticipation can be adaptive in that emotions such as anxiety or disgust have been shown to impair decision-making (Lerner, Small, & Loewenstein, 2004; Preston, Buchanan, Stansfield, & Bechara, 2007), even when physiological responses properly signal disadvantageous alternatives (Miu, Heilman, & Houser, 2008).

Emotional regulation

Emotion regulation refers to the processes by which individuals influence which emotions they have, when they have them, and how they experience and express them (Gross, 2002). Due to the fact emotions are multicomponent processes that unfold over time, emotion regulation involves changes in 'emotion dynamics' (Thompson, 1990), or the latency, rise time, magnitude, duration, and offset of responses in behavioural, experiential, or physiological domains. Emotion regulation also involves changes in how response components are interrelated as the emotion unfolds, such as when increases in physiological responding occur in the absence of overt behaviour (Gross, 2002).

Emotion can also have 'knock-on' effects on other aspects of cognitive functions, such as decision-making. The decision effects of emotion vary according to the way in which a person regulates the emotion experience (Heilman et al., 2010).

A number of recent studies (O'Doherty & Bossaerts, 2008; Rangel, Camerer, & Montague, 2008; Seymour & Dolan, 2008) suggest that the emotional impact of potential future decisions can be anticipated. This type of anticipation can be adaptive in that emotions such as anxiety or disgust have been shown to impair decision-making (Lerner et al., 2004; Preston et al., 2007), even when physiological responses properly signal disadvantageous alternatives (Miu et al., 2008). Two specific emotional regulation strategies have been extensively investigated over the past decade (Heilman et al., 2010): cognitive reappraisal and expressive suppression.

Cognitive reappraisal is an antecedent-focused emotional regulation strategy that alters the trajectory of emotional responses by changing the meaning of the situation.

Expressive suppression is a response-focused strategy that involves inhibiting behaviours (e.g. facial expressions, verbal utterances, gestures) associated with emotional responding (Gross & Thompson, 2007). Whereas both reappraisal and suppression decrease the expression of emotions, their effectiveness in decreasing the experience of emotion differs due to their timing with respect to the emotion-generating process. In particular, reappraisal and suppression effectively decrease the experience of positive emotions, but only the former is as effective in reducing the experience of negative emotions (Gross, 1998; Gross & Levenson, 1997). In addition, reappraisal diminishes emotion at an early stage and without the need for sustained effort over time, whereas suppression involves active efforts to inhibit prepotent emotional responses (Gross, 2002; Muraven, Tice, & Baumeister, 1998).

Challenge and threat

Challenge and threat interpretations have been suggested to represent the complex and simultaneous interplay of affective, cognitive, and physiological processes (Blascovich & Mendes, 2000). These states involve positive and negative feelings and emotions; and cognitively form what Lazarus (1991) described as 'core relational themes'. Physiologically these states refer to approach/avoidance or appetitive/aversive states.

The biopsychosocial model of challenge and threat (Blascovich, 2008) is a theoretical framework that explains variations in performance in situations where individuals are motivated to attain self-relevant goals (motivated performance situations; e.g. exam taking, acting on stage, and medical surgery). The challenge and threat process begins in a situation where the individual expects/is expected to perform. When performers are engaged in such tasks, they evaluate the demands of the task and whether they possess the necessary resources to cope effectively with those demands (Seery, 2011). Those performers who evaluate that they have sufficient resources to cope with the demands of a task (a challenge evaluation) tend to perform better than individuals who evaluate that they do not possess the required resources to meet the demands of the task (a threat evaluation; Seery, 2011). Empirical and predictive studies in psychology have shown that a challenge evaluation is typically associated with superior performance compared to a threat evaluation (e.g. Blascovich, Seery, Mugridge, Norris, & Weisbuch, 2004; Mendes, Blascovich, Hunter, Lickel, & Jost, 2007; Moore, Vine, Wilson, & Freeman, 2012; Seery, Weisbuch, Hetenyi, & Blascovich, 2010; Turner, Jones, Sheffield, & Cross, 2012). It has also been reported that challenge and threat evaluations can have a direct effect on the performance of both novel motor tasks and trained motor tasks under elevated pressure. Evaluating a task as more of a challenge (as opposed to a threat) has been associated with superior visual attentional control and performance (Vine, Freeman, Moore, Chandra-Ramanan, & Wilson, 2013). Empirical and predictive studies in psychology across a range of tasks and contexts have shown that a challenge state facilitates performance whereas a threat state hinders performance (Moore et al., 2012). For example, Blascovich and colleagues (2004) reported that baseball and softball players who displayed cardiovascular markers of challenge during a three-minute sport-relevant speech four to six months prior to the start of the season performed better during the subsequent season than players who displayed markers of threat.

A range of mechanisms have been suggested to explain how a challenge or threat state influences performance. A challenge state is said to be associated with both positive and negative emotions, whereas a threat state is associated with only negative emotions (Jones, Meijen, McCarthy, & Sheffield, 2009; Skinner & Brewer, 2004). Furthermore, emotions are proposed to be interpreted as facilitative for performance in a challenge state but debilitative in a threat state (Jones et al., 2009; Skinner & Brewer, 2004). It has been suggested that challenge states might well result in superior performance by promoting more favourable emotional responses (greater levels of positive emotions) and interpretation of emotions (more facilitative for performance; Moore et al., 2012). It has also been suggested that a challenge state may also be associated with more effective attentional control compared to a threat state (Blascovich et al., 2004; Jones et al., 2009; Skinner & Brewer, 2004).

Theory of challenge and threat states in athletes

The theory of challenge and threat states in athletes (TCTSA; Jones et al., 2009), has sought to build upon the biopsychosocial model of challenge and threat by integrating research on the appraisal, emotional response (intensity and direction), autonomic arousal, and performance consequences of competition. The broad basis for this theory is that a dichotomy exists between performers who perceive a competitive situation as a challenge (positively) and those who perceive it as a threat (negatively). This dichotomy is intuitively appealing because it supports the commonly held belief that some performers will rise to the demands of competition and perform well, while some fade and perform poorly.

The TCTSA (Jones et al., 2009) draws predominantly on the biopsychosocial model of challenge and threat (Blascovich & Mendes, 2000), the model of adaptive approaches to competition (Skinner & Brewer, 2004), and the control model of debilitative and facilitative competitive state anxiety (Jones, 1995) to understand the performers' responses to competition.

In this model appraisals are composed of three inter-related constructs, namely self-efficacy, perceived control, and goal orientation, all three of which determine a perceived challenge or threat state and a performer's consequential effort, attention, decision-making, and physical functioning. In essence, a perceived challenge state promotes energy efficiency through glucose delivery and culminates in successful performance, but a perceived threat state restricts blood flow to the muscles and brain which compromises the mobilization of attention and decision-making and results in less effective performance (Dienstbier 1989; Jones et al., 2009). The TCTSA (Jones et al., 2009) has a theoretical foundation that provides a potential framework for stress management to maximize performance (Turner & Jones, 2014). An applied strategy building upon this model would seek to promote self-efficacy, perceived control, and a goal-focused approach, with the overall aim being to promote a challenge state that motivates sport performance (Turner et al., 2013). It has also been suggested that a strategy that seeks to combine imagery with a "challenge strategy" (Turner & Jones, 2014) can be beneficial to performance.

Summary

It is important to recognize that the very nature of many performance environments means that it is highly likely that a range of positive and negative emotions will be experienced over time. Understanding the antecedents and characteristics of these responses enables performers to better cope with or channel the responses they experience, to maximize the potential for positive performance outcomes. In some performance domains some emotions are useful for performance. In others (such as surgery) all emotions can be a hindrance to performance. It is about understanding what the specific context is and what is required for success.

Study questions

1. To what extent do you feel that emotions are crucial to sports performance? Are some emotions more productive than others?
2. What strategies might you use to reduce the intensity of emotions experienced?
3. How can the theory of challenge and threat states in athletes be used to underpin the development and preparation of highly effective performers?

Further reading

Jones, G. (2012). Emotion regulation and performance. In S. M. Murphy (Ed.), *The Oxford handbook of sport and performance psychology*. Oxford: Oxford University Press.
A very good overview of emotions and emotional regulation. The chapter in particular explores the theoretical basis for explaining emotion regulation.
Jones, M. V., Meijen, C., McCarthy, P. J., & Sheffield, D. (2009). A theory of challenge and threat states in athletes. *International Review of Sport and Exercise Psychology, 2*, 161–180.
This article outlines the theory of challenge and threat states in athletes, presenting in much greater detail the components of the theory and the implications for performance.

7

RESILIENCE

Introduction

In the last 10–15 years there has been an increasing interest in resilience across a range of performance domains. From a performance perspective, researchers and practitioners are interested in understanding what resilience is, the factors that predict resilience, and how performers can become more resilient. Individuals who perform at a reasonably high level for an extended period of time will likely experience a number of stressors, adversities, and failures (Galli & Gonzalez, 2015; Mellalieu, Neil, Hanton, & Fletcher, 2009; Tamminen, Holt, & Neely, 2013). It is the ability of the performer to cope with these setbacks that increasingly appears to be an important predictor of future performance success.

While there has been an increasing focus on psychological resilience in the literature there has also been a growth in interest in a range of related and often overlapping concepts including: hardiness, grit, and mental toughness.

This chapter will seek to clarify what resilience is. It will also seek to clarify the link between resilience and related terms such as mental toughness, hardiness, and grit. The chapter will also explore the concepts of optimism and pessimism and consider the implications for performance.

What is resilience?

A number of definitions of psychological resilience have been suggested in the literature. Best, Garmezy, and Masten (1990) suggested that resilience is "the process of, capacity for, or outcome of successful adaptation despite challenging or threatening circumstances" (p. 426). This definition suggests three ways that resilience has been conceptualized (Reich, Zautra, & Hall, 2010): (i) as a positive outcome (i.e. something people 'do' or 'achieve'); (ii) as an innate part of individuals' personality (i.e. something people 'have'); or (iii) as a process (i.e. a capacity developed over time as people interact with their environment).

Psychological resilience has also been described as "the role of mental processes and behaviour in promoting personal assets and protecting an individual from the potential negative effect of stressors" (Fletcher & Sarkar, 2012a, p. 675). More recently psychological resilience has been suggested to be an important phenomenon that seeks to provide an explanation how individuals can positively adapt to adverse events (Morgan, Fletcher, & Sarkar, 2015). Indeed, the ability for performers to withstand stressors has been highlighted to be a prerequisite for performance excellence (Hardy, Jones, & Gould, 1996).

In seeking to understand performer perceptions and experiences of resilience Galli and Vealey (2008) interviewed ten performers from across eight different sports. The performers reported that positive adaptation occurred gradually and often required numerous shifts of thought. Moreover, the findings suggested that the resilience process operated over time and involved a variety of factors including personal resources and sociocultural influences. In a similar study, Fletcher and Sarkar (2012b) interviewed 12 Olympic champions in an attempt to understand the relationship between psychological resilience and optimal sport performance. The results suggested that a number of psychological factors worked to 'protect' high-level performers from negative stressors. Specifically: relating to a positive personality, motivation, confidence, focus, and perceived social support were suggested to influence the individual's challenge appraisal and meta-cognitions. These processes promoted facilitative responses that preceded higher levels of performance.

Adversity

The concept of resilience is often seen as being inextricably linked to the concept of adversity. Luthar and Cicchetti (2000) defined adversity as typically encompassing "negative life circumstances that are known to be statistically associated with adjustment difficulties" (p. 858). Collins and MacNamara (2012) speculated that talented youth performers can often benefit from, or even need, a variety of challenges to facilitate eventual adult performance; or, as they summarized in the title of their article: "Talent Needs Trauma" (p. 907). This ability to cope with adversity appears to be a key factor in both determining and predicting future successful performance outcomes. Resilience is cited as a key factor in determining how well individuals cope with setbacks and challenges grouped under adversity. There is also a view in the literature that adversity has unnecessarily been labelled as a negative phenomenon, whereas it can be a positive one. Particularly as it offers the opportunity for the performer to develop and grow in response to the challenges faced (Howells & Fletcher, 2015).

Factors influencing resilience

Despite some progress in the study of resilience, ambiguity in its definition and conceptualization have to date limited clear application in the performance domain

(Fletcher & Sarkar, 2013). A number of authors have highlighted difficulties associated with attempts to operationalize and measure resilience in sport and non-sport settings (e.g. Atkinson, Martin, & Rankin, 2009; Fletcher & Sarkar, 2013; Sarkar & Fletcher, 2013; Windle, 2011). Also, resilience may be correlated with other related psychological constructs such as coping (Campbell-Sills, Cohan, & Stein, 2006; Leipold & Greve, 2009; Rutter, 2012), hardiness (Howe, Smajdor, & Stokl, 2012; Windle, 2011), mental toughness (Gucciardi & Gordon, 2009), and post-traumatic growth (Westphal & Bonanno, 2007).

One way in which the impact of resilience has been conceptualized relates to explanatory style. Two significant studies have explored the effect of explanatory style (i.e. optimistic vs pessimistic) on performance following failure. Seligman, Nolen-Hoeksema, Thornton, and Thornton (1990) manipulated failure in a sample of 33 university swimmers by falsely notifying them that their time on a time trial in their best event was 1.5–5 seconds (depending on the event) slower than their actual time. All swimmers swam a second trial 30 minutes later. The results demonstrated that swimmers with an optimistic explanatory style swam a time that was at least as fast on a second trial as their actual time on the first. Martin-Krumm, Sarrazin, Peterson, and Famose (2003) further extended this research by considering the factors that have the potential to mediate the relationship between performance and explanatory style in high school students who had experienced failure on a basketball dribbling task. Failure in this context was manipulated by telling the students that they did not perform well on the task compared to other students. Participants with an optimistic explanatory style performed better on the second trial than the first, and those with a pessimistic style did not improve their performance. In this study, the effect of explanatory style on basketball dribbling performance after failure was mediated by state anxiety (an indicator of stress) and by success expectations. The presence of an optimistic style was positively correlated to expectations for success before the second trial, and lower state anxiety that in turn was positively related to dribbling improvement. This suggests that developing an optimistic explanatory style could help to facilitate more resilient appraisals.

Implications for performance

In seeking to enhance resilience a range of training programmes have been designed and implemented across a range of performance domains including: educational settings (Boniwell & Ryan, 2012; McGrath & Noble, 2003); the military (Reivich, Seligman, & McBride, 2011); and in sport (Schinke & Jerome, 2002).

One example of a resilience development programme within the educational domain is the Bounce Back and Thrive! Programme (McGrath & Noble, 2003). This programme for classroom resiliency focuses on developing key competencies such as responsible decision-making, social awareness, relationship skills, and self-management to help students overcome sadness, frustrations, and hard times during development. This has in turn been suggested to help students to cope more effectively.

From a military perspective the programme designed and implemented for the United States (US) Army offers a specific example. Researchers in the military domain have been interested in the influence of resilience on negative outcomes for soldiers such as experiencing post-traumatic stress episodes (see Hammermeister, Pickering, McGraw, & Ohlson, 2012 for a review). As a result, the US Army developed a Master Resilience Training (MRT) programme as part of the Comprehensive Soldier Fitness Performance and Resilience Enhancement Programme (CSF-PREP, now CSF2 for Comprehensive Soldier and Family Fitness; Reivich et al., 2011). The MRT programme is composed of four 'modules' that are designed to build and enhance resilience for soldiers on the programme. The first module focuses on core competencies related to resilience, such as self-regulation and optimism; with the second module focusing on developing mental toughness through cognition-based activities such as identifying negative thoughts and problem solving. The third and fourth modules seek to strengthen individual character strengths and to enhance social relationships. The MRT modules are supported by a range of evidence that cites the importance of developing individual characteristics and strong social relationships in structured environments with at-risk children (Best et al., 1990; Werner & Smith, 1992).

In the sports performance domain one specific example of a resilience development programme is that developed by Schinke and Jerome (2002); based on Seligman's (1991) learned helplessness framework. The programme focused on developing three general optimism skills in national team sports performers: evaluating personal assumptions (e.g. the typical thoughts that performers bring to a situation), disputing negative thoughts (e.g. becoming aware of negative thinking and using positive self-talk to overcome it), and decatastrophizing (e.g. trying to find optimism despite a setback). Teaching and fostering optimism is important as it has been suggested to be an important building block for resilience (Martin-Krumm et al., 2003; Seligman et al., 1990), which would appear to make optimism a needed skill in building resilience. Schinke and Jerome's preliminary data on the effectiveness of teaching optimism in national team sports performers reported that 16 of the 20 performers achieved major world championship medals for the first time post involvement in the programme.

A number of key principles/recommendations can be drawn from these specific development programme examples. Intervention programmes should be designed to develop protective factors and develop competencies, including: optimism, problem-solving skills, self-regulation skills, positive self-view, and achievement goals in socially supportive environments (e.g. Best et al., 1990; Galli & Vealey, 2008; Werner & Smith, 1992). Once these protective factors are developed, practitioners can simulate adversity for performers in a caring and safe environment and work with them to develop and practice adaptive responses. Fletcher and Sarkar (2012a) have suggested a number of specific steps to develop resilience. These include: develop a positive personality, optimize motivation, strengthen confidence, maintain focus, recognize the availability of social and support. Fletcher and Sarkar (2012b) further suggested six 'top tips' for developing resilience for sustained performance. These included: view setbacks as an opportunity for mastery and growth; be proactive in your own personal development; be sensitive to different types of motivation; build your confidence from multiple sources; focus on what you can control; and take specific steps to obtain the support you need.

Mental toughness

Over the last 20 years there has been an ever-increasing focus on the concept of mental toughness across a range of performance domains. Mental toughness is a term that has been used to describe the ability of performers to continue to strive toward and achieve their goals in psychological circumstances where others fail (Hardy, Bell, & Beattie, 2013). The term has historically been a heavily used 'lay' term, but there have been attempts over the last decade to try and develop a more rigorous conceptualization. There has been much disagreement in the literature regarding the conceptualization and measurement of mental toughness; though there does appear to be a degree of consensus among mental toughness academics that mental toughness is a dispositional construct that allows individuals to deal with obstacles, distractions, pressure, and adversity from a wide range of stressors (Clough & Strycharczyk, 2012; Gucciardi & Gordon, 2011; Jones, Hanton, & Connaughton, 2002; Hardy et al., 2013). Most conceptualizations of mental toughness are multi-dimensional in nature and focus on some collection of attitudes, cognitions, emotions, and values that are suggested to enable performers to behave in such a way as to achieve their goals in the face of challenges and adversity. There are though different perceptions about what these characteristics are. For Jones et al. (2002), these characteristics are confidence, determination, focus, and perceived control. For Gucciardi, Gordon, and Dimmock (2009), the key characteristics are thriving through challenge, sport awareness, tough attitude, and desire for success. For Clough and Strycharczyk (2012), the core characteristics are challenge appraisals, perceived control, commitment, and confidence. As a result, there is currently a lack of real consensus regarding what the specific characteristics of mental toughness are. It is also unclear how mental toughness fits with other similar concepts such as hardiness, coping with adversity, grit, and resilience.

Across a range of performance domains mental toughness is suggested to facilitate thriving in challenging, adverse, and pressure situations (Bull, Shambrook, James, & Brooks, 2005). It has also been reported to predict how successfully performers cope with performance-based stressors (Nicholls, Levy, Polman, & Crust, 2011). Also, there is a suggestion that the enhancement of mental toughness at an early age is an important factor in the development of future performance (Bell, Hardy, & Beattie, 2013; Gucciardi & Jones, 2012).

Hardiness

One way to achieve greater resilience, according to Bonanno (2004), is to develop what Kobasa (1979) conceptualized as hardiness. Hardiness has been described as a personality style that can help an individual to cope, withstand, and actively engage in transformational coping when faced with stressful events (Quick, Wright, Adkins, Nelson, & Quick, 2013). Hardiness is described to be the presence of three resilient attitudes: commitment, control, and challenge (Maddi, Harvey, Khoshaba, Lu, Persico, & Brow, 2006). *Commitment* is described as the tendency to involve oneself in a task or situation; *control* is the tendency to feel and act as if oneself is influential within the specific context; and *challenge* is suggested to be the belief that change rather than stability is normal in life and that change offers the opportunity to grow rather than a threat to security (Kobasa, Maddi, & Khan, 1982). As a result, it is proposed that as this personality style develops it forms a pathway for resilience in stressful environments (Maddi, 2006).

Hardiness has also been suggested to be important because it can act as a buffer to major life stressors (Maddi et al., 2006). High levels of hardiness have been associated with lower psychological distress and higher quality of life (Hoge, Austin, & Pollack, 2007). Performers who are high in hardiness have been described as having increased commitment, sense of control, and belief that change is a good thing (Johnsen, Eid, Pallesen, Bartone, & Nissestad, 2009). Hardiness has also been associated with resilience, good health, and good performance under a range of stressful conditions and has also been suggested to be a potentially valuable personality style for highly demanding situations and occupations (Bartone, Roland, Picano, & Williams, 2008). Previous psychological research has established hardiness as a dispositional factor in preserving and enhancing performance, and physical and mental health despite stressful circumstances (Maddi et al., 2006). In the field of sports performance few studies have examined the effect of hardiness on sport performance (e.g. Golby & Sheard, 2004; Maddi & Hess, 1992). However, the few studies that have done suggest positive links to performance. Finally, hardiness has also been suggested to be an important factor in influencing recovery and rehabilitation from injury (Salim, Wadey, & Diss, 2016; Wadey, Evans, Hanton, & Neil, 2012).

Grit

Another related personality trait that has been of interest in recent times is the psychological construct of grit. Grit has been described within the extant literature as trait-level perseverance and passion toward long-term goals (Duckworth, Peterson, Matthews, & Kelly, 2007). According to this description, grit entails working obstinately toward challenges while sustaining effort and interest in the activity over years in spite of disappointment, hardship, and plateaus (Duckworth et al., 2007). Although certain performers may change goals and the right direction forward in the wake of disappointment or boredom, gritty performers possess the fortitude to continually work towards their goal(s) even without immediate feedback or recognition. As a construct, grit is suggested to predict perseverance and achievement over and beyond the measure of talent. This suggests that grit may differentiate successful from less successful performers. Duckworth and

Quinn (2009) explored the ability of grit to differentiate individuals' retention in specific programmes, through multiple studies with varying populations. Participants who demonstrated higher levels of grit were more likely to pursue further education (Duckworth & Quinn, 2009), less likely to withdraw from military training programmes (Duckworth & Quinn, 2009; Eskreis-Winkler, Shulman, Beal, & Duckworth, 2014), more likely to keep their jobs (Eskreis-Winkler et al., 2014), and more likely to stay married (Eskreis-Winkler et al., 2014). Also, it has been reported that individuals with higher reported levels of grit engaged in more deliberate practice compared to lower scoring individuals (Duckworth, Kirby, Tsukayama, Berstein, & Ericsson, 2011). All of this suggests that grit has the potential to directly impact upon performance by moderating commitment to deliberate practice. Recent research has also highlighted a link between grit, sport-specific engagement, and perceptual-cognitive expertise (Larkin, O'Connor, & Williams, 2016).

Optimism and pessimism

An individual's general outlook (optimistic or pessimistic) has been highlighted as being important as it can have an impact on accomplishment, health, and well-being (Carver, Scheier, & Segerstrom, 2010; Forgeard & Seligman, 2012). Carver and Scheier (2001) described those individuals with a positive outlook (optimists) as those who expect good experiences in the future, and those with a negative outlook (pessimists) as those who expect bad experiences. Optimism is a cognitive construct (expectancies regarding future outcomes) that also relates to motivation: optimistic people exert effort, whereas pessimistic people disengage from effort (Carver & Schier, 2014).

Individuals develop explanatory styles that are methods of interpreting both positive and negative events (Buchanan & Seligman, 1995). Generally speaking, dispositional optimists are people who have positive expectations for their future (He, Cao, Feng, Guan, & Peng, 2013; Zhao, Huang, Li, Zhao, & Peng, 2015). In recent decades, many researchers have discovered that dispositional optimism is a protective factor for general mental health.

Optimism has mainly been analysed from two theoretical perspectives. First, there is the dispositional theory proposed by Scheier and Carver (1985), which focuses on the expectations that performers have for the events that can happen to them. In this sense, a performer with favourable expectations will increase his or her effort to achieve a goal (García & Díaz, 2010). In this model, optimism and pessimism are generalized expectations, considered to be stable dispositions, or in other words, traits (Ferrando, Chico, & Tous, 2002). Second, optimism has also been studied using the theory of explanatory style, which was developed by Abramson, Seligman, and Teasdale (1978) and has its origins in attribution theory (Weiner et al., 1971). The explanatory styles in this approach refer to the way performers explain what happens to them (Isaacowitz, 2005; Shapcott, Bloom, Johnston, Loughead, & Delaney, 2007). The performer's way of explaining their own experiences demonstrates an explanatory style that, from a theoretical point of view, has three fundamental dimensions: permanence, pervasiveness, and personalization (Abramson et al., 1978; Seligman, 2004).

Dispositional optimism and pessimism (Scheier & Carver, 1987) are typically assessed by asking individuals whether they expect future outcomes to be beneficial or negative (Scheier & Carver, 1992). It is suggested that individuals higher in dispositional optimism cope better in pressure situations because of greater psychological adjustment (Scheier & Carver, 1985). Also, performers with an optimistic explanatory style when facing adversity are more likely to view it as a challenge to be overcome (Peterson, 2000) and develop more confidence for future adversity (Seligman, 1991). Individuals high in optimism have positive expectancies and believe they have control over their future (Scheier & Carver, 1992; Scheier, Carver, & Bridges, 2001). Unlike hardiness, which can be developed at any time throughout life, optimism is typically seen as a stable personality trait that is developed during childhood (Scheier & Carver, 1992; Seligman, 1991). Optimism has been primarily studied in relation to its effect on health and well-being. For example, optimistic individuals report higher overall quality of life and satisfaction, as well as a more adaptive coping style, as compared to pessimistic individuals (Harju & Bolen, 1998; Hatchett & Park, 2004). The link between optimism and adaptive coping has also been supported in performers (Grove & Heard, 1997).

Summary

The ability to cope with challenges, setbacks, and adversity is a core aspect of performance. The nature of the environment demands an ability to cope with adversity for longevity of success. There have been significant advances in this area of psychology in recent years although a greater understanding of how resilience, mental toughness, hardiness, and grit co-exist or relate to each other is required to better understand the best way to cope with these emergent challenges.

Study questions

1. To what extent do you feel that resilience (coping with adversity) can be taught/developed rather than emerging in response to the experience of adversity?
2. In what way do the concept of grit, hardiness, mental toughness, and resilience relate to each other?
3. How important do you feel having an optimistic view of the future is to effective performance under pressure?

Further reading

Fletcher, D., & Sarkar, M. (2013). Psychological resilience: A review and critique of definitions, concepts, and theory. *European Psychologist, 18*, 12–23.

This article provides an in-depth overview of the concept of resilience, its key features, and supporting theoretical frameworks.

Gucciardi, D. F., & Gordon, S. (2011). *Mental toughness in sport: Developments in research and theory*. Abingdon: Routledge.

The book provides a comprehensive overview of the concept of mental toughness, its development, and key challenges in its conceptualization.

8

AGEING AND EXPERIENCE

Introduction

As individuals age both physical and psychological performances suffer. For many this decline begins in the mid to late twenties and continues as a steady decline through until around the age of 60. After this point this decline becomes more severe. However, with this being the case how is it that some top-level performers in many sports and performance domains appear to be able to buck this trend, and to continue to be successful with their advancing years?

Much of the existing literature exploring age-related decline (e.g. Bortz & Bortz, 1996) suggests an inevitable decline following 'peak performance' but with little attention given to how long the period of peak performance lasts. There also appears to have been a shift in the associated timescale in recent years. Research studies focused on sports performance for example have shown that performance in skilled sports tasks can be maintained at a much better rate than was previously the case (Baker, Koz, Kung, Fraser-Thomas, & Schorer, 2012). While this is encouraging for the longevity of performers at the highest level there has been little investigation of the length of time performers can aspire to remain at the top of their game (Baker et al., 2012).

The amount of time it takes to become an expert can vary depending on the discipline and complexity of the task; the age at which people achieve expertise will also vary based upon the activity. For some elite performers maturation occurs 'early' and peak performance may be attained in the late teens. By contrast 'late' maturers will not reach peak performance capacity until their mid–late twenties. Regardless of the age that peak performance is attained most elite performers show signs of decline in their overall physical and psychological performance in their early thirties (Faulkner, Davis, Mendias, & Brooks, 2008). Despite this some very late maturers and exceptionally gifted performers can still outperform much younger competitors at an elite level of performance up to 40 years of age even though they are demonstrating a decrease in their own overall performance levels (Faulkner et al., 2008).

For explosive activities, such as those that depend more heavily on reaction time and raw power (e.g. sprinting) performers consistently peak in their early twenties. For sports like golf and baseball that are more cognitive in nature peak performance occurs in the late twenties or early thirties (Horton, Baker, & Schorer, 2008). For activities that rely more heavily on complex motor skills the window of peak performance is generally later in life, and consists of a longer time frame (Horton et al., 2008). But with the acknowledged decrease in physical and psychological performance how is it that some performers can maintain higher levels of performance for longer? Is it that they are not declining (in absolute terms) at the same rate as others, or are there other mediating factors? This chapter will explore factors that determine career length in performance domains, and will seek to clarify the process by which physical and psychological decline takes place. The chapter will also explore the impact that expertise and accumulated experience can have, and also consider the implications for performance.

Career length

A number of authors across a range of performance domains have sought to explore and understand performance across the lifespan. Simonton (1999) for example, conducted research exploring lifespan creative outputs in the arts and sciences. However, in non-sporting domains the way career length is defined can be problematic. For example, Simonton (1997) described career length to be the length of time an individual has been making an active contribution to their domain. This definition suggests that individual performance (productivity) achieves a minimum standard rather than achieving higher levels of performance.

There has been limited research to date exploring career length in sport, and the length of time performers can aspire to be at 'the top of their game' (Baker et al., 2012). Of those studies, even fewer have focused on skill acquisition, and lifespan development. One exception to this is Abrams, Barnes, and Clement (2008) who did explore the performance statistics of college basketball players to determine the extent to which they predicted career length in the National Basketball Association (NBA). These results predicted length of career for some basketball positions (e.g. guards and forwards) but not for others (e.g. centres). Baker et al. (2012) explored career lengths in baseball, basketball, American football, and ice hockey. Their results, contrary to the findings of Abrams et al. (2008), reported no differences in career length across positions in basketball. What they did find though is that the players with the longer careers had better levels of performance. Ice hockey reported a similar outcome, in terms of no differences between positions, but longer careers being attributed to better performance over time. Significant position differences were reported in American football, with quarterback and defensive skill positions more likely to have longer careers than offensive skill positions or defensive linemen.

Baseball also reinforced this trend of better performance existing amongst those with longer careers. These findings suggest that the key factor influencing career length in sport (excluding confounding variables such as injury) is the maintenance of a high level of performance. As such, understanding the decline that takes place, and factors that mediate this effect (at least in the short-term) is crucial to be able to extend career-length at the elite level. Also, there is the potential for the factors that contribute to performance to vary in their influence over time. Early physical/physiological advantages are then complemented by the development of expertise through the accumulation of knowledge and expertise.

Deterioration due to ageing

Cognitive decline

There is little age-associated decline in some mental functions – such as verbal ability, some numerical abilities, and general knowledge. However, other mental functions such as memory, executive functions, processing speed, and reasoning (so-called 'fluid' mental abilities) do appear to decline with advancing age (Deary et al., 2009). A slowing of the speed of information processing appears to account for a substantial proportion of age-associated decline in all affected cognitive domains, and this slowing has begun by the time many individuals enter their thirties (Der & Deary, 2006).

While there have been many reports over the last 100 years of age-related difference in cognitive functioning, there is still disagreement about the age at which cognitive decline begins (Salthouse, 2009). One school of thought suggests that age-related cognitive decline begins relatively early in adulthood. The measures used to support this view are the age trends in a variety of neurobiological variables that can be assumed to be related to cognitive functioning. Among the variables that have been found to exhibit nearly continuous age-related declines in cross-sectional comparisons beginning when adults are in their mid twenties are: measures of regional brain volume (Allen, Burss, Brown, & Damasio 2005; Fotenos, Snyder, Girton, Morris, & Buckner, 2005; Pieperhoff et al., 2008); myelin integrity (Hsu et al., 2008; Sullivan & Pfefferbaum, 2006); cortical thickness (Magnotta et al., 1999; Salat et al., 2004); serotonin receptor binding (Sheline, Mintun, Moerlein, & Snyder, 2002); striatal dopamine binding (Erixon-Lindroth et al., 2005; Volkow et al., 2000); accumulation of neurofibrillary tangles (Del Tredici & Braak, 2008), and the concentrations of various brain metabolites (Kadota, Horinouchi, & Kuroda, 2001).

This cognitive decline over time appears to be supported by changes in mean data relating to IQ (Intelligence Quotient) scores across different age groups. The decline in IQ scores is reported to be just over one standard deviation (or 16 points) from the age of 25 to 65 (Horton et al., 2008). Overall, normal ageing is reported to take a toll on the speed and efficiency of cognitive, perceptional, and psychomotor functions (Krampe & Charness, 2006). This age-based neural decline has also been suggested to explain differences in decision-making ability. While it is generally agreed that the accumulation of experience can help experts to make successful decisions earlier, it is suggested that there is a tipping point at which older adults are unable to compensate for their age-based neural decline by using their decision-making experience (Worthy, Gorlick, Pacheco, Schnyer, & Maddox, 2011).

Physical/physiological decline

As well as experiencing cognitive decline with age, there is also a well-established view that physical/physiological performance capacity also decreases. For example, there is a well-documented age-related decline in physical fitness levels (Weston, Castagna, Impellizzeri, Rampinini, & Breivik, 2010). Motor perform-ance, which can be evaluated by force control capabilities, is known to reduce in adults as they age (Lee et al., 2015). Force control refers to a motor skill governed by the neuromuscular system in activating and coordinating muscles and limbs (Wise & Shadmehr, 2002). Bortz and Bortz (1996) proposed that 0.5 per cent per year after peak performance represented a general biomarker of the ageing process. This number was based on a range of age-related outcomes including the rate of DNA repair, fingernail growth, and various physiological systems (Horton, Baker, & Wier, 2015).

Endurance performance in running events decreases with age in a curvilinear fashion. In general, peak endurance running performance is maintained until roughly 35 years of age, followed by a modest decrease until 50–60 years of age (Tanaka & Seals, 2003), with progressively steeper reductions after that. The overall reduction in peak performance with age tends to be greater in sprint rather than endurance events (Tanaka & Seals, 2008). These findings are also supported in swimming, with the rates of performance decline with age being greater in the long duration rather than the shorter duration distances. Also, there appear to be gender differences in this decline with female swimmers experiencing a greater decline in the shorter duration events than males (Donato et al., 2003).

In sports such as golf, performers 'peak' later than performers in more aerobically based sports. This suggests that there is a reduced reliance on physical/physiological condition, and as such performance is less constrained by biological systems and more reliant on acquired skills (Baker, Deakin, Horton, & Pearce, 2006). As a result, performance can be maintained with advancing age to a greater extent in golf compared with sports such as running, swimming, and rowing (Baker et al., 2006). It has also been suggested the sports involving skills with a requirement for a finer degree of motor control need a longer period of skill acquisition, and as a result might be more resilient to age-related decline than physiological capacities (Baker et al., 2006).

There is also an interesting interaction between the environment, the physical performance, and skills of the performer. For example, Faulkner et al. (2008) reported that in elite basketball the ability to shoot is not lost at least prior to the age of 40. This finding though has also been viewed in the free-throw perform-ances of older vs younger players, and the stability of older player shooting performance over time. In game-play situations where the older player is being guarded by younger players the 40-year-old player will find it more difficult to get themselves free for a high quality shot. As a result, overall successful performance reduces even though skill execution remains good.

Enhanced knowledge and expertise

It is widely acknowledged that the accumulation of knowledge and expertise can have a significantly positive impact upon performance. In terms of decision-making performance experts are seen to have a number of advantages over less expert opponents. Indeed, domain knowledge is seen as an important aspect of the cognitive system, and a key determinant of cognitive performance (Hambrick & Engle, 2002). Domain knowledge is seen as a modifiable component of the cognitive system. It emerges from the psychological 'knowledge is power' principle, that suggests that it is the accumulation of knowledge rather than fixed intelligence or thinking factors that underpin success (Feigenbaum, 1989).

Domain knowledge is seen as the primary determinant of success in cognitive endeavours, whereas 'basic' cognitive abilities play a less important role. It would appear that this is a good place to start in seeking to understand how high-level performers appear to resist the relentless decline with age.

Also, there is evidence to suggest that with advancing age performers can become 'smarter' when it comes to the volume and type of practice undertaken. So, while the training patterns of older performers differ to younger performers (i.e. training for fewer hours per week) the level of training is substantial enough to maintain superior performance levels (Starkes, Weir, Singh, Hodges, & Kerr, 1999; Wier, Kerr, Hodges, McKay, & Starkes, 2002). Indeed, while older performers practice for fewer hours per week they train 'smarter' in the fact that they focus on the most important aspects of practice (Horton et al., 2015). This perspective is consistent with Baltes and Baltes (1990) who suggested that when resources are limited the individual copes by using a combination of selection (i.e. a conscious choice of where they invest resources), optimization (i.e. making choices that optimize performance), and compensation (i.e. adapting to accommodate for restrictions).

Maintaining performance levels with ageing

In the literature there are three main explanations for how expert performers can maintain superior performance in the face of declining abilities: (1) preserved differentiation, (2) compensation, and (3) selective maintenance (Horton et al., 2008; Horton et al., 2015). The preserved differentiation account is a genetic explanation of superior performance. It suggests that the ultimate level of achievement is constrained by innate capabilities. According to this perspective experts have always had superior abilities and an innate capacity, and these abilities are fixed. Also, these capacities facilitate higher performance levels across all stages of the life span. Crucially, these advantages existed prior to the development of higher performance levels and help to sustain performance across the age spectrum (Horton et al., 2015). However, to date there is no real evidence to support the view that experts are genetically different to the rest of the population (Horton et al., 2008). Compensation is seen as a mechanism that helps experts to maintain superior performance as general capabilities decline. It is suggested that experts acquire domain-specific compensatory skills to offset decline in other areas. Crucially, experts acquire mechanisms that permit them to circumvent the specific limitations in general processing only in those tasks relevant to their domain (Krampe, 2002). Experts show similar age-related decline in general measures of processing speed and performance, but showed reduced decline in the efficiencies or the speed at which they performed skill-related tasks (Krampe & Baltes, 2002). In support of this view, Salthouse (1984) conducted research with expert typists. Results showed that the typing performance of the older experts was equivalent to that of younger typists even though choice reaction time, finger tapping speed, and performance on the digital symbol substitution test all declined. Salthouse suggested that the older typists compensated for these declines by scanning further ahead in the text. In basketball, ageing players might develop other aspects of their game (i.e. modifying their jump shot) to compensate for a loss in jumping ability. Also, ageing golfers can compensate for a decline in power performance (e.g. distance driving) by improving their short game (Baker, Deakin, Horton, & Pearce, 2007).

Results from a study by Schorer and Baker (2009) exploring the perceptional performance of former world-class handball goalkeepers suggests performance is maintained in the face of advancing age. The ability to anticipate performance through the use of advanced visual cue information remains stable over time.

Finally, selective maintenance suggests that experts can maintain high levels of performance through sustained practice. This practice is also 'smarter' in that it is concentrated on the most relevant components of the task (Krampe & Ericsson, 1996). This approach suggests that domain-specific skills that are acquired through deliberate practice can be maintained for a greater period of time. This view is supported by research conducted by Krampe and Ericsson (1996) who reported that the measure that more strongly correlated with performance in older pianists was the amount of time they had spent in deliberate practice. However, contemporary models of skilled performance have challenged the ascendency of the deliberate practice approach (Horton et al., 2015). There is now significant research across multiple performance domains supporting the perspective that time spent in high quality deliberate practice is a robust predictor of performance (Bloom, 1985; Chase & Simon, 1973; Ericsson, Krampe, & Tesch-Römer, 1993).

This suggests that continued engagement in deliberate practice is a fundamental prerequisite for sustaining performance in most performance domains (Horton et al., 2008). Interesting research conducted by Starkes, Weir, and Young (2003) suggests that in masters swimmers and runners there is tendency to reduce the overall number of hours spent training, and a tendency to narrow the focus to specifically endurance-focused training. It is possible that this is the most efficient use of training time and also crucially an approach that can also minimize the possibility of sustaining injury.

Summary

The accumulation of expertise is important for effective performance. It is also true that this accumulation and extension of expertise can help to maintain performance at the highest levels. Indeed, evidence suggests that under the age of 40 experience can counter the effects of declining physical and psychological performance. Understanding what decline occurs and how best to manage these reductions in fundamental performance are important to maximize career length, and ultimately achieved performance levels over time.

Study questions

1. What are the factors for ageing performers to consider if they wish to maintain high levels of performance with increasing age?
2. What is the impact of ageing on cognitive performance once performers enter their thirties?
3. In what ways does physical performance decrease with age? Is the impact of these decrements uniform across performance domains?

Further reading

Horton, S., Baker, J., & Wier, P. (2015). Career length, aging, and expertise. In J. Baker & D. Farrow (Eds.), *Routledge handbook of sport expertise*. Oxford: Routledge.
An important book chapter that explores the relationship between age, experience, and performance.

9
CONFIDENCE

Introduction

Self-confidence is frequently cited as an important part of successful performance and has been suggested to influence behaviours, attitudes, and goal attainment (Cox, Shannon, McGuire, & McBride, 2010). Building on this association, it has been suggested that to achieve excellent performance outcomes a high degree of self-confidence is required (Vealey & Chase, 2008). Research has consistently reported self-confidence to be one of the most influential cognitive determinants of sport performance (Craft, Magyar, Becker, & Feltz, 2003; Moritz, Feltz, Fahrbach, & Mack, 2000; Woodman & Hardy, 2003), with elite performers stating that confidence is the most important ingredient in mental toughness and helps them to stay resilient in the face of challenges and setbacks.

Further support has been provided by Martens, Vealey, and Burton (1990) who theorized a positive linear relationship between self-confidence and performance. Similarly, Vealey's (1986, 2001) sport confidence model posits a positive relationship between confidence and performance. All of which suggests an inextricable link between confidence and performance. International-level elite sports performers have identified self-belief as fundamental when defining and developing mental toughness (Connaughton, Wadey, Hanton, & Jones, 2008; Jones, Hanton, & Connaughton, 2002). One of the most consistent findings in the peak performance literature is the direct link between high levels of self-confidence and successful sporting performance (Zinsser, Bunker, & Williams, 2006). Previous research has also found a significant association between confidence and flow in sport (Koehn, Morris, & Watt, 2013) and between flow and performance (Koehn & Morris, 2012).

This chapter will explore what confidence is and in particular consider the different theoretical conceptualizations that currently exist. The chapter will also explore overconfidence and robust/resilient confidence, and also consider the implications for practice.

What is confidence?

Three major conceptualizations of confidence have been suggested in the broader psychology literature: self-efficacy, self-confidence, and sport confidence.

Self-efficacy

Self-efficacy theory was first introduced by Bandura (1977) to both explain and adapt human behaviour. Self-efficacy was defined by Bandura (1997, p. 3) as "beliefs in one's capabilities to organize and execute the course of action required to produce given attainments". Broadly speaking this reflects the confidence the individual has in their ability to perform a specific task. This construct was derived from self-efficacy theory, which proposes that self-efficacy enhances performance through increasing the difficulty of self-set goals, escalating the level of effort that is expended, and strengthening persistence (Bandura, 1977, 2012; Bandura & Locke, 2003). Providing support for this view, the overwhelming majority of research has found positive relationships between self-efficacy and performance. Self-efficacy has been reported to increase performance by up to 25%, which is a stronger effect than goal setting, feedback interventions, or behaviour modifications (Sitzmann & Yeo, 2013; Stajkovic & Luthans, 1998). In addition, more than 90% of studies have found positive correlations between self-efficacy and performance at the between-persons level of analysis (Sitzmann & Ely, 2010; Stajkovic & Lee, 2001).

Bandura's (1997) theory of self-efficacy, which is rooted in social cognitive theory, predicts a positive relationship between self-efficacy and performance by drawing on four key antecedents of self-efficacy beliefs: enactive mastery experiences, vicarious experience, verbal persuasion, and physiological/affective states. It is thought that efficacy beliefs influence one's behaviours (e.g. actions), cognitions (e.g. thoughts), and affect (e.g. feelings). These influences are predicted by six main sources of information (Maddux & Gosselin, 2003). These sources (presented in Figure 9.1) are enactive mastery experiences (e.g. gaining belief from mastery and successful experiences), vicarious experiences (e.g. gaining belief from observing the successful experiences of others), verbal persuasion (e.g. gaining belief from the support of significant others including themselves), physiological and emotional states (e.g. gaining belief from associations made between performance and our physiological arousal and emotions), and imaginal experiences (e.g. referring to the performer gaining belief from imagining themselves, or others, behaving successfully).

Self-efficacy beliefs are suggested to vary along three dimensions: level, strength, and generality (Feltz, Short, & Singleton, 2008). *Level* refers to the individual's performance attainment at different levels of difficulty. *Strength* refers to the certainty of the individual's beliefs that they can achieve at these different levels of performance. *Generality* relates to the number of domains of functioning that performers judge themselves to be efficacious in and the transferability of these efficacy judgements across different tasks of activities.

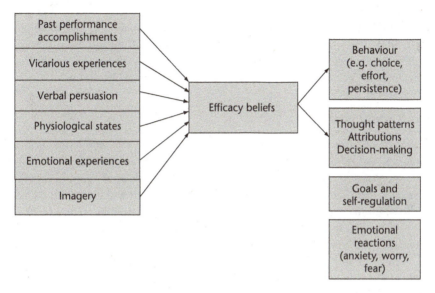

FIGURE 9.1 Overview of self-efficacy sources and outcomes

Source: adapted from Bandura, 1997.

Research has also highlighted links between self-efficacy and other performance-related measures including adaptability to new approaches (Hill, Smith, & Mann, 1987); coping with career-related events (Stumpf, Brief, & Hartman, 1987); generating new ideas and approaches (Gist, 1989); leadership performance (Wood, Bandura, & Bailey, 1990), skill acquisition (Mitchell, Hopper, Daniels, George-Falvy, & James, 1994); and newcomer adjustment to new environments (Saks, 1995). There is also an important moderating influence of task complexity in the relationship between self-efficacy and performance (Stajkovic & Luthans, 1998). Highly complex tasks require different skills for their successful execution by placing greater demands on a range of factors including: required knowledge, cognitive ability, memory capacity, behavioural facility, information processing, persistence, and physical effort (Bandura, 1997). These greater demands can, in turn, lead to a faulty assessment of task performance requirements leading to incorrect self-efficacy referent thoughts regarding the amount of effort required, and how long to sustain this effort to achieve a successful outcome (Bandura, 1986).

Self-confidence

Self-confidence is an individual's belief that he or she can be successful. Self-confidence is proposed to be context-specific to relevant tasks and it is suggested that some individuals can display this feature through a wide range of activities. Self-confidence is also similar to self-efficacy as suggested by self-efficacy theory. Self-confidence is simply described to be a self-perceived measure of one's belief in one's own abilities that is dependent upon contextual background and setting (Perry, 2011). Self-confidence is a general feature of personality; it is not a temporary attitude (Pervin & John, 2001). Similarly, Feltz (1988) further described self-confidence as a belief of a person that they can successfully achieve an activity and individuals' trust to their own judgement, ability, strength and decisions.

Sports confidence

Vealey (1986) developed a sport-specific construct of self-confidence termed 'sport confidence' defined as "the belief or degree of certainty about one's ability to be successful in sport" (p. 222). Vealey's model focuses on the notion that the interaction between dispositional or trait sport confidence and competitive goals predicted momentary/state sport confidence. The underlying theoretical focus of the model is that individual differences in trait sport confidence and competitive orientation can influence how performers perceive factors within an objective sport situation and predispose them to respond to sport situations with certain levels of state sport confidence which would affect behaviour (Short & Ross-Stewart, 2009).

The core of the sport confidence model consists of three source domains (achievement, self-regulation, social climate), sport confidence, and the ABC triangle (affect, behaviour, cognition). The three domains represent the nine sources of confidence: mastery, demonstration of ability (achievement), physical and mental preparation, physical self-presentation (self-regulation), social support, vicarious experience, coach's leadership, environmental comfort, and situational favourableness (social climate). The three source domains affect the performers' level of confidence, which in turn influences the performers' affect (e.g. anxiety and flow), behaviour (e.g. effort and persistence), cognitions (e.g. decision-making), and, finally, performance. These nine sub-scales form the structure for the Sources of Sport Confidence Questionnaire (SSCQ; Vealey, Hayashi, Garner-Holman, & Giacobbi, 1998).

Vealey (2001) also developed the 'integrative model of sport confidence' designed to provide a framework for the extension of understanding and the design of applied interventions. The model (see Figure 9.2) outlines a range of factors that both influence and determine sport confidence. At the core of the individual in the model are affect, cognition, and behaviour. Other key internal factors highlighted include self-regulation, social climate, and achievement. Performance is highlighted as being an important factor, as are the culture of the organization and the personal characteristics of the individual.

Negative effects of high confidence

While high levels of confidence are generally viewed as a good thing, there is evidence to suggest this is not always the case. For example, in their study of pistol shooters, Gould, Petlichkoff, Simons, and Vevera (1987) revealed a negative

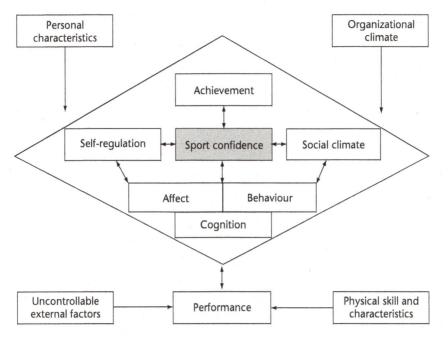

FIGURE 9.2 Integrative model of sport confidence

Source: adapted from Vealey, 2001.

relationship between self-confidence and shooting performance. Similarly, Hardy, Woodman, and Carrington (2004) found that high self-confidence was associated with depressed golf performance scores (see also Woodman & Hardy, 2005). One explanation for such findings is that high confidence can lead to risk-taking (Campbell, Goodie, & Foster, 2004) and/or complacency (Jones, Swain, & Hardy, 1993), which in turn may hinder performance. Woodman, Akehurst, Hardy, and Beattie (2010) reported that in their group of 'skippers' performance improved when self-confidence decreased. These results support Bandura and Locke's (2003) view that some self-doubt can help performance. The role of effort though in this relationship remains to be further clarified.

Overconfidence

Overconfidence is the tendency to place an irrationally excessive degree of confidence in one's abilities and beliefs (Grinblatt & Keloharju, 2009). There is evidence to suggest that individuals are not very good at estimating their performance on trivial topics, topics that are likely novel to them or outside the realm of their expertise. More interesting, though, is that individuals often tend to be biased toward over- and not underestimation. Even more interesting is that this tendency does not disappear with experience. Overconfidence has been identified among clinical psychologists, physicians, nurses, investment bankers, engineers, entrepreneurs, lawyers, negotiators, managers, and sports performers (Barber & Odean, 2001). Further, Barberis and Thaler (2003) claim expertise actually exacerbates overconfidence. Indeed, many of the conditions faced by experts – for example, abstractly defined goals, and decisions that are low in frequency or produce noisy feedback – are exactly ones that have been linked to biased and overconfident decision-making (Malmendier & Tate, 2005).

Resilient or robust confidence

It has suggested that 'robust', 'resilient', and 'unshakeable' confidence is important for achieving successful performance outcomes (e.g. Bull et al., 2005; Jones et al., 2002, 2007; Vealey & Chase, 2008). It is this concept of stability that has, for the most part, led to researchers exploring what has been termed 'resilient confidence' (Bull et al., 2005; Vealey, 2001) in the past, and more recently 'robust sport-confidence' (Thomas, Lane, & Kingston, 2011). Specifically, in a study involving elite performers, robust sport confidence was described as a multidimensional and stable construct that allows performers to deal with setbacks and the constant psychological and environmental challenges that occur in sport (Thomas et al., 2011). In addition, the construct was found to have six key characteristics: It is multidimensional (i.e. made up of different types of confidence); malleable (i.e. responds and reacts to negative factors); durable (i.e. stable over time); a strong set of beliefs (i.e. the athlete truly believes in their ability); developed (i.e. not innate but developed over time); and protective (i.e. acting as a buffer against negative factors). Thomas et al. (2011) further suggested that these characteristics may serve as a foundation from which stable sport confidence can be developed and as a result could have important implications for performers and psychologists alike.

Enhancing self-efficacy

Bandura (1997) outlined six specific sources of self-efficacy that could be used to underpin interventions to enhance efficacy beliefs: past performance accomplishments, observation, verbal instruction, physiological states, emotional states, and imaginal states (see Figure 9.2).

Past performance accomplishments are suggested to exert the greatest influence on efficacy beliefs (Bandura, 1997), this is because they are experiences of the individual performer.

It has been suggested that the old adage 'success builds confidence' can be effective in enhancing self-efficacy (Short & Ross-Stewart, 2009). So, following this line of thought developing practice and performance environments in which the performer experiences success are important (Feltz et al., 2008). The rationale here is to develop efficacy beliefs by a gradual increase in skill improvement (Feltz & Weiss, 1982). This is in part similar to the goal-setting literature that highlights the importance of goal attainment in enhancing perceptions of confidence. The use of performance and process goals in particular is seen as important in this process (Filby, Maynard, & Graydon, 1999). There has been some suggestion in the literature that you can help to achieve this success by modifying the practice environment to increase the likelihood of success (e.g. Chase, Ewing, Lirgg, & George, 1994). While this might enhance self-efficacy levels it could also have a negative long-term effect on skill execution by changing the nature of the task performed. There is also a suggestion in the literature that changing the way performers attribute success and failure could impact upon efficacy beliefs (Maddux & Lewis, 1995; Weiner, 1985).

Vicarious experiences involve the performer observing and comparing themselves to others. Importantly though efficacy beliefs will be influenced by who the comparison is with (Schultz & Short, 2006). Bandura (1997) suggested the more formidable the opponent looks the lower the efficacy beliefs will be. Interestingly, Bandura also suggested that the mere presence of a very confident-looking opponent can be enough to undermine skill execution. There is also evidence to suggest that the body language and clothing of the opposition can also have an impact (Buscombe, Greenlees, Holder, Thelwell, & Rimmer, 2006; Greenlees, Bradley, Holder, & Thelwell, 2005).

Imagery experiences have been suggested to be impactful as they mimic real experience, and as a result can be used to build, maintain, and regain self-efficacy (Short & Ross-Stewart, 2009). However, it has been highlighted that the function of the imagery intervention needs to be clearly focused on either building, maintaining, or regaining self-efficacy (for further information on imagery see Chapter 12).

Verbal persuasion is generally seen as a less potent source of self-efficacy compared with some of the other outlined sources. Also, it is important to recognize that the debilitative effects of verbal persuasion are more powerful than the enabling effects (Bandura, 1997).

Physiological states have been suggested to impact upon efficacy beliefs when the performer associates aversive physiological arousal with poor behavioural performance, a perceived lack of competence, and perceived failure (Maddux & Lewis, 1995). The most important physiological states for active performers include: arousal, strength, fitness, fatigue, and pain (Short & Ross-Stewart, 2009). Interventions that seek to influence these perceptions seek to influence the performers' appraisal of the experienced physical sensations.

The most effective approaches to enhancing efficacy beliefs have been suggested to be a combination of more than one source of efficacy information (Short & Ross-Stewart, 2009).

Enhancing confidence

Vealey and Vernau (2010) developed a model for building confidence in athletes. While there is significant crossover with the approaches highlighted in the previous section to enhance self-efficacy there were also some additions. Vealey and Vernau highlighted four main sources of confidence that they termed: physical training and preparation (perspiration); self-regulation for productive responses (regulation); inspirational social forces (inspiration); and achievement and experience (validation).

The authors also suggested that self-confidence is 'nested' within a range of social contexts, and that it is important to account for all of those different types of confidence. So, for an individual in a sports team this could include self-confidence, role confidence, coach confidence, team confidence, and organizational confidence. The model also subjects two routes to developing confidence. The first focuses on the four sources of confidence outlined that then underpins strong resilient beliefs about the performer's abilities. The second route focuses on building physical and mental skills that leads to effective energy management, productive thinking, and an optimal focus.

Implications for performance

From a conceptual perspective, Vealey (2001) highlighted the need to identify a variety of sources of confidence to maximize the ability of the performer to draw on a salient source at any given time. Vealey further suggested that the sources most important to the performer should be targeted when designing interventions to enhance confidence. Vealey's model has received support (e.g. Hays, Maynard, Thomas, & Bawden, 2007; Wilson, Sullivan, Myers, & Feltz, 2004), most notably in implying the proposition that the performers' characteristics and organizational culture influence their sources of sport confidence. Indeed, Hays et al. (2007) conducted a study involving elite team and individual athletes and identified both types and sources of confidence. From the nine sources of confidence reported, there were some sources overlapping with those initially outlined by Vealey et al. (1998) but also further sources of confidence unique to the culture of world-class sport (e.g. trust, competitive advantage, and innate factors). Taken together, the findings support the proposition that the sources and types of confidence will influence performers' confidence levels and will vary depending on the organizational culture of the particular performance domain. Although there are intervention techniques aimed at increasing confidence, such as goal setting (Kingston & Hardy, 1997); imagery (Garza & Feltz, 1998); self-talk (Hatzigeorgiadis, Zourbanos, Mpoumpaki, & Theodorakis, 2009); hypnosis (Barker & Jones, 2006); and modelling (McAuley, 1985), it is also unclear if these traditional techniques are effective at building and maintaining robust sport-confidence. Indeed, Thomas et al. (2011) implied the need to shift from a traditional view that higher levels of confidence should be developed to more of a focus on developing the strength of the belief across several sources to maintain robust sport confidence over time. One potential strategy to build and maintain robust sport confidence is to help performers to become more aware of, and develop, their own unique strengths. Knowledge of a unique strength and how it can be used appears to help performers enter competition with a perceived competitive advantage (Linley, 2008). For this to happen most effectively, the process requires the integration of the performer, the psychologist, and the coach/mentor, because unique strengths are not solely psychological but relate to the performers' strategic, technical, and physical conditioning elements of performance (Beaumont, Maynard, & Butt, 2015).

Vealey and Vernau (2010) also suggested four broad categories from which confidence could be drawn including: physical training, the use of self-regulatory strategies (self-talk, imagery, energy management, behaviour monitoring) to habituate productive responses in the performance domain; gain inspiration and support from others (e.g. team members, leaders, family); and to progressively gain experience of achieving in a diverse range of contexts.

Summary

There is now extensive evidence that suggests confidence is correlated with performance. However, while this is the case there also appear to be optimal levels of confidence beyond which performance can suffer. The development of robust self-confidence appears key in achieving long-term performance success. This is important as a loss of confidence can be difficult to reverse. For example, Hays, Thomas, Maynard, and Bawden (2009) reported that elite performers can struggle to regain confidence if it was lost in the pressurized environment of competition. This finding supports Vealey and Chase's (2008) suggestion that confidence remains a work in progress for performers and is a fragile construct. As a result, performers need to understand what factors influence and determine their levels of confidence and design an environment in which confidence/efficacy beliefs are continually being enhanced, even in the face of setbacks and failure.

Study questions

1. To what extent do you feel that high levels of confidence are always desirable for effective performance?
2. What strategies can be adopted to enhance the development and maintenance of robust self-confidence?

Further reading

Hays, K., Maynard, I., Thomas, O., & Bawden, M. (2007). Sources and types of confidence identified by world class sports performers. *Journal of Applied Sport Psychology, 19*, 434–456.
>   An important article that explores the sources of confidence for high-level performers.
Short, S., & Ross-Stewart, L. (2009). A review of self-efficacy based interventions. In S. D. Mellalieu & S. Hanton (Eds.), *Advances in applied sport psychology*. Abingdon: Routledge. This chapter provides a very detailed overview of applied intervention approaches that have been adopted to develop self-efficacy.
Thomas, O., Lane, A., & Kingston, K. (2011). Defining and contextualizing robust sport-confidence. *Journal of Applied Sport Psychology, 23*, 189–208.
>   Another interesting article that seeks to develop and clarify the concept of robust self-confidence and its importance in continued performance success.

10

PSYCHOPHYSIOLOGY

Introduction

For the last century there has been increasing interest in being able to measure and understand differences in cognitive functioning. Measures of electrocardiographic activity (i.e. a measure of cardiac activity), and electroencephalographic activity in particular (i.e. a measure of cortical activity) have long-standing associations with understanding information processing and response programming (Cooke, 2013). The long-held view is that successful performance outcomes are related to specific cortical measures. These data could be used to help to prepare for, and even predict performance.

Both cross-sectional and longitudinal studies of elite-level performers have suggested that superior performance is characterized by efficiency of cerebral–cortical processing. Comparisons of expert and novice performers across a range of domains have revealed that expert performers exhibit increased neural efficiency relative to novices (Del Percio et al., 2009; Hatfield, Landers, & Ray, 1984; Haufler, Spalding, Santa Maria, & Hatfield, 2000), and that efficiency has been shown to increase with motor learning (Kerick, Douglass, & Hatfield, 2004).

This chapter will introduce the field of psychophysiology and specifically explore EEG, ECG, and eye tracking. The chapter will also explore how these measures through biofeedback and neurofeedback approaches can be utilized to better prepare the performer for the 'real world' environment.

Psychophysiology

Psychophysiology as a field of study is related to both the anatomy and physiology of the body. Crucially, it is also concerned with psychological phenomena such as the experience and behaviour of individuals in the physical and social environment

(Cacioppo, Tassinary, & Berntson, 2007). Contemporary definitions of psycho-physiology emphasize the mapping of the relationships between mechanisms under-lying psychological and physiological events (Ackles, Jennings, & Coles, 1985; Hugdahl, 1995). Cacioppo et al. (2007) further defined psychophysiology as "the scientific study of social, psychological, and behavioural phenomena as related to and revealed through physiological principles and events in functional organisms" (p. 7). Psychophysiology is built upon the assumption that human perception, cog-nition, emotion, and action are all embodied phenomena, and the physical/physiological responses can be used as measures to understand human nature. As such, psychophysiology represents a top-down approach that differs from the bot-tom-up approach of psychobiology. Although psychophysiology is relatively new as a formal discipline, interest in the interrelations between physiological and psycho-logical events can be traced back to the ancient Egyptians and Greeks. Psychophysi-ology considers a wide range of phenomena utilizing a varied range of measurement techniques. Particular areas of interest include: electroencephalography, electrocardi-ography, electrodermal activity, pupillary responses, and eye movements. This chapter will specifically explore EEG, ECG, and tracking eye movements. This approach to measuring psychological processes can be particularly useful as it can "provide an objective and relatively non-invasive method of examining the complex processes involved in performance as they take place" (Collins, 2002, p. 12).

Electroencephalography (EEG)

The electrical activity of neurons in the brain produces currents that reach the surface of the scalp. This in turn can be used as a broad indicator of cognitive activ-ity. EEG provides a non-invasive method of recording the voltage differences of these scalp potentials. EEG measures are used across a wide range of domains to understand varying aspects of human functioning. Examples include neuromarket-ing (understanding shopping habits and decision-making); social interactions; med-icine (e.g. monitoring epilepsy and sleep patterns); understanding brain processes (e.g. attention, learning, and memory); clinical and psychiatric studies (to evaluate treatment effectiveness, and impaired functioning); brain computer interfaces, and sports performance.

EEG measurement requires the attachment of electrodes to internationally standardized locations on the scalp. These electrodes are generally made of highly conductive silver (Ag) or silver chloride (AgCl) although other metals such as tin, gold, and platinum are also used. These electrodes are attached to the scalp using conductive paste with impedances generally kept below 5 kX. Prior to attaching the electrodes the skin is usually prepared with an abrasive paste to reduce skin impedance (Burbank & Webster, 1978; Seitsonen, Yli-Hankala, & Korttila, 2000). The number of active electrodes can range from one, which is sufficient for neuro-feedback training, to multiple electrodes necessary for source localization with the number of electrodes typically varying from 32 to 128 (Nunez & Srinivasan, 2006). Electrode placement is standardized to aid comparison between studies and overtime. The international method of electrode placement is the '10–20 system' (Jasper, 1958). A differential amplifier measures the voltage difference between inputs from the active and reference electrodes, with the resulting signal amplified and displayed as a channel of EEG activity. A signal that is common to both inputs is thus automatically rejected in what is known as common mode rejection (CMR). 'Noise' shared across electrodes is thus effectively eliminated leaving only the (hopefully neural) activity specific to the active electrode. In sporting applications, the reference tends to be from electrodes placed on the mastoid (the bone behind the ear), occasionally the ear lobes or the average of all (common average montage) or surrounding (Laplacian montage) electrodes in multi-channel setups.

The EEG signal is picked up by electrodes placed on the scalp and transmitted to a differential amplifier in order to amplify the potentials that are severely attenuated by their passage through the skull (Thompson, Steffert, Ros, Leach, & Gruzelier, 2008). This signal is continuously sampled (recorded) at a high rate (typically 256 Hz but often more) to provide a high temporal resolution. An analogue bandpass filter is used to filter the raw EEG signal and typically possesses a lower cut-off of 0.5 Hz and a higher cut-off of 50 Hz. The 50 Hz filter helps eliminate electrical noise originating from 50/60 Hz mains power. These filters also affect the processing of nearby frequencies so care must be taken to ensure the cut-off frequencies do not lie too close to the frequencies under investigation. This is not generally an issue in the performance-focused research as the frequencies of interest are usually between 4 and 20 Hz. After amplification and filtering, the EEG signal is sent to a computer where it can be processed as continuous data and, if desired, its spectral parameters compared with some criterion measure. This is the approach adopted by EEG-biofeedback training in sports and other performance domains that rewards desirable changes in specific frequency bands. An alternative approach in seeking to understand EEG data is the study of event-related potentials (ERPs). These ERPs usually consist of data epochs of short duration reflecting the cortical response to a specific external stimulus. In order to offset data noise, many ERPs (often hundreds) are averaged to provide a favourable signal-to-noise ratio.

The EEG signal can be split into different categories based upon the signals frequency, which is measured in Hertz (Hz). Frequency bands include: Delta (1–3 Hz), Theta (4–7 Hz), Alpha (8–12 Hz), Beta (13–30 Hz), and Gamma (31–50 Hz). Slower waves such as delta are typically associated with sleep while faster beta waves are linked to a 'relaxed focus or mental readiness'. In a theoretical sense, elevations in alpha power have been commonly interpreted to reflect a reduction in non-essential cortical processes (Klimesch, 1999; Pfurtscheller, Stancak, & Neuper, 1996). More specifically, low-alpha frequencies (8–10 Hz) are conventionally used to index general cortical activity, whereas high-alpha frequencies (10–13 Hz) are thought to reflect task-relevant cortical activity (Pfurtscheller & Lopes da Silva, 1999). The observed power of specific frequency bands, coupled with the expression of their spatial topography, has been used to infer various psychological processes. For example, verbal–analytical and visuospatial processes have been generally attributed to the left and right temporal lobes, respectively (Cohen, 1993).

Implications for performance

There have been a significant number of studies over the past 30 years that have explored differences between expert and novice performers. Expert marksmen have been shown to exhibit greater alpha (8–13 Hz) power in the left temporal region (T3) relative to novices during the seconds prior to shot execution (Hatfield et al., 1984; Haufler et al., 2000; Hunt, Rietschel, Hatfield, & Iso-Ahola, 2013). Moreover, alpha power in the left and right temporal (T4) regions has been shown to increase over the course of an intensive target-shooting training protocol (Kerick et al., 2004).

Research in the motor control literature has also indicated that most voluntary self-paced movements are preceded by a reduction (desynchronization) in EEG alpha power that is strongest in the hemisphere contralateral to the active limb, or occurs across both hemispheres in the case of bimanual tasks (Leocani, Toro, Manganotti, Zhuang, & Hallett, 1997; Pfurtscheller & Aranibar, 1979; Pfurtscheller & Lopes da Silva, 1999). For instance, in a recent study of preparation for action in expert golfers, Babiloni et al. (2008) reported that EEG alpha power reduced in both hemispheres during the four seconds preceding putts. Moreover, this reduction in EEG alpha power was greater ahead of putts that were holed when compared to putts that were missed.

Loze, Collins, and Holmes (2001), in comparing best and worst shots in expert air-pistol shooters, reported increased occipital EEG power during epochs 1–3 for the best shots. Loze et al. argued this suppression of visual attention for best shots represented a shift from 'attentional' to 'intentional' processes. Various recent studies have explored the alpha power characteristics exhibited by sports performers in various environments. Janelle and colleagues (2000) reported that expert marksmen exhibited a significant increase in left hemisphere alpha power (a more relaxed state) compared with the right hemisphere, as well as asymmetrical patterns of alpha and beta activity in both hemispheres. Landers et al. (1994) reported that the amounts of alpha activity across both hemispheres at the beginning of learning were relatively low. However, as the participants become more skilled, an increase in alpha activity was evident in the left hemisphere while activity in the right hemisphere remained constant. All of these studies suggest a link between alpha power, particularly in the left hemisphere, and the pre-performance state.

A more recent approach to exploring EEG relating to performance is to assess coherence (Cooke, 2013). Recent studies (Babiloni et al., 2011; Deeny, Hillman, Janelle, & Hatfield, 2003; Zhu, Poolton, Wilson, Maxwell, & Masters, 2011) suggest that coherence can be used as an indicator of verbal-analytic information processing, and preparation for action. However, more research focusing on coherence is required to better understand this phenomenon.

Electrocardiography and heart rate measures

The electrocardiogram (ECG) is a method of assessing cardiac activity that involves placing electrodes on the skin, to detect electrical activity generated by the heart

(Andreassi, 2006). In terms of psychophysiology, the ECG is most used to measure variability in heart rate (Cooke, 2013). Measures such as the power of heart activity in low (0.02–0.06 Hz), mid (0.07–0.14 Hz), and high (0.15–0.50 Hz) frequency power bands can be used to provide an insight into the emotional and motivational state of a performer (Kreibig, 2010; Mulder, 1992). Heart rate variability (HRV) as indexed by spectral analysis of the cardiac signal, has been shown to reflect changes in mental effort (Montano et al., 2009; Mullen, Hardy, & Tattersall, 2005). Specifically, it has been suggested that these changes represent increases in the intensity of attentional processing associated with shifts from automatic to controlled processing (Mulder, 1992). Carlstedt (2004) suggested that heart activity can be viewed as the window into mind–body interactions, further concluding that heart rate (HR), and more importantly variation in HR have been shown to be an important measure of attention and cognitive activity. This is also supported by Sandman, Walker, and Berka (1982) who reported that HR and blood pressure (BP) were the physiological parameters that best differentiated the cognitive-perceptual process.

This link between HR and cognitive activity has been explained on the basis of brain-heart interactions where HR Deceleration (HRD) has been found to release the cortex from the inhibitory control of the baro-receptors; conversely, HR acceleration (HRA) has been shown to stimulate baro-receptor activity and thereby inhibit cortical activity (Sandman et al., 1982). Indeed, HR and BP are thought to inhibit cortical activity, thereby decreasing attention, whereas HRD and lowered BP are thought to facilitate attentional processes (Lacey & Lacey, 1978; Sandman et al., 1982). EEG studies have helped to confirm this link.

Phasic changes in HR have most commonly been examined immediately prior to performance. Elite golfers have shown HR deceleration across the five inter-beat intervals preceding the putt, with the execution of the putt coinciding with the time at which HR was slowest (Boutcher & Zinsser, 1990; Hassmén & Koivula, 2001). This deceleration in HR has also been reported prior to other types of golf shots (Cotterill & Collins, 2005). This effect is suggested to be more pronounced in elite performers (Hassmén & Koivula, 2001; Tremayne & Barry, 2001). Boutcher and Zinsser (1990) reported that both elite and novice golfers can exhibit HR deceleration, although the deceleration was more pronounced for elite golfers, a conclusion also supported by Neumann and Thomas (2011). The observation of more pronounced HR deceleration at higher skill levels has also been found in other sports, such as pistol shooting (Tremayne & Barry, 2001), rifle shooting (Hatfield, Landers, & Ray, 1987), and darts (Radlo, Steinberg, Singer, Barba, & Melnikou, 2002), although it was not found in one study on archery (Salazar et al., 1990). Lacey and Lacey's (1974, 1980) intake–rejection hypothesis provides a framework to explain the relationship between HR changes and motor skill performance. According to this hypothesis, a deceleration in HR is associated with decreased feedback to the brain and results in a more effective external focusing of attention and superior performance. Laboratory-based studies have supported this conceptualization (Lacey & Lacey, 1974). Support has also been found during self-paced sporting tasks. For example, Radlo et al. (2002) asked novices to throw darts at a target while focusing attention externally at the target or internally on their movements. The external focus condition was associated with a pronounced deceleration in HR immediately before the throw, whereas the internal focus condition was associated with an acceleration of HR. Moreover, performance was better in the external focus condition than in the internal focus condition.

The relationship between interbeat interval (IBI) duration and performance has been investigated in a number of studies. Radlo et al. (2002) specifically focused on level of performance, comparing the four best and four worst shots for four epochs prior to dart release, finding that the good shots had significantly longer when compared to the poor shots immediately prior to dart release. Carlstedt (2004) also reported differences in IBI duration when comparing games won vs games lost in a tennis case study. Games won were characterized by higher mean IBIs than games lost. Boutcher and Zinsser (1990) measured IBI between heartbeats immediately prior to, during, and post completing a putting task. The IBI increased significantly prior to performance. Boutcher and Zinsser concluded that there was a greater cardiac deceleration associated with superior putting performance.

Eye tracking

Eye tracking is a set of methods and techniques used to detect and record ocular movement. Research focused on eye movements has increased over time with continued advances in eye-tracking technology and psychological theory on the relationship between eye behaviour and cognitive processes. Eye trackers provide the opportunity to explore a number of factors in the performance domain including: comparing the visual strategies and spatial awareness of elite vs amateur performers; highlighting where successful performers direct their visual attention prior to skill execution; and comparing the performer's visual search strategies during successful and unsuccessful performance. Eye-tracking techniques can broadly be divided into diagnostic or interactive techniques. In its diagnostic role, eye-tracking equipment can be used to provide objective and quantifiable evidence of the performer's visual and attentional processes (Duchowski, 2002). Conversely eye tracking can be used as an interactive system responding to or interacting with the performer based on observed eye movements (Mele & Federici, 2012).

Most contemporary studies specifically seek to explore fixations, saccades, and smooth pursuits (Bojko, 2013). Fixations are defined by an absence of movement. This is where the eye stays relatively still to allow for visual perception to take place (Holmqvist et al., 2011). Fixations usually last between 200 ms and 300 ms, and there is a general assumption (Bojko, 2013; Duchowski, 2007; Vickers, 2009) that when we measure a fixation we also measure attentional focus. In between these fixations for visual perception there are movements called saccades. Saccades are rapid shifts in the line of sight made to bring the fovea (the centre of best vision) from one specific location to the next. A saccade is in essence, a rapid movement from one fixation to another (Kowler, 2011). This technique is a useful and efficient strategy used by the brain to sample the visual environment. Saccades are extremely quick movements (the quickest movement the body can produce) and usually only take 30–80 ms to complete. During a saccade the eye moves at such a high speed that the visual system is technically blind (Holmqvist et al., 2011). Another important factor relating to eye movements is smooth pursuit. Smooth pursuits occur when the eyes slowly track an object, for example, an aeroplane flying across the sky. Strictly speaking, smooth pursuits are not under voluntary control (Kowler, 2011); they cannot be performed unless the eyes have something to follow. Other less commonly recorded eye movements, which can only be detected by highly sensitive eye-tracking technology, include microsaccades, tremors, drifts, and glissades. Micro-saccades, tremors, and drifts exist within fixations. Drifts are the slow movements away from the centre of the fixation that the eye makes automatically. Microsac-cades are the actions we complete to bring the drift back to the centre of the fixa-tion (Martinez-Conde, Macknik, & Hubel, 2004). Tremors are very small movements of the eye that we make during the fixation; this is because it is impossible to keep our eyes 100 per cent still. Finally, a glissade is a movement that the eye produces to correct for an overshot saccade. For example, if we move from point A to point B, and overshoot point B, a glissade will bring the fixation back to the intended target (Weber & Daroff, 1972).

For example, Campbell and Moran (2014) reported significant differences between elite and amateur golfers when it came to reading greens before a putt. Their findings suggest that the professional golfers used a more economical gaze pattern consisting of fewer fixations of longer duration, when compared to amateur and club players (Campbell & Moran, 2014). Using this information to teach golfers how to successfully read the green could have a substantial impact on their overall performance, after all putting accounts for about 40 per cent of the shots played in a typical round (Gwyn & Patch, 1993).

Research has highlighted differences between experts and novices in terms of their visual search behaviour, with experts focusing more than novices on information-rich areas of the visual display (Campbell & Moran, 2014; Hodges, Starkes, & MacMahon, 2006). In sports such as soccer, field hockey, and tennis elite performers have been found to direct their gaze appropriately sooner, make more predictive eye movements, and fixate on relevant features for longer than non-elite performers (Ward & Williams, 2003; Williams, Ward, & Chapman, 2003; Wil-liams, Ward, Smeeton, & Allen, 2004). In cricket the eye movements and field of gaze of batsmen associated with accurately judging the timing and placement of a ball bowled by a fast bowler were recorded using a head-mounted eye camera and were found to differ according to skill level (Land & McLeod, 2000). The term 'quiet eye' has been used to describe the final fixation on the target prior to the initiation of the movement needed to execute the task (Vickers, 1996). It was pro-posed by Vickers that differences in visual behaviour attributable to expertise are most notable in tasks involving physical movement and the control of multiple systems in natural settings (Vickers, 1996).

Biofeedback

According to Blanchard and Epstein (1978, p. 2), biofeedback can be described as

> A process in which an individual learns to reliably influence physiological responses of two kinds: either responses which are not ordinarily under voluntary control or responses which ordinarily are easily regulated but for which regulation has 'broken down', due to some reason (e.g. trauma or disease).

The term 'biofeedback' refers to external psychophysiological feedback, physiological feedback, or augmented proprioception. Biofeedback is used extensively in medical settings. For example, surface electromyography (sEMG) is used extensively to monitor disorders such as tension headaches, chronic pain, spasmodic torticollis (chronic neck pain), and temporomandibular joint dysfunction (jaw pain). EEG is used often for ADHD, epilepsy, and for monitoring sleep (Frank, Khorshid, Kiffer, Moravec, & McKee, 2010).

The basic function of biofeedback is to provide individuals with information about what is going on inside their bodies, including their brains (Bar-Eli, 2002). It has been suggested that (Pusenjak, Grad, Tusak, Leskovsek, & Schwarlin, 2015) biofeedback training of psychophysiological responses can enhance performance. Heart rate variability biofeedback training can also be used, for example Lehrer et al. (2013) have specifically developed a protocol for HRV biofeedback.

Neurofeedback

Neurofeedback is a sophisticated form of biofeedback that is based on specific aspects of cortical activity. This technique requires the performer to learn to modify some aspect of his/her cortical activity. This may include learning to change the amplitude, frequency, and/or coherence of distinct electrophysiological components of the brain (Vernon, 2005). The goal of neurofeedback training is to teach the individual what specific states of cortical arousal feel like and how to activate such states voluntarily.

Neurofeedback training provides individuals with real-time information about their level of cortical activity via sounds or visual displays (Hammond, 2007). Based on principles derived from operant learning theory (Skinner, 1963), rewarding positive reinforcement, such as a change in the pitch of a tone, is provided when a desired level of cortical activity is achieved. Electroencephalography (EEG) is perhaps the most common brain imaging method that is used to provide neurofeedback training (Vernon, 2005). There have been a number of studies investigating whether EEG neurofeedback training can facilitate performance in sport, and while the evidence concerning the effectiveness of EEG neurofeedback is not conclusive, it is certainly encouraging (e.g. Arns, Kleinnijenhuis, Fallahpour, & Breteler, 2007; Kavussanu, Crews, & Gill, 1998; Landers et al., 1991; Rostami, Sadeghi,

Karami, Abadi, & Salamati, 2012). For instance Landers et al. (1991) investigated the effects of neurofeedback in 16 experienced archers. Landers et al. (1991) reasoned that archery performance should be associated with activation of the right hemisphere of the brain, which is associated with visual-spatial processing, and deactivation of the left hemisphere of the brain, which is associated with verbal-analytic processing (Hatfield, Landers, & Ray, 1984; Landers et al., 1994). Landers et al. measured EEG activity and archery performance in pre- and post-test sessions, separated by approximately 60 minutes of neurofeedback training during which the archers watched their relative left- and right-hemisphere activity on a visual display. Results highlighted that performance improved from the pre-test to the post-test in eight archers who were rewarded when they reduced cortical activity over their left hemisphere. In contrast, performance deteriorated.in the remaining eight archers, who were rewarded when they reduced cortical activity over their right hemisphere.

In a review of the evidence supporting neurofeedback training, Vernon (2005) offered a note of caution regarding the strength of supporting evidence. Vernon concluded that the evidence was equivocal and that future research needs to measure pre- and post-EEG baselines to monitor changes resulting from neurofeedback training. Also, where possible, to utilize a moving baseline measurement of the EEG to control for possible changes in physiological arousal. Finally, to always include a non-contingent control group, ideally one that receives everything that the experimental group receives.

Summary

Psychophysiological measures offer real potential to better understand the links between measureable cortical activity and performance. Biofeedback and neuro-feedback offer the potential to provide real-time objective data to help performers to achieve the optimal cortical states both prior to and during performance. However, while the evidence to date offers potential for the future the authenticity of some of these findings is a matter of concern. Much of this research, by the nature of the measures and equipment used, has been laboratory-based. Several sport and exercise studies suggest that laboratory-based findings do not automati-cally hold in training and competition situations under field conditions (Reinecke et al., 2011; Riley et al., 2008); results can often be comparable but not directly equivalent. As a result it is crucial the research embraces more ecologically valid and representative designs in seeking to better understand preparation for and responses in the real performance environment.

Study questions

1. The use of EEG as a real-time measure offers potential to better understand what is happening in the brain. What limitations currently exist in maximizing the potential of this measure?

2. How could neurofeedback be integrated into preparation for performance for specific performance domains?

3. What differences are reported in the literature in visual search strategies between expert and novice performers?

Further reading

Andreassi, J. L. (2006). *Psychophysiology: Human behaviour and physiological response* (5th edn). London: Lawrence Erlbaum Associates.

The book provides a comprehensive overview of psychophysiology with specific chapters exploring a range of different psychophysiology modalities.

Cooke, A. (2013). Readying the head and steadying the heart: a review of cortical and cardiac studies of preparation for action in sport. *International Review of Sport and Exercise Psychology*, 1–17.

This article provides a comprehensive review of research focused on EEG and cardiac responsiveness in relation to preparation for performance.

11

DEVELOPING MOTOR SKILLS

Introduction

Across all performance domains the acquisition and development of key skills is a fundamental requirement for future success. Motor skill acquisition refers to the process by which movements produced alone, or in a sequence, come to be performed effortlessly through repeated practice and interactions with the environment (Willingham, 1998). Such motor behaviours are used on a daily basis, and are thus important for our activities in everyday life (e.g. playing a musical instrument such as the piano, grasping small objects, or practicing sports). Many of these motor behaviours though also underpin performance.

While researchers continue to discuss the specific elements essential for developing expertise (e.g. Baker & Davids, 2006; Tucker & Collins, 2012). Most agree that expert-level performance is not possible without a long-term commitment to training and practice (Baker & Young, 2014; Howe, Davidson, & Sloboda, 1998; Starkes, 2000). Though what, how, and how much appear to still be up for debate.

From a performance perspective, researchers have demonstrated an expertise effect for perceptual-cognitive skills (Ward, Ericsson, & Williams, 2013; Williams, Hodges, North, & Barton, 2006), and sport-specific engagement (Ford et al., 2012; Roca, Williams, & Ford 2012; Williams et al., 2012). Retrospective recall techniques have been used to identify the time invested by skilled and less skilled performers in sport-specific activities such as competition, training, and play. Findings have demonstrated that elite performers generally accumulate significantly more hours of sport-specific engagement compared to less skilled players (Roca et al., 2012). Furthermore, researchers using video-based assessments have demonstrated perceptual-cognitive skills such as decision-making, situational probability assessment, and pattern recognition, differentiate skilled and lesser skilled performers (Ward et al., 2013).

This chapter will explore the process of skill development, first considering the cortical and central nervous system changes that take place. The chapter will then consider both traditional and ecological approaches to skill acquisition and development before considering the key factors that influence this process.

Cortical and CNS changes

During recent years, a number of studies have highlighted that several brain structures forming the cortico–striatal (CS) or the cortico–cerebellar (CC) anatomical systems are crucial for mediating the acquisition and execution of motor skills as they reach the various stages of learning (Doyon, 1997; Hikosaka, Nakamura, Sakai, & Nakahara, 2002). Studies using functional brain imaging technology such as positron emission tomography (PET) and functional magnetic resonance imaging (fMRI), in particular, have enabled researchers to better understand the plastic changes that occur within these neural systems as performance improves with practice on motor tasks (Doyon & Benali, 2005).

Traditional concepts of the nervous system plasticity responsible for these skills have assumed that this plasticity occurs in only a few very specific locations and by only a limited number of mechanisms, and as a result have focused most attention on the cortex, cerebellum, and closely related brain regions. However, recent evidence indicates that this traditional view is not correct. Research suggests that activity-dependent plasticity is ubiquitous in the central nervous system (CNS). New appreciations of the many kinds of synaptic and neuronal plasticity, of their presence in many different areas, and of the frequency with which they occur, has overturned the traditional view of a hardwired CNS that acquires skills through only a few mechanisms at only a few specialized sites. Activity-dependent plasticity is now recognized as a feature of the entire CNS (Wolpaw, 2007), and as a result suggests a far more flexible and reactive system (Ganguly & Poo, 2013).

Skill acquisition and motor learning

The acquisition of skill relates to the concept of learning, broadly described by Kerr (1982) as a relatively permanent change in performance resulting from practice or past experience. The acquisition of perceptual-motor expertise in different performance domains (e.g. clinical, physical education, music, and sport coaching) can be viewed as a complex, contextualized process (Uehara, Button, Falcous, & Davids, 2016). A number of approaches have been suggested that seek to explain this process of skill acquisition, which can broadly be termed traditional (information processes), or ecological dynamics approaches.

Traditional approaches

Traditional approaches to skill acquisition have been underpinned by a top-down information processing perspective. Fitts and Posner (1967) suggested that the learning of a movement progresses through three interrelated phases: the cognitive phase, the associative phase, and the autonomous phase. The cognitive phase involves the performer identifying and developing the specific components of a skill. The associative phase involves the lining of the component parts into a smooth action, in a process involving deliberate practice. The autonomous phase involves continued rehearsal of the skill so it becomes automatic.

Similarly, Gentile (1972) proposed a two-stage model. In the first stage the learner works to develop a movement coordination pattern to learn to differentiate between regulation and non-regulation conditions. In the second stage learners adapt their movement pattern, increase consistency of goal achievement, and perform with an economy of effort. Extending this line of thought, Dreyfus and Dreyfus (1986) suggested a five-stage model of skill acquisition in adults including: novice, advanced beginner, competence, proficiency, and expertise. *Novices* seek to decompose the task environment into context-free features. The novice then develops rules for determining action based on these features. *Advanced beginners* utilize monitoring to ensure behaviours increasingly conform to the established rules. *Competence* relates to the individual understanding the environment (which is no-longer context-free) by developing 'aspects' which are then associated with specific actions. *Proficiency* involves exposing the learner to a wide variety of 'whole' situations. Each whole situation is linked to a long-term goal. *Expertise* sees a significant improvement of mental processing. The learner develops an analytical principle (rule) to connect understanding of the situation to a specific action.

Recently though, questions have been raised over traditional approaches to motor behaviour, which have emphasized the role of internal representations in information processing and cognitive neuroscientific accounts (e.g. Davids & Araújo, 2010; Zelaznik, 2014).

The Mesh approach

Influential characterizations of skill acquisition in both psychology and philosophy depict this process as progression from an initial cognitive phase to an expert phase in which performance is largely automatic (Dreyfus & Dreyfus, 1986; Fitts & Posner, 1967). Indeed, this traditional view highlights a shift from cognitive control to automatic processes that subsequently does not require conscious cognitive control. However, Christensen, Sutton, and Mcilwain (2016) questioned this approach suggesting that cognitive and automatic processes both make a major contribution to skilled action. Contrary to traditional information-processing models Christensen et al. suggested a hybrid 'Mesh' model where cognitive control is used to focus on strategic aspects of performance with automatic processes more concerned with implementation. One of the cognitive functions associated with cognitive control in this view is the flexible integration of information concerning the situation. In skills and expertise research this has been conceptualized as situation awareness, and can involve explicit inferences (Endsley, 1995). The Mesh approach suggests that 'Mesh' cognitive control contributes directly to skill execution by way of the influence of situation awareness on action. The influence of cognitive control on execution is not through 'step-by-step' control of the movement but through selection of action type, determination of the perceptual-motor configuration, and the parameterization of the action (Christensen et al., 2016). Strategic focus, action slips, increased attention in response to challenge, and increased cognitive effort in response to challenge in this approach are all suggestive of cognitive control.

Deliberate practice

Anders Ericsson introduced the psychological concept of deliberate practice (Ericsson et al., 1993), proposing that it was not simply training of any type, but a prolonged engagement in 'deliberate practice' that was necessary for the attainment of expertise. Deliberate practice in this context refers to activities that require cognitive or physical effort, do not lead to immediate personal, social, or financial rewards, and are undertaken with the purpose of improving performance. Although the concept of deliberate practice was advanced using data from musicians, Ericsson and his colleagues have indicated that it applies to the acquisition of expertise in all areas of human endeavour, with the domain of sport often used to exemplify the relationship between types of practice and attainment. In particular, they proposed that between-group differences in skilled performance (e.g. expert compared to less-expert groups) are predominantly related to differences in the amount of deliberate practice accumulated over long periods of time.

In two studies, Ericsson et al. (1993) recruited musicians with different levels of accomplishment and asked them to estimate the amount of deliberate practice they had engaged in per week for each year of their musical careers. On average, the cumulative amount of deliberate practice was much higher for the most-accomplished groups of musicians than for the less-accomplished groups. For example, at age 20, the average for the 'best' violinists was more than 10,000 hours, whereas the averages were about 7,800 hours for the 'good' violinists and about 4,600 hours for the least accomplished group. Ericsson et al. (1993) similarly explained that "individual differences in ultimate performance can largely be accounted for by differential amounts of past and current levels of practice" (p. 392) and that "the differences between expert performers and normal adults reflect a life-long period of deliberate effort to improve performance in a specific domain" (p. 400).

Although deliberate practice is important, growing evidence indicates that it is not as important as Ericsson and colleagues (Ericsson, 2007; Ericsson et al., 1993; Ericsson & Moxley, 2012) have previously argued. Gobet and Campitelli (2007) found a large amount of variability in total amount of deliberate practice among master-level chess players – from slightly more than 3,000 hours to more than 23,000 hours. In a recent reanalysis of previous findings, Hambrick et al. (2014) found that deliberate practice accounted for about one-third of the reliable variance in performance in chess and music. Thus, in these domains, a large proportion of the variance in performance is explainable by factors other than deliberate practice (Macnamara, Hambrick, & Oswald, 2014).

Hambrick et al. (2014) further highlighted two popular myths regarding deliberate practice. The first myth is that people require very similar amounts of deliberate practice to acquire expert performance. Gladwell (2008) wrote in *Outliers* that Ericsson et al.'s (1993) "research suggested that once a musician has enough ability to get into a top music school, the thing that distinguishes one performer from another is how hard he or she works. That's it" (p. 39). Similarly, Syed (2010) wrote in his book *Bounce* that top performers had devoted thousands of additional hours to the task of becoming master performers. But that's not all. Ericsson also found that there were no exceptions to this pattern: nobody who had reached the elite group without copious practice, and nobody who had worked their socks off but failed to excel (pp. 12–13). Such categorical claims have been shown to be false. The evidence suggests that some individuals reach an elite level of performance without large volumes of practice, while other individuals fail to do so despite significant practice. The second myth is that it requires at least 10 years, or 10,000 hours, of deliberate practice to reach an elite level of performance. Ericsson et al. (2007) explained this idea as follows: "Our research shows that even the most gifted performers need a minimum of ten years (or 10,000 hours) of intense training before they win international competitions" (p. 119). Subsequently, Gladwell (2008) proposed in *Outliers* that "Ten thousand hours is the magic number of greatness" (p. 41). More recently, the Nobel laureate Daniel Kahneman (2011) wrote in his book *Thinking, Fast and Slow* that "Studies of chess masters have shown that at least 10,000 hours of dedicated practice … are required to attain the highest levels of performance" (p. 238). But the data indicate that there is an enormous amount of variability in deliberate practice – even in elite performers. One player in Gobet and Campitelli's (2007) chess sample took 26 years of serious involvement in chess to reach a master level, while another player took less than two years to reach this level. As a result, while deliberate practice is important, it does not appear to be the defining factor it has been suggested to be.

Ecological dynamics of skill acquisition

In recent decades, the dominant research philosophy within motor learning has been questioned through emerging theories, namely ecological psychology and dynamical systems theory under the umbrella of the constraints-led approach (Davids, Button, & Bennett, 2008). The associated framework of 'ecological dynamics' conceptualizes movement coordination as an emergent property resulting from interacting individual, task, and environment constraints (Seifert, Button, & Davids, 2013) rather than a top-down rules-based system. Co-ordination emerges in complex neurobiological systems (i.e. between muscles, joints, and limbs of the body) during learning and performance (Davids, Araújo, Vilar, Renshaw, & Pinder, 2013).

Ecological dynamics is a systems-oriented theoretical rationale for understanding the emergent relations in a complex system formed by each performer and a performance environment. This approach has identified the individual-environment relationship as the relevant scale of analysis for modelling how processes of perception, cognition, and action underpin expert performance in sport (Davids et al., 2013; Zelaznik, 2014).

According to Bernstein (1967) the acquisition of movement coordination is "the process of mastering redundant degrees of freedom of the moving organ, in other words its conversion to a controllable system" (p. 127). Building on this point, the theory of ecological dynamics advocates that the relevant scale of analysis for understanding behaviour is the performer-environment relationship, and not the description of the environment or the activities of the learner, separately (Araújo & Davids, 2011). Based on this perspective the most relevant information for performance and learning in dynamic environments arises from continuous performer-environment interactions (Araújo et al., 2006; Travassos, Araújo, Duarte, & McGarry, 2012; van Orden, Holden, & Turvey, 2003).

Gibson (1986) suggested that individuals are surrounded by 'banks' of energy flows that have the potential to act as specifying information variables to constrain the coordination of actions in performance environments. The critical information that is inherent in the environment then serves to continuously shape decision-making, planning and organization, and goal-directed behaviour. One example of this in practice would be a basketball player dribbling the ball and moving in a synchronized way with the environment (Cordovil et al., 2009).

As a result, skill acquisition programmes in sport, therefore, should aim to develop an enhanced coupling of an individual's perception and action sub-systems to achieve intended task goals (Davids et al., 2013). One of the ways in which this can be achieved is to help the performer to understand information sources and how to harness them for action (Davids et al., 2013). From the ecological dynamics perspective the development of expertise requires learning how to identify and use opportunities for action to then achieve their performance goals. Crucial in designing practice from this perspective is the representative design of the learning environment (see Chapter 13 for further details).

Factors influencing motor skill development

It has been well established that an individual's focus of attention can have important implications for motor performance (e.g. Beilock et al., 2002; Gray, 2004; Jackson, Ashford, & Norsworthy, 2006; Land, Frank, & Schack, 2014; Wulf, 2007). That is, what an individual focuses on during the execution of a motor task can greatly influence the quality and accuracy of the movement. To this extent, research has demonstrated that an external focus of attention (e.g. focusing on the effects of the movement on the environment) can lead to greater performance accuracy (Wulf & Su, 2007), reduced attentional/working memory demands (Wulf, McNevin, & Shea, 2001), reduced brain and muscle activity (Zachry, Wulf, Mercer, & Bezodis, 2004), reduced susceptibility to choking under pressure (Land & Tenenbaum, 2012), and overall better outcome performance (McNevin, Shea, & Wulf, 2003), compared to an internal focus (i.e. attention directed to the performer's own body movements), or irrelevant focus (i.e. attention directed to stimuli not pertaining to the task). Furthermore, one's focus of attention may also play an important role during the learning of a new motor skill. Research has indicated significant differences in motor skill acquisition as a result of how one focuses their attention (e.g. external or internal focus of attention) during learning (see Wulf, 2007). Traditionally, motor learning has been assumed to benefit from attention directed to the step-by-step components of skill execution (Wulf & McNevin, 2003). Instructions and feedback, therefore, are typically given to novices regarding various aspects of their movements. However, recent research suggests that skill acquisition is facilitated when attention is directed externally to the effects of one's movement on the environment, and not the movements themselves (Castaneda & Gray, 2007).

Information in dynamic performance domains changes instantaneously. The ecological dynamics perspective highlights how performers perceive properties of performance environments as opportunities to act (i.e. affordances) (Gibson, 1986). Affordances capture the fit between individual performer constraints and relevant properties of specific performance environments. Perceiving an affordance is to perceive how one can act under specific performance conditions, which need to be simulated carefully in training tasks. In team environments individuals couple actions to relevant properties of particular performance environments, such as the distance to a teammate/opponent (Travassos et al., 2012), goal, or target area (Travassos et al., 2012; Vilar, Araújo, Davids, & Travassos, 2012) and location of the ball relative to a teammate/opponent (Travassos et al., 2012). Affordances are dynamic, continuously changing across on-going performer-performer(s) interactions, providing the rationale for a more extensive focus on SSCG in team games training. Affordances could be designed into training tasks by faithfully sampling key properties of performance environments. Athletes can learn how to guide their actions according to the informational specificity of each performance context.

Summary

For all performance domains the acquisition and development of important motor skills is a fundamental requirement for future success. As such understanding the process by which this development takes place is important to be able to maximize skill development that is a prerequisite for performance. The learning environment and learning/developmental activities can then be designed to take advantage of this knowledge of the process and influencing factors. This in turn can serve to develop skilled performance and expertise in a quicker and more efficient manner. Also, by understanding the process of skill acquisition/development ultimately higher levels of competence and expertise can be achieved.

Study questions

1. What are the key differences between traditional and ecological dynamics approaches to motor skill development?

2. To what extent does the Mesh approach answer some of the criticisms levelled at traditional models of skill development?
3. How important is deliberate practice in the achievement of performance expertise?

Further reading

Araújo, D., Davids, K., & Hristovski, R. (2006). The ecological dynamics of decision making in sport. *Psychology of Sport and Exercise, 7*, 653–676.

This article provides a good overview of the ecological dynamics approach and the implications for practice.

Davids, K., Button, C., & Bennett, S. (2008). *Dynamics of skill acquisition: A constraints-led approach*. Champaign, IL: Human Kinetics.

The article outlines how a constraints-led approach can be implemented in seeking to enhance skill acquisition.

Hodges, N., & Williams, M. A. (2012). *Skill acquisition in sport: Research, theory and practice*. Abingdon: Routledge.

The book provides a detailed overview of the skill acquisition literature, also articulating current understanding and future challenges from a traditional perspective.

12

PSYCHOLOGICAL STRATEGIES TO ENHANCE PERFORMANCE UNDER PRESSURE

Introduction

While there are many performance-focused interventions that are used by sport and performance psychologists in practice, evidence suggests a key set of skills that can help to underpin performance. These skills ideally should be embedded in development programmes to ensure they are as well developed as the motor skills ultimately underpinning performance. The structured approach adopted to the development of these skills is referred to as psychological skills training, and the systematic development of relevant psychological skills has been associated with enhanced performance outcomes (Behncke, 2004; Birrer & Morgan, 2010).

This chapter will explore what mental skills training is and considers the evidence supporting the development of imagery, cognitive restructuring, self-talk, relaxation techniques, goal setting, and concentration/focusing strategies.

Psychological skills training

Psychological skills training (PST) refers to the systematic and consistent practice of mental or psychological skills for the purpose of enhancing performance, increasing enjoyment, or achieving greater sport and physical activity self-satisfaction (Weinberg & Gould, 2007, p. 250). Based on this perspective, PST should be developed in a systematic, goal-oriented, planned, controlled, and evaluated manner (Seiler & Stock, 1994). Some authors (Seiler & Stock, 1994; Vealey, 2007) who have focused on PST have differentiated between psychological skills as the desired outcome (e.g. increased self-confidence and enhanced attentional focus) and psychological methods or techniques (e.g. imagery and self-talk) as the means to promote the desired outcomes through the systematic application of these techniques. Research across a number of domains has shown that psychological skills training can be effective in enhancing the individual's performance and positively influencing cognitive and affective states (Williams & Krane, 2001).

In the last two decades, a variety of specific intervention techniques have been promoted to help performers develop psychological skills to enhance their performance (Weinberg & Williams, 2001). Employing a combination of intervention techniques has been shown to be particularly effective in sports including: tennis (Daw & Burton, 1994), cricket (Spittle & Morris, 1997), and gymnastics (Kazemi, Khaberi, & Farokhi, 2003).

A range of specific psychological skills have been cited in a range of studies as having the potential to mediate the effect that performing under pressure can have on the individual performer including: imagery, cognitive restructuring, self-talk, relaxation techniques, goal setting, and focusing/concentration.

Imagery

Imagery is one of the most popular psychological skill techniques utilized by performers and coaches/mentors to enhance performance. The frequent use of imagery has been reported to be a characteristic of those most successful performers in the domain of sport (Cumming & Williams, 2013; Martin, Moritz, & Hall, 1999). It has been described as an experience that reflects actual experience in a variety of senses (e.g. sight, taste, sound) without experiencing the real thing (White & Hardy, 1998). Holmes and Calmels (2008) in seeking to further clarify the concept defined imagery as a top-down, knowledge-driven process involving the generation or regeneration of parts of a brain representation or neural network. They further explain that imagery is primarily under the conscious control of the individual. This allows individuals to experience or re-experience situations in their mind by retrieving information from long-term memory (Cumming & Williams, 2013).

Imagery ability is defined as "an individual's capability of forming vivid, controllable images and retaining them for sufficient time to effect the desired imagery rehearsal" (Morris, Spittle, & Watt, 2005, p. 60). Hall (1998) explained that everyone has the ability to generate an image, but this may differ between individuals in terms of vividness, controllability, kinesthetic feelings, ease, and emotional experience. Studies confirm that imagery abilities are not universal across individuals and patterns of activation move from the frontal area to more posterior parts of the brain in good imagers (Debarnot, Sperduti, Di Rienzo, & Guillot, 2014). Individuals may have varying capacities to generate images depending on imagery mode (Goss, Hall, Buckolz, & Fishburne, 1986; Guillot et al., 2009) and/or perspective (Williams et al., 2012). Studies have also shown that mental imagery is an ability that improves with practice, and, as initially proposed by Paivio (1985) it is a function of experience interacting with genetic (biological) variability (i.e. physiological differences among individuals and within the same individual overtime).

Motor imagery can be described as the mental execution of a movement without any overt movement or muscle activation (Lotze & Halsband, 2006). Several studies have reported improvements in performance with motor imagery practice (Feltz & Landers, 1983; Holmes & Calmels, 2008; Murphy, 1994; Stevens & Stoykov, 2003).

Within performance domains, the two main (but not the only) modalities of movement imagery that performers use to enhance performance outcomes are visual and kinaesthetic. Visual imagery involves seeing the movement and can be experienced from two different perspectives: external and internal. External visual imagery involves watching yourself perform the movement as if from another person's point of view. Whereas, internal visual imagery involves viewing the movement through your own eyes as if actually performing the movement (Morris et al., 2005). Kinaesthetic imagery refers to imaging the feelings and sensations associated with the movement. Although internal, external, and kinaesthetic imagery have been identified as separate constructs (Roberts, Callow, Hardy, Markland, & Bringer, 2008; Williams et al., 2012), combining visual and kinaesthetic imagery is thought to be most beneficial for enhancing performance (Williams et al., 2012).

Cognitive restructuring

This technique refers to a structured, collaborative therapeutic approach in which distressed individuals are taught how to identify, evaluate, and modify the faulty thoughts, evaluations, and beliefs that are considered responsible for their psychological disturbance (Dobson & Dozois, 2010; Hollon & Dimidjian, 2009).

Cognitive restructuring techniques have been applied across a broad range of contexts and have been shown to reduce depression (Marcotte, 1997); increase self-esteem (Schilder, 2002); and reduce anxiety (Sud, 1993). Cognitive restructuring is a useful method for controlling symptoms of depression (and anxiety) and is based on the premise that what causes these feelings is not the situation itself but, rather, the interpretation of the situation. So, by changing the interpretation of the system the individual can then influence their associated thoughts and behaviours. Indeed, Meyers, Whelan, and Murphy (1996) highlighted the effectiveness of cognitive restructuring in enabling sports performers to achieve higher levels of performance.

Burns (1989) outlined a six-step process to implementing cognitive restructuring. First, to identify the problematic or upsetting situation. Second, to record the associated negative feelings. Third, record your automatic thoughts. Fourth, to analyse these thoughts. Fifth, to construct realistic and balanced thoughts. Sixth, to evaluate this restructuring process.

Self-talk

Self-talk techniques are based on the use of specific verbal cues that aim to facilitate learning and enhancing performance, through the activation of appropriate responses. Such techniques have been implemented in a variety of motor and performance tasks ranging from fine (Van Raalte et al., 1995) to gross (Hamilton,

Scott, & MacDougall, 2007). A recent meta-analysis (Hatzigeorgiadis, Zourbanos, Galanis, & Theodorakis, 2011) more emphatically stressed the effectiveness of self-talk interventions in sport. An overall effect size of 0.48 was identified, indicating that self-talk can meaningfully facilitate learning and enhance performance in sport tasks.

Hardy and colleagues (2009) proposed a conceptual framework that theorized the factors believed to underpin the self-talk–performance relationship. Adopting a throughput perspective, the authors argued that self-talk improves motor skill execution via four possible mechanisms (cognitive, motivational, behavioural, and affective). Cognitive mechanisms were described as encompassing informational processing and attentional control. Performers have reported using self-talk for a variety of attention-based outcomes (e.g. concentration; Chroni, Perkos, & Theodorakis, 2007), and in addition, experimental studies have indicated that manipulating self-talk may be a useful adjunct strategy to alter attentional foci (Bell & Hardy, 2009) and decrease interfering thoughts (Hatzigeorgiadis, Theodorakis, & Zourbanos, 2004). Motivational mechanisms relate to a focus on self-efficacy (Bandura, 1997) and persistence or long-term goal commitment. Self-talk use has been associated with persistence and subsequent higher performance on challenging tasks (Chiu & Alexander, 2000).

Behaviour mechanisms refer to the direct impact of self-talk on behaviour. Researchers have identified improvements in both subjectively and objectively assessed technique resulting from self-talk (Anderson, Vogel, & Albrecht, 1999; Edwards, Tod, & McGuigan, 2008). It has also been suggested that during early phases of skill learning, novices may 'talk' themselves through movements (Coker & Fischman, 2010; Fitts & Posner, 1967). Affective mechanisms relate to the potential impact that affect can have on performance. A number of studies have highlighted a link between cognitive content and affect (e.g. Beck, 1976; Lazarus, 1991), and in turn, affect and performance (e.g. Beedie et al., 2000). Evidence suggests that self-talk may also serve to increase self-confidence in performers (Johnson, Hrycaiko, Johnson, & Hallas, 2004; Landin & Hebert, 1999; Perkos, Theodorakis, & Chroni, 2002).

Relaxation techniques

Relaxation techniques can be divided into two specific categories: muscle to mind, and mind to muscle. Muscles to mind techniques include breathing exercises and Jacobson's progressive muscular relaxation approach. Mind to muscle techniques include meditation, autogenic approaches, and imagery approaches, each of which is unique, but also have the same effect on physiological variables in the body (Alwan, Zakaria, Rahim, Hamid, & Fuad, 2013). Procedures like progressive muscular relaxation, autogenic training, imagery, and meditation seek to decrease oxygen consumption, heart rate, and respiration (Cox, 2007; Dusek et al., 2008; Stefano, Fricchione, Slingsby, & Benson, 2001). Described as the 'gold standard' of relaxation techniques (Weinberg, 2010a), progressive muscle relaxation seems best suited to self-paced activities where there are natural breaks in performance. Davidson and Schwartz's (1976) matching hypothesis reinforces the appropriateness of such a technique to address the muscular tension and increased heart rate that can be present in pressured environments. The major criticisms of progressive muscle relaxation have predominantly focused on the technique's lack of utility in a performance environment (Balague, 2005; Morris & Thomas, 1995). However, this criticism is perhaps a little superficial as once the technique is well learnt, performers should be able to scan their bodies for feelings of tension and subsequently relax specific muscles (Batey & Symes, 2016).

Goal setting

Goal setting has been advocated as "a highly consistent and a robust performance enhancement strategy" (Burton & Naylor, 2002, p. 463). Research suggests that goal setting is particularly effective in enhancing performance and positively affecting behaviour when focusing on a combination of outcome, performance, and process goals (Filby, Maynard, & Graydon, 1999; Gould, 2001). There is evidence that goal setting can be highly effective in influencing behaviour, motivation, and performance. Indeed a number of meta-analyses in the psychology literature (Burton, Naylor, & Holliday, 2001; Kyllo & Landers, 1995) have consistently reported strong to moderate effects of goal-setting use on overall performance. Goal setting is particularly effective as it influences performance in four distinct ways. First, goals direct attention to important elements of the skills and tasks being performed. Second, goals prolong the efforts of the individual and team. Third, goals prolong player and team persistence. Finally, goals foster the development of new learning and problem-solving strategies (Weinberg & Gould, 2007).

Within the goal-setting literature there are generally two main classifications of goals. First, goals are either classified as being outcome, performance, or process focused. Second, goals are referred to as being short-term or long-term. Outcome goals focus on the ultimate outcomes linked to a positive performance, and are in the main, focused on winning. Unfortunately achieving this type of goal is not necessarily within the performer's control as the outcome also depends on a range of environmental factors, including the performance of others. Performance goals are linked to the explicit performance of individual performers. Process goals are usually focused on how a particular skill is executed. This type of goal is equally useful in both practice and the performance domain. There is evidence to suggest that using a combination of goal strategies (outcome, performance, and process goals) can produce significantly better results than just relying on one type of goal (Filby et al., 1999). As well as the three different types of goals outlined above, there is also a distinction drawn between short-term and long-term goals. Long-term goals are seen as ultimate goals. For Olympic athletes it could be winning a medal at the next Olympics in four years' time. Short-term goals are more immediate and provide the stepping-stones for achieving the long-term goals. Burton (1992) made reference to a goal-setting 'staircase' with the short-term goals helping you to climb closer to the ultimate long-term goals. A successful performer should set a mixture of both short-term and long-term goals to be most effective. Indeed, research has revealed that both short-term and long-term goals are needed to maintain motivation and performance in the long-term (Weinberg, Butt, & Knight, 2001).

Research across performance domains has clearly demonstrated that just setting goals alone does not necessarily ensure improvements in performance or productivity. Instead, it is recognized that certain principles need to be followed to maximize the effectiveness of the goals that may have been set. Weinberg (2010b) highlighted the following findings from a range of performance-related goal-setting research in seeking how to be most effective in using goal setting to enhance performance:

- Performance is enhanced when goals are moderately difficult and challenging, but also realistic.
- Goal setting can help to provide a focus for both the teams and the individual team members.
- Motivation and commitment are higher if the team accepts the set goals.
- Goals, and feedback relating to these goals, produce better performances than just setting goals.
- Barriers to goal achievement are usually categorized as physical, psychological, or external.
- Goals should be prioritized (either order of importance or preference).
- Performance and process goals should be emphasized the most.
- A number of factors negatively affect goal achievement including time pressure, stress, tiredness, and social relationships.
- Both short-term and long-term goals are important.

A number of sources within the broader psychology literature advocate the SMART approach to goal setting (Bull, Albinson, & Shambrook, 1996), referring to effective goals as being specific (S), measurable (M), action-related (A), realistic (R), and timetabled (T). Possibly the most important, and often overlooked, aspect of goal setting is the evaluation and re-evaluation of progress and achievement. This evaluation allows current progress to be monitored and for changes to be made if required, maximizing the potential for the goal(s) to be realized.

Concentration/focusing

Concentration is an attentional process that involves the ability to focus on the task at hand while ignoring a range of competing stimuli (distractions). Cognitive research has consistently the importance of concentration and shows that it is vital in any field of skilled performance (Moran, 2012). According to Wulf (2007) and Wulf, Shea, and Lewthwaite (2010), the accuracy and quality of skilled actions depend significantly on what the performer focuses on while executing their skills.

Concentration/focusing strategies are another core component of many psychological skills development programmes. The general rationale here is that distractions should be kept to a minimum or eliminated with only relevant information allowed into the performer's attentional space (Kimiecik & Jackson, 2002).

It is important where possible to adopt a positive rather than a negative strategy in this regard. Examples of negatively focusing strategies include the notion of 'thought stopping', a process of stopping negative thoughts and replacing them with positive ones. While a number of authors have advocated this approach (Sheard & Golby, 2006; Zinsser et al., 2006) it is very difficult to do. So, instead of focusing on what not to get distracted by performers should focus on what to concentrate on. A subtle but important difference. That said it is still important to understand the sources of distraction, which in turn can help to foster effective concentration strategies. Many attentional researchers (e.g. Johnston & Dark, 1986) distinguish between 'external' (data-driven or bottom-up) and 'internal' (concept-driven or top-down) processes. The former involve sensory activity while the latter entail cognitive processing (Howe, Warm, & Dember, 1995). 'External' distractions are described as stimuli from the environment, which diverts the performer's attention away from its intended direction. Typical distractors in this category include (i) visual distraction, (ii) noise, (iii) weather and playing conditions, and (iv) the behaviour and tactics of opponents. Indeed, Dalloway (1993) suggested mastery over thoughts, fears and worries (i.e. internal noise) frequently poses a greater challenge than overcoming external distractions. Moran (1996) in his 'losing concentration in sport' chapter highlighted five aspects to internal distraction, these are: (i) regrets, (ii) fortune telling, (iii) inadequate motivation, (iv) fatigue, and (v) anxiety.

In order to counter these distractions Kremer and Moran (2008) highlighted five key principles for effective concentration: decide to concentrate (it won't just happen); focus on one thought at a time; do exactly what you are thinking; focus only on factors you can control; and focus outward when you get nervous. A range of practical strategies have been developed to improve the performer's ability to concentrate including: pre-performance routines (for further detail see Chapter 3); trigger words (a form of self-talk); visualization (imagery); goal setting, and simulation training. Simulation training (i.e. practising under conditions that replicate key aspects of an impending challenge) has been suggested to help skilled performers to concentrate (Moran, 2012) more effectively in the real performance domain.

Summary

While specific situations often demand individualized psychological solutions the development and implementation of the broad strategies and techniques in this chapter can go a long way to ensuring performers are well prepared to cope with the challenges that their specific performance domain holds. As with the development of motor skills these psychological skills need to be developed and practised on a regular basis to ensure that they are well learnt and almost habitual in their deployment. Environments that are designed to help foster the performers of the future should seek to embed the development and understanding of these key psychological skills to ensure future performers are as well prepared as they can be to cope with the challenges they will face.

Study questions

1. To what extent do you believe the key psychological skills should be embedded in performance development environments?
2. What factors could limit the effectiveness or application of imagery-focused interventions in a wider context?
3. While many individuals are aware of the importance of effective goal-setting practice is still variable. What factors impact upon the application of goal-setting theory for performance?

Further reading

Gould, D. (2001). Goal setting for peak performance. In J. M. Williams (Ed.), *Applied sport psychology: Personal growth to peak performance* (4th edn, pp. 190–205). Mountain View, CA: Mayfield.

This chapter presents a good overview of goal-setting theory, and practice strategies for the successful setting and monitoring of goals to enhance performance.

Vealey, R. S. (2007). Mental skills training in sport. In G. Tenenbaum & R. C. Eklund (Eds.), *Handbook of sport psychology* (3rd edn, pp. 287–309). Hoboken, NJ: John Wiley & Sons.

The chapter offers a good overview of psychological skills training and its application within a sporting environment.

13

PRACTISING FOR PERFORMANCE

Introduction

In many performance domains individuals must adapt to the constraints of a dynamic environment, with commensurate variable conditions and situations, while performing under different emotional states that constrain their cognitions, perceptions, and actions (Headrick, Renshaw, Davids, Pinder, & Araújo, 2015). As a result the preparatory activities of any performer need to incorporate the full range of variables to maximize preparation for performance. A criticism of performers historically has been that they have focused too much on skill development at the expense of skill deployment. That is to say insufficient attention has been given to the transfer from practice to the performance domain. In particular limited attention has been given to the design of the practice domain to facilitate optimal performance in the performance domain and to increase the probability of highly effective and efficient skill execution, all of which increases the likelihood of positive performance outcomes.

This chapter will explore the concepts of preparation and practice, and the development of habitual responses to specific triggers and environmental conditions. The chapter will also consider the importance of representative task design, the links between preparation and performance, and how to maximize this transfer from practice to performance.

What is preparation and practice?

Preparation for the performance environment is a crucial aspect of the actual performance itself. This concept of preparation is related to but also different from the notion of skill learning through deliberate practice (see Chapter 11 for further information). Having the technical ability to execute required skills is important, but executing the right skills at the right time is of paramount importance. Careful preparation is crucial to success; "that is not to say that everything will go according to plans, but the precondition for departing from your plan is that you have a plan" (Anders Fogh Rasmussen, Secretary General, NATO: quoted from Wedell-Wedellsborg, 2015).

One example of this notion of 'preparation for performance' is that of the French Military Health Service Tactical Combat Casualty Care (TCCC) programme. Following a review of the conditions of modern combat the French Military Health Service developed a programme to best prepare its Medical Personnel to perform in the combat arena (Pasquier et al., 2014). The medical practitioners in the programme are highly skilled medical personnel, but the French military recognized that the ability to perform these complex skills in the 'real world' environment was crucial. The programme develops a deep understanding of appropriate techniques, and crucially considers the environment in which the techniques need to be applied. The programme also requires the medical staff to apply these techniques in 'real' simulated environments. Parallels can be drawn here with many performance domains and the need, where possible, to simulate the 'real' performance environment. Often the aim is to develop habitual responses to key environment stimulus.

By contrast practice refers more to the process of repetition of actions (repeating) associated with skill learning and development. Practice in itself does not lead to high quality performance (Ericsson et al., 1993). Ericsson and colleagues clarified that deliberate practice (activities that require cognitive or physical effort), does not lead to immediate personal, social, or financial rewards. But it is undertaken with the purpose of improving performance, as it is ultimately what is required for highly consistent and flawless/near-flawless skill execution. The repetitive nature of practice also underpins the development of habitual responses (or habits) to specific stimuli. The nature of good quality preparation is to ensure that the stimuli or cues that are being responded to are consistent with the performance environment.

Habit formation

What are habits?

The more an action or a skill is repeated in a certain way (such as throwing a ball) the more the action becomes 'reinforced' and as a result the brain develops a tendency to respond in that particular way to a stimulus (ball in your hand). Over time the more reinforcing that takes place the stronger that tendency to respond in a certain way (habit) becomes (strengthening the association between stimulus and response). Habits are generally described in psychology as the learning of sequences of actions that have become automatic responses to specific situations, which may be functional in order to satisfy specific needs, or to obtain certain goals (Aarts, Paulssen, & Schaalma, 1997). Habits are characterized by a goal-directed type of automaticity, and habitual behaviours are instigated by a specific goal-directed state of mind in the presence of triggering stimulus cues. The reason why understanding habits is so important is that they both underpin and determine our behaviour. Researchers in psychology have suggested that deliberate intention (what you would like to do) may become irrelevant in guiding a response when behaviours have been repeatedly performed in the past and have become habitual (Triandis, 1980). Indeed, it is suggested that while there is an interaction between intention (what you would like to do) and habit (what you have programmed yourself to do), it is ultimately the ingrained actions (habits) that have the greatest influence (Aarts et al., 1997). This relationship is particularly true under conditions of pressure. The ability to think through different courses of action is further reduced and because of this the performer becomes even more likely to respond in a habitual way. As a result, it is important to ensure that performers develop the right habits to help them to perform effectively under pressure.

There is consensus in the literature that habits are acquired through the incremental strengthening of the association between stimulus and response. Repetition of a behaviour in a consistent context progressively increases the automaticity with which the behaviour is performed when the situation is encountered (Verplanken, 2006; Wood & Neal, 2007). 'Automaticity' in this context is evidenced by the behaviour displaying some or all of the following features: efficiency, lack of awareness, unintentionality, and uncontrollability (Bargh, 1994). Essentially, the more you practise the greater the association between the action and the goal. What is learnt in preparation and practice then forms the foundation of the automatic responses that take place in the performance environment. When performing any action the individual learns about the favourable and unfavourable consequences of the action. If the action resulted in a positive outcome the performer is more likely to repeat it. As a result, decisions are strongly influenced by previous experiences, a process that ultimately underpins habit formation. Habit strength increases as a result of repetitions of positive reinforcements. This is one of the reasons why a performer who is successful early on in their career may be developing bad habits that will constrain performance in the future (Aarts et al., 1997). When it comes to performing under pressure habitual behaviours are then triggered by a specific goal-directed state of mind that occurs in the presence of relevant triggering stimulus cues from the environment. Often though this strong association between the goal and the action is overlooked in many practice settings, often manifesting itself in preparation environments that do not mirror the performance environment. This is because principles of training specificity suggest that training demands should replicate match requirements to ensure optimal adaptation (Reilly, Morris, & Whyte, 2009).

Historically there has been a lack of the application of this principle in preparatory training across a range of performance settings. One such example is cricket, and in particular the use of bowling machines in preparation. Pinder and colleagues (2009) have demonstrated that removing the information available in a bowler's delivery action (running up and bowling the ball) can lead to detrimental performance changes in batter's timing and coordination. This is turn has the potential to reduce performance success in the real performance environment.

Verplanken (2006) suggested that complex behaviours achieve lower levels of automaticity than simple behaviours. The main assumption underlying this process-oriented approach towards habits is that frequent and consistent behavioural choices made to attain the same goal determines the formation of an association between a goal and an action, and thus, a habit (Aarts & Dijksterhuis, 2000).

Historically, habits have been measured by assessing the frequency of past behaviours (Ajzen, 2002; Sheeran, 2002). However, this assumes that the relationship between repetition and automaticity is linear, which is unlikely because it implies that every repetition, whether early on in the habit formation process or after a large number of repetitions, would result in the same increase in automaticity.

Changing existing habitual responses

Habitual responses once developed can be very difficult to change. The reason for this is that habits are formed through significant repetition. This repetition underpins the whole process of learning, and the more an action is repeated the stronger the resulting association between the stimulus and that specific response. Many efforts to change behaviour are characterized either by complete failure or by short-term success followed by relapse (see Polivy & Herman, 2002 for a review). The defining quality of habitual responses is that a history of reinforcement means that the learned response is elicited relatively automatically when the associated cue is encountered (Webb, Sheeran, & Luszczynska, 2009). As a result, seeking to reverse this process can be problematic.

One self-regulatory strategy that has been proposed to support individuals in managing the critical stimulus in such a way that they are able to act on their counter-habitual intentions is to furnish one's intentions with 'implementation intentions' (Adriaanse, De Ridder, & De Wit, 2009). Implementation intentions specifying the replacement of a habitual response with an alternative response in a critical situation can overrule habits. These implementation intentions are simple action plans stipulating where, when, and how one will perform an intended behaviour, which have been found to promote goal-directed action (Gollwitzer, 1999). Instead of simply specifying an end state the performer aims to reach, as is the case for intentions ("I intend to achieve X"), implementation intentions specify the where, when, and how of reaching this end state and take the form of "If I am in situation X, then I will perform goal directed behaviour Y" (Gollwitzer, 1999, p. 495). Recent studies have provided compelling evidence for the notion that implementation intentions that link a critical cue for a habitual response to an alternative response can effectively overrule habitual responses (Adriaanse et al., 2011).

Representative practice/preparation design

Egon Brunswik proposed the term 'representative design' as an alternative to systematic design more than half a century ago (Brunswik, 1956). He advocated the study of psychological processes at the level of organism–environment relations, an ideal focus for psychologists interested in performance-related research and practice (Pinder, Davids, Renshaw, & Araújo, 2011). In recent years the concept of representative design has become entangled with another of Brunswik's terms, ecological validity (Araújo, Davids, & Passos, 2007), which has been inadvertently adopted to refer to the generalizability of experimental designs in sport psychology and other sports sciences.

Brunswik (1956) advocated that for the study of organism–environment interactions (such as those observed in visual anticipation in research), 'cues' (or perceptual variables) should be sampled from the organism's typical environment so as to be representative of the environmental stimuli from which they have been adapted, and to which behaviour is intended to be generalized (Brunswik, 1956).

For performers, coaches, mentors, and support staff focused on achieving high levels of performance, representative design equates to the design of practice and preparation environments. As in experiments, the constraints of preparation and practice need to adequately replicate the performance environment so that they allow performers to detect opportunities for action and couple actions to key information sources within those specific settings (Pinder et al., 2011). A related and important concept that also requires consideration at this point is that of Action Fidelity (Araújo et al., 2007; Stoffregen, Bardy, Smart, & Pagulayan, 2003). In the context of flight simulations, Stoffregen et al. (2003, p. 120) described action fidelity as the "fidelity of performance", and proposed that fidelity exists when there is a transfer of performance from the simulator to the simulated system. In this respect, practice, preparation, and learning tasks could be viewed as simulations of the performance environment that need to be high in action fidelity (in much the same way that video designs in experimental settings are simulations of the performance context that is the subject of generalization). The degree of action fidelity that exists can be measured by analysing task performance in detail, and comparing the different environments.

The representative nature of preparation tasks is crucial as research suggests that the use of 'modified' activities can change the demands of the task. For example, Vickery, Dascombe, Duffield, Kellett, and Portus (2013) highlighted that the use of a 'small-sided game' playing environments can significantly influence the activity demands and resulting physiological responses in sports such as football and rugby. This is similar to the changes in activity demands that result from the use of bowling machines in cricket (Pinder, Renshaw, & Davids, 2009). These changes make the environment less information rich, which impacts upon information perception and processes.

Links between preparation and performance

When considering the links between preparation and performance a number of factors can be used to explore the similarities between the two environments. In cricket Petersen, Pyne, Dawson, Kellett, & Portus (2011) have demonstrated that in comparison to matches, the physiological demands on players have historically been typically lower when performing game simulations and skill sessions. This suggests that there are real differences between the requirements of the practice and performance environments. Effective preparation for performance is crucial in helping the individual cope with the pressures and stress of the performance context (Cotterill, 2015). The maintenance of an optimal psychological state during the pre-performance period in particular has been highlighted as a key factor determining performance (Kao et al., 2013). Arora et al. (2010) in considering the performance environment of surgeons highlighted that the operating room can be a highly pressurized environment in which surgeons encounter various stressors, including technical complications, equipment failure, time pressures, distractions, evaluative threat, and performance anxiety. In this environment it has been suggested that effective preparation is crucial in determining the surgeon's ability to cope with these stressors (Arora et al., 2010). In particular effective preparation has been suggested to enhance the surgeon's ability to cope with evaluative pressure, time pressure, and distractions (Arora et al., 2010). But to be effective the preparatory environment needs to reflect these specific demands.

Cotterill (2015) conducted research to explore the preparatory techniques adopted across a range of performance domains. The participants were 18 'performers', drawn from sporting, musical, performing arts, and medical domains. The results suggest that there are similarities in both behavioural and mental preparation strategies adopted across performance professions. This reinforces the view that the importance of preparation to perform is recognized across a number of performance domains (Broomhead et al., 2012; Burke, 2010; Cotterill et al., 2010; Hammermeister, Pickering, & Lennox, 2010).

Strategies to enhance preparation for performance

The starting point here is to understand the specific challenges that exist in the real performance environment. If performers, coaches, and mentors understand these performance challenges they can design and set up scenarios and challenges that, as accurately as possible, replicate the real performance environment and the existing constraints/influencing factors.

This point returns to whether the performer is learning the skill (practice) or preparing to perform (preparation). If the performer is learning the skill they need repetition to get better at the skill (deliberate practice). When preparing to perform the individual needs to be able to, as much as possible, replicate the demands of performance (Pinder et al., 2011). Often, it is left to the individual performer to really make the practice scenario as realistic as possible. Anything you do that is outside of the real performance environment is never exactly the same. As such it is the responsibility of the performer to create the real scenario in their head. This requires the performer to push to achieve the performance and intensity levels required. Anyone can perform flawlessly when the pressure is off, but can they do it when it counts? The best performers in preparation mode will have a specific scenario in their head and will have a clear idea of what the required outcome is. Then, after every practice they will evaluate their performance against this target, with only the best being acceptable. In this way the performers learn to execute the skill, but also how to execute the skill in the right situation with the appropriate control.

So as mentioned at the start of this section, understanding the challenges of the real performance environment can ensure that the performers prepare in a way that increases the individual's ability to execute the skills when it matters under pressure. So what are these factors? The more closely the practice domain can mirror the real performance environment the better. So, using the sport of cricket as an example, practising in the middle of a prepared grass pitch, with batters, a wicket keeper, bowlers, umpires, and the appropriate number of fielders in real game scenarios is about as realistic as possible. Or considering dramatic or musical performances, practising on a stage running a full 'dress rehearsal' in front of a crowd is the ultimate practice (Vickery et al., 2013).

Although typically focusing on soccer-based team sports, past research has suggested that the use of small-sided games allows players to simultaneously develop decision-making and technical ability, along with metabolic conditioning, while simulating match conditions (Dellal et al., 2008; Gabbett, 2006; Gamble, 2004). A small-sided games approach to cricket training has been developed and termed 'Battlezone' (Renshaw, Chappell, Fitzgerald, Davison, & McFadyen, 2010). Renshaw et al. (2010) proposed that Battlezone allows players to acquire cricket-specific skills in an intensive match-simulation environment. Such a training environment may facilitate a greater transference of learnt skills into match play (Renshaw et al., 2010). It is also important in team-focused sports to replicate real match constraints to facilitate the development of shared mental models, which in turn will underpin collective team decision-making during performance (Giske, Rodahl, & Høigaard, 2014).

In sport, performers must adapt to the constraints of dynamic performance environments, with commensurate variable conditions and situations, while performing under different emotional states that constrain their cognitions, perceptions, and actions (Jones, 2003; Lewis, 2004). As a result the preparation environments must as much as possible reflect the key constraints. Indeed, an ecological dynamics approach to enhancing expertise recognizes the need for individuals to form mutual functional relationships with specific performance environments during practice and training (Araújo & Davids, 2011; Davids et al., 2013; Seifert et al., 2013).

Summary

Preparing for performance and the performing environment is as important as the development of expert skills in the first instance. One without the other significantly reduces the probability of high quality performance outcomes. The representative nature of the practice environment will determine the degree to which the performer can apply their underpinning motor skills in the performance context.

Consideration should be given to the constraints and sources of information that are present in the performance environment and how these can be replicated, or as much as possible reproduced in practice. More research is needed to better understand how this can successfully be achieved, and in particular specific case studies of approaches adopted would be particularly beneficial to the development of an evidence-based approach to preparation for performance.

Study questions

1. What variables are crucial in order to replicate (as much as possible) the task and environmental demands of the performance environment?
2. What are the implications for future success of developing inefficient/non-optimal technique (habits) in the development phase?
3. How can practitioners effectively seek to develop a representative design for preparation sessions, and maximize action fidelity?

Further reading

Pinder, R. A., Davids, K., Renshaw, I., & Araujo, D. (2011). Representative design and functionality of research and practice in sport. *Journal of Sport and Exercise Psychology, 33*, 146–155.

This article explores the important concept of representative design in particular detail and offers a range of practical recommendations for research and for applied practice.

Vickery, W., Dascombe, B., Duffeld, R., Kellett, A., & Portus, M. (2013). The influence of field size, player number, and rule changes on the physiological responses and movement demands of small-sided games for cricket training. *Journal of Sports Sciences, 31*, 629–638.

An interesting article that considers the real implications of the practice environment in relation to the 'real' demands of competition.

14

FUTURE DEVELOPMENTS IN RESEARCH AND PRACTICE

Introduction

While knowledge and understanding relating to the core aspects of performance psychology has developed significantly in recent years there still remain many unanswered questions. Indeed, advances in both understanding and technology have opened up a number of areas of investigation that were not previously explorable. This chapter will seek to summarize key limitations in current knowledge and gaps in understanding highlighted throughout the book and offer a number of important future directions for performance psychology research.

Conceptualization of performance psychology

Historically there has been a significant bias in the literature relating to the conceptualization of performance psychology. While at a general level in psychology the study of performance covers a range of psychological domains – such as human performance (Matthews et al., 2000) – from an applied perspective there has been a dominant link between sport and performance. This has often resulted in the two things being seen to be inextricably linked. For example, in the 'history of sport and performance psychology' chapter by Kornspan (2012) the content is almost exclusively sport psychology. Similarly, Hays (2012) suggests three sources that inform the field of performance psychology: applied sport psychology, psychotherapy, and consultation and coaching – both of these perspectives are still dominated by a sport psychology perspective. There is relevant literature that is emerging in other domains of psychology, but as yet there is still some way to go before performance psychology can be seen as a coherent field in its own right.

While there have been some recent attempts to contextualize performance psychology and the psychology of performance, greater clarity is still required to provide a stronger foundation and framework for this field of study. More specifically, performance psychology should be seen as a broader field of study that encompasses performance in sport, business, medicine, the military, the performing arts, etc.; that is underpinned by coherent psychological principles that run across all of these different performance domains.

Performance under pressure

There has been a rapid development of understanding concerning the choking (under pressure) phenomenon in recent years, particularly within the domain of sports performance. Question marks can be raised though about how well understanding has progressed in other performance domains. Also, while the importance of coping strategies is acknowledged in the performance literature, there is still to date, limited research that has sought to explore the nature of these performance-specific strategies, the impact they have, and crucially how best to develop their implementation by the individual performer.

There is increasingly literature available on the use of pre-performance routines to cope with pressure and to enhance performance (Cotterill, 2010). However, there is currently little literature reporting on how these routines can or should be developed, and whether they are stable over time (Cotterill, 2011). A greater focus on the design, implementation, and successful use of routines in ecologically valid environments is required to enhance the use of routines in the future to enhance performance.

While the importance of coping strategies and resources is acknowledged in the relevant literature, there is still to date, limited research that has sought to explore the nature of these performance-specific strategies, the impact they have, and crucially how best to develop their implementation by the performer. Future research should specifically explore the coping strategies used in the performance domain, the effect they have, and crucially how to maximize their impact.

In terms of developing the individual performer's ability to cope under pressure acclimatization training offers real potential to better prepare performers for the performance environment (Nieuwenhuys & Oudejans, 2011). But to date there has been variable success in producing a positive effect on performance utilizing this approach (Beseler et al., 2016). So, while offering a potential solution to developing the performer's ability to cope under pressure acclimatization training needs significantly greater investigation with increasingly ecologically valid study designs. Also, more research is required that seeks to explore the use of this technique in a more diverse range of performance domains.

Decision-making

There is a strong consensus within the literature regarding the importance of effective decision-making in facilitating high levels of performance. However, there is currently a lack of an overall model that successfully integrates classical decision-making, naturalistic decision-making, and ecological approaches to decision-making. Although it might be that each of these three main approaches to understanding decision-making in sport (CDM, NDM, Ecological) actually focus on different types of decisions in the performance domain, so in a sense all could explain some of the processes involved. As a result, a unifying theory of decision-making might offer a more complete explanation.

In terms of decision-making there is also currently a lack of consensus regarding how intuitive decisions occur. Some experts suggest that intuitive decisions are the result of an awareness of some phenomenological internal and discriminative physiological state that evolves from non-conscious stimulus (Perrig & Wippich, 1995). Other authors assume that these physiological states may be induced rather than preceded by intuitive decisions (Hogarth, 2001). With intuitive decisions highlighted to be crucial within performance settings a greater understanding of the process underpinning these decisions is important.

There is also currently little research that has specifically sought to assess the impact of domain-specific knowledge on decision-making performance (Schläppi-Lienhard & Hossner, 2015). One study that has explored domain-specific knowledge is that conducted by Schläppi-Lienhard and Hossner (2015) exploring decision-making in expert beach volleyball players. The study found that beach volleyball players reported similar gaze patterns that may be generalized as: reception-set-approach-body-direction-position in relation to the ball-shoulder-elbow-arm-wrist/hand-ball. This suggests an optimal gaze pattern in beach volleyball defence (Schläppi-Lienhard & Hossner, 2015). If this is true it would suggest you could then seek to 'train' optimal gaze behaviour strategies instead of waiting for them to organically emerge through engagement with the performance environment. As a result, further research is required to explore this and whether it is transferable to other domains.

Psychophysiology

The continued advancement and increased flexibility and robustness of technology for psychophysiological research is opening up new and exciting avenues for research.

The recent focus on assessing coherence in relation to sports performance (Cooke, 2013) offers potential to better understand key underlying factors represented in the psychophysiological signals measured. Recent studies (Babiloni et al., 2011; Deeny, Hillman, Janelle, & Hatfield, 2003; Zhu, Poolton, Wilson, Maxwell, & Masters, 2011) have suggested that coherence can be used as an indicator of verbal-analytic information processing, and preparation for action. More research though is required to better understand coherence and its relationship to performance. In particular, in seeking to better understand what is happening during the preparation phase for performance and to better understand (rather than describe) differences in the pre-performance period between good and poor performance at the highest level.

As the psychophysiological evidence base continues to expand and biofeedback/ neurofeedback equipment becomes more portable, reliable, and operatable, there will be increased use of these sources of information in relation to preparation for performance. However, it is important to ensure that practice is underpinned by a strong empirical rationale and compelling evidence. In a review of the state of evidence supporting neurofeedback training, Vernon (2005) offered a note of caution regarding empirical evidence to date. Vernon concluded that the literature to date was equivocal and that future research needs to measure pre- and post-EEG baselines to monitor changes resulting from neurofeedback training. Also, where possible, researchers need to utilize a moving baseline measurement of the EEG to control for possible changes in physiological arousal. Finally, Vernon suggested to always include a non-contingent control group, ideally one that receives everything that the experimental group receives.

Resilience

The concept of resilience has received significant attention in recent years, with an increasingly strong relationship reported between resilience and (coping with) adversity. While this is encouraging, the proliferation of related concepts needs further clarifying or rationalizing. In particular the relationship between resilience, hardiness, grit, adversity, and mental toughness needs greater clarification to reduce confusion, and to enhance the practical applicability of the associated knowledge and evidence base.

Cognition

Interest in meta-cognition has also increased in recent years, though this is not as well developed in relation to performance psychology. While the conceptualization of meta-cognition appears to be robust further study is required to understand how to develop and enhance meta-cognitive knowledge and meta-cognitive skills. It has also been suggested that a more in-depth understanding of the impact of pressure on high-level cognition is required, and that a systematic investigation of these effects would have both theoretical and practical benefits (Werner, 2016).

Also, active problem solving and creativity are seen as desirable cognitive traits within many performance settings. While a general conceptualization of these factors exists there needs to be greater exploration of how these key cognitive skills can be developed, enhanced, and applied within a range of performance domains.

Ageing

Broadly speaking there is a well-developed understanding of age-related decline within the psychology literature, particularly in relation to general population cognitive and physical/physiological decline. There is though less research exploring these performance reductions in performance-focused groups – particularly relating to cognitive decline. There has been limited research to date exploring career length in sport, and the length of time performers can aspire to be at 'the top of their game' (Baker et al., 2012). This is also true across a number of other perform-ance domains. Of those studies, even fewer have focused on skill acquisition, and lifespan development. Finally, the mechanisms that underpin the maintenance of performance with ageing need to be further clarified, and greater light shed on the prevalence or interaction between the current explanations for this process: pre-served differentiation, compensation, and selective maintenance (Horton, Baker, & Wier, 2015).

Confidence

There have been significant advances in relation to understanding confidence and performance in recent years, in particular the recognition that robust/resilient con-fidence is crucial for performance under pressure. It is interesting to note though that performance increases have also been reported after a reduction in levels of self-confidence (Woodman, Akehurst, Hardy, & Beattie, 2010). This supports Bandura and Locke's (2003) suggestion that some self-doubt can help performance. The role of effort though in this relationship remains to be further clarified. Also, further exploration of this effect is required to better understand the specific con-texts and whether this effect is robust and repeatable over time.

With the increasing recognition of the importance of robust self-confidence in achieving long-term success, further detail regarding how to develop it is required. This is particularly important as the reversal of potential reductions in confidence is often difficult to achieve. For example, Hays et al. (2009) reported that elite per-formers can struggle to regain confidence if it was lost in the pressurized environ-ment of competition. This finding supports Vealey and Chase's (2008) suggestion that confidence remains a work in progress for performers and is a fragile construct. The next step in terms of knowledge in this area is to provide greater empirical support for strategies and approaches to both develop and maintain levels of confi-dence in the face of performance pressures.

Practising for performance

Current understanding suggests that the representative nature of the practice and preparation environments are key to the development and implementation of effective performance skills. However, to date while there is an increasingly strong theoretical rationale (Headrick et al., 2015; Pinder et al., 2011) there are still limited cases that demonstrate how this can be achieved. In particular there is a limited range of evidence that demonstrates how specific manipulations of the environ-ment can be applied that still replicate the key demands of performance while also acknowledging the difficulty in replicating the performance environment exactly. So future research needs to provide empirical support for specific approaches to enhancing preparation for performance.

Summary

Performance psychology, like many other emergent disciplines within psychology, has borrowed significantly from other domains. While this is useful in developing fundamental theoretical frameworks and knowledge the field needs to continue to develop its own literature base. In particular this would mean seeking to interrogate existing models and theories from a performance-focused perspective, and to engage in research that both encompasses and compares different performance domains. Crucially, a greater understanding is required in terms of the practical application of this knowledge to ensure the development of a strong evidence base from which the ability to perform when it counts can be both developed and further enhanced.

REFERENCES

Aarts, H., & Dijksterhuis, A. P. (2000). The automatic activation of goal-directed behaviour: The case of travel habit. *Journal of Environmental Psychology, 20*, 75–82.

Aarts, H., Paulssen, T., & Schaalma, H. (1997). Physical exercise habit: On the conceptualization and formation of habitual health behaviours. *Health Education Research, 12*, 363–374.

Abernethy, B., Wood, J. M., & Parks, S. (1999). Can the anticipatory skills of experts be learned by novices? *Research Quarterly for Exercise and Sport, 70*, 313–318.

Abrams, W., Barnes, J., & Clement, A. (2008). Relationship of selected pre-NBA-career variables to NBA players' career longevity. *The Sport Journal: United States Sports Academy, 11*, 1.

Abramson, L. Y., Seligman, M. E. P., & Teasdale, J. D. (1978). Learned helplessness in humans: Critique and reformulation. *Journal of Abnormal Psychology, 87*, 49–74.

Ackles, P. K., Jennings, J. R., & Coles, M. G. H. (1985). *Advances in psychophysiology* (Vol. 1). Greenwich, CT: JAI.

Adriaanse, M. A., De Ridder, D. T. D., & De Wit, J. B. F. (2009). Finding the critical cue: Implementation intentions to change one's diet work best when tailored to personally relevant reasons for unhealthy eating. *Personality and Social Psychology Bulletin, 35*, 60–71.

Adriaanse, M. A., Gollwitzer, P. M., De Ridder, D. T. D., de Wit, J. B. F., & Kroese, F. M. (2011). Breaking habits with implementation intentions: A test of underlying processes. *Personality and Social Psychology, 37*, 502–513.

Ahituv, N., Igbaria, M., & Sella, A. (1998). The effects of time pressure and completeness of information on decision-making. *Journal of Management Information Systems, 15*, 153–172.

Ahmed, L., & de Fockert, J. W. (2012). Focusing on attention: The effects of working memory capacity and load on selective attention. *PLoS ONE, 7*, 1–10.

Ajzen, I. (2002). Residual effects of past on later behavior: Habituation and reasoned action perspectives. *Personality and Social Psychology Review, 6*, 107–122.

Alain, C., & Proteau, I. (1977). Perception of objective probabilities in motor performance. In B. Kerr (Ed.), *Human performance and behavior* (9th edn, pp. 1–5). Banff, Alberta: SCAPS.

Alder, D., Ford, P. R., Causer, J., & Williams, A. M. (2016). The effects of high- and low-anxiety training on the anticipation judgments of elite performers. *Journal of Sport & Exercise Psychology, 38*, 93–104.

Aldwin, C. M. (1994). *Stress, coping, and development: An integrative perspective.* New York: Guilford Press.

Alison, L., van den Heuvel, C., Waring, S., Crego, J., Power, N., Long, A., & O'Hara, T. (2013). Immersive simulated learning environments for researching critical incidents: A knowledge synthesis of the literature and experience of studying high-risk strategic decision making. *Journal of Cognitive Engineering and Decision Making, 7*, 255–272.

Allen, J. S., Burss, J., Brown, C. K., & Damasio, H. (2005). Normal neuroanatomical variation due to age: The major lobes and a parcellation of the temporal region. *Neurobiology of Aging 2005, 26*, 245–1260.

Alwan, M., Zakaria, A., Rahim, M. A., Hamid, N. A., & Fuad, M. (2013). Comparison between two relaxation methods on competitive state anxiety among college soccer teams during pre-competition stage. *International Journal of Advanced Sport Sciences Research, 1*, 90–104.

Ames, A. (2000). ACNS energy metabolism as related to function. *Brain Research Reviews, 34*, 42–68.

Amiel, S. A. (1994). Nutrition of the brain: Macronutrient supply. *Proceedings of the Nutrition Society, 53*, 401–405.

Amiel, S. A., Archibald, H. R., Chusney, G., & Glae, E. A. M. (1991). Ketone lowers hormone responses to hypoglycaemia – evidence for acute and cerebral utilization of a non-glucose fuel. *Clinical Science, 81*, 189–194.

Anderson, A., Vogel, P., & Albrecht, R. (1999). The effect of instructional self-talk on the overhand throw. *Physical Educator, 56*, 215–221.

Andreassi, J. L. (2006). *Psychophysiology: Human behavior and physiological response* (5th edn). London: Lawrence Erlbaum Associates.

Anshel, M. H., Kim, K. W., Kim, B. H., Chang, K. J., & Eom, H. J. (2001). A model for coping with stressful events in sport: Theory, application, and future directions. *International Journal of Sport Psychology, 32*, 43–75.

Araújo, D., & Davids, K. (2011). What exactly is acquired during skill acquisition? *Journal of Consciousness Studies, 18*, 7–23.

Araújo, D., Davids, K., Bennett, S., Button, C., & Chapman, G. (2004). Emergence of sport skills under constraints. In A. M. Williams & N. J. Hodges (Eds.), *Skill acquisition in sport: Research, theory and practice* (pp. 409–433). London: Routledge.

Araújo, D., Davids, K., & Hristovski, R. (2006). The ecological dynamics of decision-making in sport. *Psychology of Sport and Exercise, 7*, 653–676.

Araújo, D., Davids, K., & Passos, P. (2007). Ecological validity, representative design, and correspondence between experimental task constraints and behavioral setting: Comment on Rogers, Kadar, and Costall (2005). *Ecological Psychology, 19*, 69–78.

Araújo, D., Davids, K., & Serpa, S. (2005). An ecological approach to expertise effects in decision-making in a simulated sailing regatta. *Psychology of Sport and Exercise, 6*, 671–692.

Arns, M., Kleinnijenhuis, M., Fallahpour, K., & Breteler, R. (2007). Golf performance enhancement and real-life neurofeedback training using personalized eventlocked EEG profiles. *Journal of Neurotherapy, 11*, 11–18.

Arora, S., Sevdalis, N., Nestel, D., Woloshynowych, M., Darzi, A., & Kneebone, R. (2010). The impact of stress on surgical performance: A systematic review of the literature. *Surgery, 147*, 318–330.

Ashford, K. J., & Jackson, R. C. (2010). Priming as a means of preventing skill failure under pressure. *Journal of Sport and Exercise Psychology, 32*, 518–536.

Atkinson, P. A., Martin, C. R., & Rankin, J. (2009). Resilience revisited. *Journal of Psychiatric & Mental Health Nursing, 16*, 137–145.

Atkinson, R. C., & Shiffrin, R. M. (1968). Human memory: A proposed system and its control processes. In K. Spence & J. Spence (Eds.), *The psychology of learning and motivation* (Vol. 2, pp. 89–195). New York: Academic Press.

Babiloni, C., Del Percio, C., Iacoboni, M., Infarinato, F., Lizio, R., Marzano, N., & Eusebi, F. (2008). Golf putt outcomes are predicted by sensorimotor cerebral EEG rhythms. *Journal of Physiology, 586*, 131–139.

Babiloni, C., Infarinato, F., Marzano, N., Iacoboni, M., Dassu, F., Soricelli, A., & Del Percio, C. (2011). Intra-hemispheric functional coupling of alpha rhythms is related to golfer's performance: A coherence EEG study. *International Journal of Psychophysiology, 82*, 260–268.

Baddeley, A. D. (1997). *Human memory: Theory and practice.* Hove: Psychology Press.

Baddeley, A. D. (2007). *Working memory, thought, and action.* Oxford: Oxford University Press.

Baddeley, A. D., & Hitch, G. J. (1974). Working memory. In G. A. Bower (Ed.), *Recent advances in learning and motivation* (Vol. 8, pp. 47–89). New York: Academic Press.

Baddeley, A. D., Lewis, V., Eldridge, M., & Thomson, N. (1984). Attention and retrieval from long-term memory. *Journal of Experimental Psychology: General, 113*, 518–540.

Bader, G. G., & Engdal, S. (2000). The influence of bed firmness on sleep quality. *Applied Ergonomics, 31*, 487–497.

Baker, J., Coté, J., & Abernethy, B. (2003). Sport-specific practice and the development of expert decision-making in team ball sports. *Journal of Applied Sport Psychology, 5*, 12–25.

Baker, J., & Davids, K. (2006). Genetic and environmental constraints on variability in sport performance. In K. Davids, S. J. Bennett, & K. M. Newell (Eds.), *Movement system variability* (pp. 109–132). Champaign, IL: Human Kinetics.

Baker, J., Deakin, J., Horton, S., & Pearce, G. W. (2007). Maintenance of skilled performance with age: A descriptive examination of professional golfers. *Journal of Aging and Physical Activity, 15*, 299–316.

Baker, J., Horton, S., Perce, W., & Deakin, J. M. (2006). A longitudinal examination of performance decline in champion golfers. *High Ability Studies, 16*(2), 179–185.

Baker, J., Koz, D., Kungl, A.-M., Fraser-Thomas, J., & Schorer, J. (2012). Staying at the top: Playing position and performance affect career length in professional sport. *High Ability Studies, 24*(1), 63–76.

Baker, J., & Young, B. (2014). 20 years later: Deliberate practice and the development of expertise in sport. *International Review of Sport and Exercise Psychology, 7*, 135–157.

Balague, G. (2005). Anxiety: From pumped to panicked. In S. Murphy (Ed.), *The sport psych handbook: A complete guide to today's best mental training techniques* (pp. 73–92). Champaign, IL: Human Kinetics.

Balagué, N., Hristovski, R., & Vazquez, P. (2008). Ecological dynamics approach to decision making in sport. Training issues. *Education, Physical Training, Sport, 4*, 11–22.

Baltes, P. B., & Baltes, M. M. (1990). Psychological perspectives on successful aging: The model of selective optimization with compensation. In P. B. Baltes & E. M. Baltes (Eds.), *Successful aging: Perspectives from the behavioural sciences* (pp. 1–34). Cambridge: Cambridge University Press.

Bandura, A. (1977). Self efficacy: Toward a unifying theory of behavioural change. *Psychological Review, 84*, 191–215.

Bandura, A. (1986). *Social foundations of thought and action*. Englewood Cliffs, NJ: Prentice-Hall.

Bandura, A. (1997). *Self-efficacy. The exercise of control*. New York: Freeman.

Bandura, A. (2012). On the functional properties of perceived self-efficacy revisited. *Journal of Management, 28*, 9–44.

Bandura A., & Locke, E. A. (2003). Negative self-efficacy and goal effects revisited. *Journal of Applied Psychology, 88*, 87–99.

Banks, A. P., & Millward, L. J. (2007). Running shared mental model as a distributed cognitive process. *British Journal of Psychology, 91*(4), 513–531.

Barber, B. M., & Odean, T. (2001). Boys will be boys: Gender, overconfidence, and common stock investment. *Quarterly Journal of Economics, 116*, 261–292.

Barberis, N., & Thaler, R. (2003). A survey of behavioral finance. In G. M. Constantinides, M. Harris, & R. M. Stulz (Eds.), *Handbook of the economics of finance* (pp. 1053–1121). Amsterdam: Elsevier.

Bar-Eli, M. (2002). Biofeedback as applied psychophysiology in sport and exercise: Conceptual principles for research and practice. In B. Blumenstein, M. Bar-Eli, & G. Tenenbaum (Eds.). *Brain and body in sport and exercise*. Chichester: John Wiley & Sons.

Bar-Eli, M., Plessner, H., & Raab, M. (2011). *Judgement, decision making and success in sport*. Chichester: Wiley-Blackwell.

Bard, C., Fleury, M., & Goulet, C. (1994). Relationship between perceptual strategies and response adequacy in sport situations. *International Journal of Sport Psychology, 25*(3), 266–281.

Bargh, J. A. (1994). The four horsemen of automaticity: Awareness, intention, efficiency, and control in social cognition. In R. S. Wyer & T. K. Srull (Eds.), *Handbook of social cognition: Vol. 1 basic processes* (pp. 1–40). Hove: Psychology Press.

Barker, J., & Jones, M. (2006). Using hypnosis, technique refinement, and self-modelling to enhance self-efficacy: A case study in cricket. *The Sport Psychologist, 20*, 94–110.

Barker, J. B., Neil, R., & Fletcher, D. (2016). Using sport and performance psychology in the management of change. *Journal of Change Management, 16*, 1–7.

Bartone, P. T., Roland, R. R., Picano, J. J., & Williams, T. J. (2008). Psychological hardiness predicts success in US Army Special Forces candidates. *International Journal of Selection and Assessment, 16*, 78–81.

Batey, J., & Symes, R. (2016). Ahead of the competition: Anxiety control in archery. In S. T. Cotterill, N. Weston, & G. Breslin (Eds.), *Sport and exercise psychology: Practitioner case studies* (pp. 125–148). Chichester: John Wiley and Sons.

Batey, M., & Furnham, A. (2008). The relationship between measures of creativity and schizotypy. *Personality and Individual Differences, 45*, 816–821.

Bauer, P. J. (2013). Memory. In P. D. Zelazzo (Ed.), *The Oxford handbook of developmental psychology, Vol. 1: body and mind*. Oxford: Oxford University Press.

Baumeister, R. F. (1984). Choking under pressure: Self-consciousness and paradoxical effects of incentives on skilful performance. *Journal of Personality and Social Psychology, 46*, 610–620.

Baumeister, R. F. (1997). Esteem threat, self-regulatory breakdown, and emotional distress as factors in self-defeating behavior. *Review of General Psychology, 1*, 145–174.

Baumeister, R. F., & Steinhilber, A. (1984). Paradoxical effects of supportive audiences on performance under pressure: The home field disadvantage in sports championships. *Journal of Personality and Social Psychology, 47*, 85–93.

Beach, L. R., & Lipshitz, R. (1993). Why classical decision theory is an inappropriate standard for evaluating and aiding most human decision making. In G. A. Klein, J. Orasanu, R. Calderwood, & C. E. Zsambok (Eds.), *Decision making in action: Models and methods* (pp. 21–35). New York: Ablex.

Beaumont, C., Maynard, I. W., & Butt, J. (2015). Effective ways to develop and maintain robust sport-confidence: Strategies advocated by sport psychology consultants. *Journal of Applied Sport Psychology, 27*, 301–318.

Beck, A. T. (1976). *Cognitive therapy and the emotional disorders*. Madison, WI: International Universities Press.

Beedie, C. J., Terry, P. C., & Lane, A. M. (2000). The profile of mood states and athletic performance: Two meta-analyses. *Journal of Applied Sport Psychology, 12*, 49–68.

Behncke, L. (2004). Mental skills training for sports: A brief review. *Athletic Insight, 6*, 1–19.

Beilock, S. L., & Carr, T. H. (2001). On the fragility of skilled performance: What governs choking under pressure? *Journal of Experimental Psychology: General, 130*, 701–725.

Beilock, S. L., Carr, T. H., MacMahon, C., & Starkes, J. L. (2002). When paying attention becomes counterproductive: Impact of divided versus skill-focused attention on novice and experienced performance of sensorimotor skills. *Journal of Experimental Psychology: Applied, 8*, 6–16.

Beilock, S. L., & Gray, R. (2007). Why do athletes choke under pressure? In G. Tenenbaum & R. C. Eklund (Eds.), *Handbook of sport psychology* (3rd edn, pp. 425–444). Hoboken, NJ: Wiley & Sons.

Beilock, S. L., Kulp, C. A., Holt, L. E., & Carr, T. H. (2004). More on the fragility of performance: Choking under pressure in mathematical problem solving. *Journal of Experimental Psychology: General, 133*, 584–600.

Bell, J. J., & Hardy, J. (2009). Effects of attentional focus on skilled performance in golf. *Journal of Applied Sport Psychology, 21*, 163–177.

Bell, J. J., Hardy, L., & Beattie, S. (2013). Enhancing mental toughness and performance under pressure in elite young cricketers: A 2-year longitudinal intervention. *Sport, Exercise and Performance Psychology, 2*, 281–297.

Benton, D., & Owens, D. (1993). Blood glucose and human memory. *Psychopharmacology, 113*, 83–88.

Bernstein, N. (1967). *The co-ordination and regulation of movements*. Oxford: Pergamon Press.

Beseler, B., Mesagno, C., Young, W., & Harvey, J. (2016). Igniting the pressure acclimatization training debate: Contradictory pilot-study evidence from Australian football. *Journal of Sports Behavior, 39*, 22–38.

Best, K., Garmezy, N., & Masten, A. S. (1990). Resilience and development: Contributions from the study of children who overcome adversity. *Development and Psychopathology, 2*, 425–444.

Birrer, D., & Morgan, G. (2010). Psychological skills training as a way to enhance an athlete's performance in high-intensity sports. *Scandinavian Journal of Medicine and Sports Science, 20*, 78–87.

Blanchard, E. B., & Epstein, L. H. (1978). *A biofeedback primer*. Reading, MA: Addison-Wesley.

Blascovich, J. (2008). Challenge and threat. In A. J. Elliot (Ed.), *Handbook of approach and avoidance motivation* (pp. 431–445). New York: Psychology Press.

Blascovich, J., & Mendes, W. B. (2000). Challenge and threat appraisals: The role of affective cues. In J. P. Forgas (Ed.), *Feeling and thinking: The role of affect in social cognition* (pp. 59–82). Paris: Cambridge University Press.

Blascovich, J., Seery, M. D., Mugridge, C. A., Norris, R. K., & Weisbuch, M. (2004). Predicting athletic performance from cardiovascular indexes of challenge and threat. *Journal of Experimental Social Psychology, 40*, 683–688.

Bleckley, M. K., Durso, F. T., Crutchfield, J. M., Engle, R. W., & Khanna, M. M. (2003). Individual differences in working memory capacity predict visual attention allocation. *Psychonomic Bulletin & Review, 10*, 884–889.

Bloom, B. S. (1985). *Developing talent in young people*. New York: Ballantine.

Bojko, A. (2013). *Eye tracking the user experience*. New York: Rosenfeld.

Bolger, N. (1990). Coping as a personality process: A prospective study. *Journal of Personality and Social Psychology, 59*, 525–537.

Bonanno, G. A. (2004). Loss, trauma, and human resilience: Have we underestimated the human capacity to thrive after extremely aversive events? *American Psychologist, 59*, 20–28.

Boniwell, I., & Ryan, L. (2012). *Personal well-being lessons for secondary schools: Positive psychology in action for 11 to 14 year-olds*. Oxford: The Open University Press.

Bortz, W. M., & Bortz, W. M. (1996). How fast do we age? Exercise performance over time as a biomarker. *Journal of Gerontology: Medical Sciences, 51*, 223–225.

Boutcher, S. H. (1992). Attentional and athletic performance: An integrated approach. In T. S. Horn (Ed.), *Advances in sport psychology* (pp. 251–266). Champaign, IL: Human Kinetics.

Boutcher, S. H., & Crews, D. J. (1987). The effect of a preshot attentional routine on a well learned skill. *International Journal of Sport Psychology, 18*, 30–39.

Boutcher, S. H., & Zinsser, N. W. (1990). Cardiac deceleration of elite and beginning golfers during putting. *Journal of Sport and Exercise Psychology, 12*, 37–47.

Broadbent, D. P., Causer, J., Williams, A. M., & Ford, P. R. (2015). Perceptual-cognitive skills training and its transfer to expert performance in the field: Future research directions. *European Journal of Sport Science, 15*, 322–331.

Broomhead, P., Skidmore, J. B., Eggett, D. L., & Mills, M. M. (2012). The effects of a positive mindset trigger word pre-performance routine on the expressive performance of junior high age singers. *Journal of Research in Music Education, 60*, 62–80.

Brophy, D. R. (1998). Understanding, measuring, and enhancing individual creative problem-solving efforts. *Creativity Research Journal, 11*, 123–150.

Bruce, V., Green, P. R., & Georgeson, M. A. (1996). *Visual perception: Physiology, psychology and ecology* (3rd edn). London: Lawrence Erlbaum.

Bruner, J. S. (1957). On perceptual readiness. *Psychological Review, 64*, 123–152.

Brunswik, E. (1956). *Perception and the representative design of psychological experiments* (2nd edn). Berkeley: University of California Press.

Buchanan, G. M., & Seligman, M. E. P. (1995). *Explanatory style*. Hillsdale, NJ: Erlbaum.

Bull, S. J., Albinson, J. G., & Shambrook, C. J. (1996). *The mental game plan*. Eastbourne, East Sussex: Sports Dynamics.

Bull, S. J., Shambrook, C. J., James, W., & Brooks, J. (2005). Towards an understanding of mental toughness in elite English cricketers. *Journal of Applied Sport Psychology, 17*, 209–227.

Burbank, D. P., & Webster, J. G. (1978). Reducing skin potential motion artifact by skin abrasion. *Medical & Biological Engineering & Computing, 16*, 31–38.

Burke, C. S., Salas, E., Wilson-Donnelly, K., & Priest, H. (2004). How to turn a team of experts into an expert medical team: Guidance from the aviation and military communities. *Quality and Safety in Health Care, 131*, 96–104.

Burke, V. (2010). Performing under pressure. *Management Focus, 28*, 24–25.

Burns, D. D. (1989). *The feeling good handbook*. New York: Penguin.

Burton, D. (1992). The Jekyll/Hyde nature of goals: Reconceptualizing goal setting in sport. In T. S. Horn (Ed.), *Advances in sport psychology* (pp. 267–297). Champaign, IL: Human Kinetics.

Burton, D., & Naylor, S. (2002). The Jekyll/Hyde nature of goals: Revisiting and updating goal-setting sport. In T. Horn (Ed.), *Advances in sport psychology* (2nd edn, pp. 459–499). Champaign, IL: Human Kinetics.

Burton, D., Naylor, S., & Holliday, B. (2001). Goal setting in sport: Investigating the goal effectiveness paradigm. In R. Singer, H. Hausenblas, & C. Janelle (Eds.), *Handbook of sport psychology* (2nd edn, pp. 497–528). New York: Wiley.

Buscombe, R., Greenlees, I. A., Holder, T., Thelwell, R. C., & Rimmer, M. (2006). Expectancy effects in tennis: The impact of opponent's pre-match non-verbal behaviour on male tennis players. *Journal of Sport Sciences, 24*, 1265–1272.

Butler, J. L., & Baumeister, R. F. (1998). The trouble with friendly faces: Skilled performance with a supportive audience. *Journal of Personality and Social Psychology, 75*, 1213–1230.

Cacioppi, J. T., Tassinary, L. G., & Berntson, G. G. (2007). *Handbook of psychophysiology* (2nd edn). Cambridge, UK: Cambridge University Press.

Čačković, L., Barić, R., & Vlašić, J. (2010). The nine step connection model as one of the method of dance sport psychological preparations. *Sport Science, 5*, 98–101.

Campbell, M., & Moran, A. (2014). There is more to green reading than meets the eye! Exploring the gaze behaviors of experts in a virtual golf putting task. *Cognitive Processing, 15*, 363–372.

Campbell, W. K., Goodie, A. S., & Foster, J. A. (2004). Narcissism, confidence, and risk attitude. *Journal of Behavioral Decision Making, 17*, 297–311.

Campbell-Sills, L., Cohan, S. L., & Stein, M. B. (2006). Relationship of resilience to personality, coping, and psychiatric symptoms in young adults. *Behavior Research and Therapy, 44*, 585–599.

Carlstedt, R. A. (2004). *Critical moments during competition: A mind-body model of sport performance when it counts most.* New York: Psychology Press.

Carskadon, M. A., & Dement, W. C. (2011). Monitoring and staging human sleep. In M. H. Kryger, T. Roth, & W. C. Dement (Eds.), *Principles and practice of sleep medicine* (5th edn, pp. 16–26). St Louis: Elsevier Saunders.

Carson, S., Peterson, J. B., & Higgins, D. M. (2003). Decreased latent inhibition is associated with increased creative achievement in high-functioning individuals. *Journal of Personality and Social Psychology, 85*, 499–506.

Carson, S., Peterson J. B., & Higgins, D. M. (2005). Reliability, validity, and factor structure of the Creative Achievement Questionnaire. *Creativity Research Journal, 17*, 37–50.

Carver, C. S., & Scheier, M. F. (2001). Optimism, pessimism, and self-regulation. In E. C. Chang (Ed.), *Optimism and pessimism: Implications for theory, research, and practice* (pp. 31–51). Washington, DC: American Psychological Association.

Carver, C. S., & Scheier, M. F. (2014). Dispositional optimism. *Trends in Cognitive Science, 18*, 293–299.

Carver, C. S., Scheier, M. F., & Segerstrom, S. C. (2010). Optimism. *Clinical Psychology Review, 30*, 879–889.

Castaneda, B., & Gray, R. (2007). Effects of focus of attention on baseball batting performance in players of differing skill levels. *Journal of Sport & Exercise Psychology, 29*, 60–77.

Catley, D., & Duda, J. (1997). Psychological antecedents of the frequency and intensity of flow in golfers. *International Journal of Sport Psychology, 28*, 309–322.

Cattell, R. B. (1943). The measurement of adult intelligence. *Psychological Bulletin, 40*, 153–193.

Chase, M. A., Ewing, M. E., Lirgg, C. D., & George, T. R. (1994). The effects of equipment modification on children's self-efficacy and basketball shooting performance. *Research Quarterly for Exercise and Sport, 65*, 159–168.

Chase, W. G., & Simon, H. A. (1973). The mind's eye in chess. In W. G. Chase (Ed.), *Visual information processing*. New York: Academic Press.

Chiu, S., & Alexander, P. A. (2000). The motivational function of preschoolers' private speech. *Discourse Processes, 30*, 133–152.

Christensen, W., Sutton, J., & Mcilwain, D. J. F. (2016). Cognition in skilled action: Meshed control and the varieties of skill experience. *Mind and Language, 31*, 37–66.

Christie, M. J., & McBrearty, E. M. (1979). Psychophysiological investigations of post lunch state in male and female subjects. *Ergonomics, 22*, 307–323.

Chroni, S., Perkos, S., & Theodorakis, Y. (2007). Function and preferences of motivational and instructional self-talk for adolescent basketball players. *Athletic Insight, 9*, 19–31.

Chun, M. M., Golomb, J. D., & Turk-Browne, N. B. (2011). A taxonomy of external and internal attention. *Annual Review of Psychology, 62*, 73–101.

Clough, P., & Strycharczyk, D. (2012). *Applied mental toughness: A tool kit for the 21st century.* London: Kogan Page.

Clowes, H., & Knowles, Z. (2013). Exploring the effectiveness of pre-performance routines in elite artistic gymnasts: A mixed method investigation. *Science of Gymnastics Journal, 5*, 27–40.

Cohen, N. J., & Squire, L. S. (1980). Preserved learning and retention of pattern analysing skill in amnesia using perceptual learning. *Cortex, 17*, 273–278.

Cohen, R. A. (1993). *The neuropsychology of attention.* New York: Plenum Press.

Cohen, S., & Wills, T. A. (1985). Stress, social support, and the buffering hypothesis. *Psychological Bulletin, 98*, 310–357.

Coker, C. A., & Fischman, M. G. (2010). Motor skill learning for effective coaching and performance. In J. M. Williams (Ed.), *Applied sport psychology: Personal growth to peak performance* (6th edn, pp. 21–41). Boston, MA: McGraw-Hill.

Colflesh, G. J. H., & Conway, A. R. A. (2007). Individual differences in working memory capacity and divided attention in dichotic listening. *Psychonomic Bulletin & Review, 14*, 699–703.

Collins, D. (2002). Psychophysiology and athletic performance. In B. Blumenstein, M. Bar-Eli, & G. Tenenbaum (Eds.), *Brain and body in sport and exercise.* Chichester: John Wiley & Sons.

Collins, D., & MacNamara, A. (2012). The rocky road to the top: Why talent needs trauma. *Sports Medicine, 42*, 907–914.

Connaughton, D., Wadey, R., Hanton, S., & Jones, G. (2008). The development and maintenance of mental toughness: Perceptions of elite performers. *Journal of Sports Sciences, 26*, 83–95.

Conway, A. R. A., Cowan, N., & Bunting, M. F. (2001). The cocktail party phenomenon revisited: The importance of working memory capacity. *Psychonomic Bulletin & Review, 8*, 331–335.

Cooke, A. (2013). Readying the head and steadying the heart: A review of cortical and cardiac studies of preparation for action in sport. *International Review of Sport and Exercise Psychology*, 1–17.

Cooke, A., Kavussanu, M., McIntyre, D., Boardley, I. D., & Ring, C. (2011). Effects of competitive pressure on expert performance: Underlying psychological, physiological, and kinematic mechanisms. *Psychophysiology, 48*, 1146–1156.

Cooke, N. J., Salas, E., Cannon-Bowers, J. A., & Stout, R. (2000). Measuring team knowledge. *Human Factors, 42*, 151–173.

Coombes, S. A., Janelle, C. M., & Duley, A. D. (2005). Emotion and motor control: Movement attributes following affective picture processing. *Journal of Motor Behavior, 37*, 425–436.

Cordovil, R., Araújo, D., Davids, K., Gouveia, L., Barreiros, J., Fernandes, O., & Serpa, S. (2009). The influence of instructions and bodyscaling as constraints on decision-making processes in team sports. *European Journal of Sport Science, 9*, 169–179.

Cotterill, S. T. (2010). Pre-performance routines in sport: Current understanding and future directions. *International Review of Sport & Exercise Psychology, 3,* 132–154.

Cotterill, S. T. (2011). Experiences of developing pre-performance routines with elite cricket players. *Journal of Sport Psychology in Action, 2,* 81–91.

Cotterill, S. T. (2012). *Team psychology in sports: Theory and application.* Abingdon: Routledge.

Cotterill, S. T. (2014). Developing decision-making for performance: A framework to guide applied practice in cricket. *Journal of Sport Psychology in Action, 5,* 88–101.

Cotterill, S. T. (2015). Preparing for performance: Strategies adopted across performance domains. *The Sport Psychologist, 29,* 158–170.

Cotterill, S., & Collins, D. (2005). Heart rate deceleration characteristics across shot types in golf. *Journal of Sports Science, 23,* 173–174.

Cotterill, S. T., & Discombe, R. (2016). Enhancing decision-making in sport: Current understanding and future directions. *Sport and Exercise Psychology Review, 12,* 54–68.

Cotterill, S. T., & Moran, A. (2016). Concentration and performing under pressure. In S. T. Cotterill, N. Weston, & G. Breslin (Eds.), *Sport & exercise psychology: Practitioner case studies* (pp. 37–54). Chichester: John Wiley & Sons.

Cotterill, S. T., Sanders, R., & Collins, D. (2010). Developing effective pre-performance routines in golf: Why don't we ask the golfer? *Journal of Applied Sport Psychology, 22,* 51–64.

Cox, R., Shannon, J., McGuire, R., & McBride, A. (2010). Predicting subjective athletic performance from psychological skills after controlling for sex and sport. *Journal of Sport Behavior, 33,* 129–145.

Cox, R. H. (2007). *Sport psychology: Concepts and applications.* New York: McGraw-Hill.

Craft, L. L., Magyar, T. M., Becker, B. J., & Feltz, D. L. (2003). The relationship between the Competitive State Anxiety Inventory-2 and sport performance: A metaanalysis. *Journal of Sport & Exercise Psychology, 25,* 44–65.

Craik, F. I. M., Govoni, R., Naveh-Benjamin, M., & Anderson, N. D. (1996). The effects of divided attention on encoding and retrieval processes in human memory. *Journal of Experimental Psychology: General, 125,* 159–180.

Cremandes, J. G., Tashman, L. S., & Quartiroli, A. (2014). Initial considerations: Developing the pathway to become a sport, exercise and performance psychology professional. In J. G. Cremandes & L. S. Tashman (Eds.), *Becoming a sport, exercise, and performance psychology professional: A global perspective* (pp. 3–12). New York: Psychology Press.

Croskerry, P. (2002). Achieving quality in clinical decision-making: Cognitive strategies and detection of bias. *Academic Emergency Medicine, 9,* 1184–1204.

Csikszentmihalyi, M. (1975). *Beyond boredom and anxiety.* San Francisco: Jossey-Bass.

Csikszentmihalyi, M. (1990). *Flow: The psychology of optimal experience.* New York: Harper and Row.

Csikszentmihalyi, M. (2002). *Flow: The psychology of optimal experience* (2nd edn). New York: Harper & Row.

Cumming, J., & Williams, S. E. (2013). Introducing the revised applied model of deliberate imagery use for sport, dance, exercise, and rehabilitation. *Movement & Sport Sciences, 82,* 69–81.

Cutrona, C. E., & Russell, D. W. (1990). Type of social support and specific stress: Toward a theory of optimal matching. In B. R. Sarason, I. G. Sarason, & G. R. Pierce (Eds.), *Social support: An interactional view* (pp. 319–366). New York: Wiley.

Czech, D. R., Ploszay, A. J., & Burke, K. L. (2004). An examination of the maintenance of preshot routines in basketball free throw shooting. *Journal of Sport Behavior, 27,* 323–329.

Dalloway, M. (1993). *Concentration: Focus your mind, power your game*. Phoenix, AZ: Optimal performance institute.

Daneman, M., & Carpenter, P. A. (1980). Individual differences in working memory and reading. *Journal of Verbal Learning and Verbal Behavior, 19*, 450–466.

Davids, K., & Araújo, D. (2010). Perception of affordances in multi-scale dynamics as an alternative explanation for equivalence of analogical and inferential reasoning in animals and humans. *Theory & Psychology, 20*, 125–134.

Davids, K., Araújo, D., Vilar, L., Renshaw, I., & Pinder, R. (2013). An ecological dynamics approach to skill acquisition: Implications for development of talent in sport. *Talent Development and Excellence, 5*(1), 21–34.

Davids, K., Button, C., & Bennett, S. (2008). *Dynamics of skill acquisition: A constraints-led approach*. Champaign, IL: Human Kinetics.

Davids, K., Renshaw, I., & Glazier, P. (2005). Movement models from sport reveal fundamental insights into the coordination process. *Exercise and Sport Science Reviews, 33*(1), 36–42.

Davidson, R. J., & Schwartz, G. E. (1976). The psychobiology of relaxation and related states: A multi-process theory. In D. Mostofsky (Ed.), *Behavioral control and modification of physiological activity* (pp. 399–442). Englewood Cliffs, NJ: Prentice-Hall.

Daw, J., & Burton, D. (1994). Evaluation of a comprehensive psychological skills training program for collegiate tennis players. *The Sport Psychologist, 8*, 37–57.

Deary, I. J. (1998). The effects of diabetes on cognitive function. *Diabetes Annual 11*, 97–118.

Deary, I. J., Corley, J., Gow, A. J., Harris, S. E., & Houlihan, L. M., et al. (2009). Age-associated cognitive decline. *British Medical Bulletin, 92*, 135–152.

Debarnot, U., Sperduti, M., Di Rienzo, F., & Guillot, A. (2014). Experts bodies, experts minds: How physical and mental training shape the brain. *Frontiers in Human Neuroscience, 8*, 1–17.

Deeny, S., Hillman, C. H., Janelle, C. M., & Hatfield, B. D. (2003). Cortico-cortical communication and superior performance in elite marksmen: An EEG coherence analysis. *Journal of Sport & Exercise Psychology, 25*, 188–204.

Dellal, A., Chamari, K., Pintus, A., Girard, O., Cotte, T., & Keller, D. (2008). Heart rate responses during small-sided games and short intermittent running training in elite soccer players: A comparative study. *Journal of Strength and Conditioning Research, 22*, 1449–1457.

Del Percio, C., Babiloni, C., Marzano, N., Iacoboni, M., Infarinato, F., Vecchio, F., & Eusebi, F. (2009). 'Neural efficiency' of athletes' brain for upright standing: A high-resolution EEG study. *Brain Research Bulletin, 79*, 193–200.

Del Tredici, K., & Braak, H. (2008). Neurofibrillary changes of the Alzheimer type in very elderly individuals: Neither inevitable nor benign. Commentary on 'No disease in the brain of a 115-year-old woman'. *Neurobiology of Aging, 29*, 1133–1136.

De Martino, B., Kumaran, D., Seymour, B., & Dolan, R. J. (2006). Frames, biases, and rational decision-making in the human brain. *Science, 313*, 684–687.

Der, G., & Deary, I. J. (2006). Reaction time age changes and sex differences in adulthood. Results from a large, population based study: the UK Health and Lifestyle Survey. *Psychology of Aging, 21*, 62–73.

De Weerd, P. (2003). Attention, neural basis of. In L. Nadel (Ed.), *Encyclopaedia of cognitive science* (Vol. 1, pp. 238–246). London: Nature Publishing.

DiBartolo, P. M., & Shaffer, C. (2002). A comparison of female college athletes and nonathletes: Eating disorder symptomatology and psychological well-being. *Journal of Sport and Exercise Psychology, 24*, 33–42.

Didierjean, A., & Marmèche, E. (2005). Anticipatory representation of visual basketball scenes by novice and expert players. *Visual Cognition, 12*, 265–283.

Dienstbier, R. A. (1989). Arousal and physiological toughness: Implications for mental and physical health. *Psychological Review, 96*, 84–100.

Discombe, R. M., & Cotterill, S. T. (2015). Eye tracking in sport: A guide for new and aspiring researchers. *Sport and Exercise Psychology Review, 11*(2), 49–58.

Dobson, K. S., & Dozois, D. J. A. (2010). Historical and philosophical bases of the cognitive behavioral therapies. In K. S. Dobson (Ed.), *Handbook of cognitive-behavioral therapies* (3rd edn, pp. 3–38). New York: Guilford Press.

Donato, A. J., Tench, K., Glueck, D. H., Seals, D. R., Eskurza, I., & Tanaka, H. (2003). Declines in physiological functional capacity with age: A longitudinal study in peak swimming performance. *Journal of Applied Physiology, 94*, 764–769.

Dougherty, M. R. P., & Hunter, J. E. (2003). Probability judgment and subadditivity: The role of working memory capacity and constraining retrieval. *Memory & Cognition, 31*, 968–982.

Douglas, K., & Fox, K. R. (2002). Performance and practise of elite women European tour golfers during pressure and non-pressure putting simulation. In E. Thain (Ed.), *Science and golf IV* (pp. 246–256). London: Routledge.

Doyon, J. (1997). Skill learning. *International Review of Neurobiology, 41*, 273–294.

Doyon, J., & Benali, H. (2005). Reorganization and plasticity in the adult brain during learning of motor skills. *Cognitive Neuroscience, 15*, 161–167.

Dreyfus, H. L., & Dreyfus, S. E. (1986). *Mind over machine: The power of human intuition and expertise in the era of the computer.* New York: Free Press.

Driskell, J. E., & Johnston, J. H. (1998). Stress exposure training. In J. A. Cannon-Bowers & E. Salas (Eds.), *Making decisions under stress: Implications for individual and team training* (pp. 191–217). Washington, DC: American Psychological Association.

Duchowski, A. T. (2002). A breadth-first survey of eye-tracking applications. *Behavioral Research Methods: Instruments and Computers, 34*, 455–470.

Duchowski, A. T. (2007). *Eye tracking methodology: Theory and practice* (2nd edn). London: Springer.

Duckworth, A. L., Kirby, T. A., Tsukayama, E., Berstein, H., & Ericsson, K. A. (2011). Deliberate practice spells success: Why grittier competitors triumph at the national spelling bee. *Social Psychological and Personality Science, 2*, 174–181.

Duckworth, A. L., Peterson, C., Matthews, M. D., & Kelly, D. R. (2007). Grit: Perseverance and passion for long-term goals. *Journal of Personality and Social Psychology, 92*, 1087–1101.

Duckworth, A. L., & Quinn, P. D. (2009). Development and validation of the Short Grit Scale (GRIT–S). *Journal of Personality Assessment, 91*, 166–174.

Dusek, J. A., Hibberd, P. L., Buczynski, B., Chang, H. B., Dusek, K., Johnston, J. M., Wohlhueter, A. L., Benson, H., & Zusman R. M. (2008). Stress management versus lifestyle modification on systolic hypertension and medication elimination: A randomized trial. *The Journal of Alternative and Complementary Medicine, 14*, 129–138.

Dye, L., Lluch, A., & Blundell, J. E. (2000). Macronutrients and mental performance. *Nutrition, 16*, 1021–1034.

Easterbrook, J. A. (1959). The effect of emotion on cue utilization and the organization of behavior. *Psychological Review, 66*, 183–201.

Edwards, C., Tod, D., & McGuigan, M. (2008). Self-talk influences vertical jump performance and kinematics in male rugby union players. *Journal of Sports Sciences, 26*, 1459–1465.

Eichenbaum, H., Otto, T., & Cohen, N. J. (1992). The hippocampus – what does it do? *Behavioral Neural Biology, 57*, 2–36.

Ekman, P. (1999). Basic emotions. In T. Dalgleish and M. Power (Eds.), *Handbook of cognition and emotion* (pp. 45–60). New York: John Wiley & Sons.

Elbanna, S., & Child, J. (2007). The influence of decision, environmental and firm characteristics on the rationality of strategic decision-making. *Journal of Management Studies, 44*, 561–591.

Endler, N. S., & Parker, J. A. (1989). Multidimensional assessment of coping: A critical evaluation. *Journal of Personality and Social Psychology, 58*, 844–854.

Endsley, M. R. (1995). Toward a theory of situation awareness in dynamic systems. *Human Factors, 37*, 32–64.

Engeser, S., & Rheinberg, F. (2008). Flow, performance, and moderators of challenge-skill balance. *Motivation and Emotion, 32*, 158–172.

Engle, R. W., Tuholski, S., Laughlin, J., & Conway, A. R. A. (1999). Working memory, short-term memory and general fluid intelligence: A latent variable approach. *Journal of Experimental Psychology, 128*, 309–331.

Ericsson, K. A. (1985). Memory skill. *Canadian Journal of Psychology, 39*, 188–231.

Ericsson, K. A. (2007). Deliberate practice and the modifiability of the body and mind: Toward a science of the structure and acquisition of expert and elite performance. *International Journal of Sport Psychology, 38*, 4–34.

Ericsson, K. A., & Kintsch, W. (1995). Long-term working memory. *Psychological Review, 102*, 211–245.

Ericsson, K. A., Krampe, R. T., & Tesch-Römer, C. (1993). The role of deliberate practice in the acquisition of expert performance. *Psychological Review, 100*, 363–406.

Ericsson, K. A., & Moxley, J. H. (2012). The expert performance approach and deliberate practice: Some potential implications for studying creative performance in organizations. In M. D. Mumford (Ed.), *The handbook of organizational creativity* (pp. 141–167). London: Academic Press.

Ericsson, K. A., Prietula, M. J., & Cokely, E. T. (2007). The making of an expert. *Harvard Business Review, 85*, 114–121.

Erixon-Lindroth, N., Farde, L., Robins Whalin, T. B., Sovago, J., Halldin, C., & Backman, L. (2005). The role of the striatal dopamine transporter in cognitive aging. *Psychiatry Research: Neuroimaging, 138*, 1–12.

Eskreis-Winkler, L., Shulman, E. P., Beal, S. A., & Duckworth, A. L. (2014). The grit effect: Predicting retention in the military, the workplace, school and marriage. *Frontiers in Psychology, 5*, 1–12.

Eysenck, M. W. (2001). *Principles of cognitive psychology* (2nd edn). Hove: Psychology Press.

Eysenck, M. W. (2004). *Psychology: An international perspective*. Hove: Psychology Press.

Eysenck, M. W., & Calvo, M. G. (1992). Anxiety and performance: The processing efficiency theory. *Cognition and Emotion, 6*, 409–434.

Fajen, B. R., Riley, M. A., & Turvey, M. T. (2008). Information, affordances and the control of action in sport. *International Journal of Sport Psychology, 40*, 79–107.

Faulkner, J. A., Davis, C. S., Mendias, C. L., & Brooks, S. V. (2008). The aging of elite male athletes: Age related changes in performance and skeletal muscle structure and function. *Clin. Journal of Sports Medicine, 18*, 501–507.

Feigenbaum, E. A. (1989). What hath Simon wrought? In D. Klahr & K. Kotovsky (Eds.), *Complex information processing: The impact of Herbert A. Simon* (pp. 165–180). Hillsdale, NJ: Erlbaum.

Feltz, D. L. (1988). Self-confidence and sports performance. *Exercise and Sport Science Review, 16*, 423–458.

Feltz, D. L., & Landers, D. M. (1983). The effects of mental practice on motor skill learning and performance: A meta-analysis. *Journal of Sport Psychology, 5*, 25–57.

Feltz, D. L., Short, S. E., & Singleton, D. A. (2008). The effect of self-modeling on shooting performance and self-efficacy with intercollegiate hockey players. In M. P. Simmons & L. A. Foster (Eds.), *Sport and exercise psychology research advances* (pp. 9–18). New York: Nova Science Publishers.

Feltz, D. L., & Weiss, M. R. (1982). Developing self-efficacy through sport. *Journal of Physical Education, Recreation, and Dance*, 24–26.

Ferrando, P. J., Chico, E., & Tous, J. M. (2002). Propiedades psicométricasdel test de optimismo life orientation test. *Psicothema, 14*, 673–680.

Filby, W. C. D., Maynard, I. W., & Graydon, J. K. (1999). The effect of multiple-goal strategies on performance outcomes in training and competition. *Journal of Applied Sport Psychology, 11*, 230–246.

Fitts, P. M., & Posner, M. I. (1967). *Human performance*. Belmont, CA: Wadsworth.

Flavell, J. H. (1979). Metacognition and cognitive monitoring. *American Psychologist, 34*, 906–911.

Fletcher, D., & Sarkar, M. (2012a). A grounded theory of psychological resilience in Olympic champions. *Psychology of Sport and Exercise, 13*, 669–678.

Fletcher, D., & Sarkar, M. (2012b). Developing resilience: Lessons learned from Olympic champions. *The Wave, 4*, 36–38.

Fletcher, D., & Sarkar, M. (2013). Psychological resilience: A review and critique of definitions, concepts, and theory. *European Psychologist, 18*, 12–23.

Flin, R., Slaven, G., & Stewart, K. (1996). Emergency decision making in the off shore oil and gas industry. *Human Factors, 38*, 262–277.

Folkard, S., & Monk, T. H. (1985). *Hours of work: Temporal factors in work scheduling*. Chichester: Wiley.

Folkman, S., & Lazarus, R. S. (1988). Coping as a mediator of emotion. *Journal of Personality and Social Psychology, 54*, 466–475.

Ford, P. R., Carling, C., Garces, M., Margues, M., Miguel, C., Farrant, A., Stenling, A., Moreno, J., Le Gall, F., Holmström, S., Salmela, J. H., & Williams, M. (2012). Developmental activities of elite soccer players aged under-16 years from Brazil, England, Mexico, Portugal and Sweden. *Journal of Sport Sciences, 30*, 1653–1663.

Forgas, J. P. (1992). Affect in social judgements and decisions: A multi-process model. *Advances in Experimental Social Psychology, 25*, 227–275.

Forgeard, M. J. C., & Seligman, M. E. P. (2012). Seeing the glass half full: A review of the causes and consequences of optimism. *Pratiques Psychologiques, 18*, 107–120.

Fotenos, A. F., Snyder, A. Z., Girton, L. E., Morris, J. C., & Buckner, R. L. (2005). Normative estimates of cross-sectional and longitudinal brain volume decline in aging and AD. *Neurology, 64*, 1032–1039.

Frank, D. L., Khorshid, L., Kiffer, J. F., Moravec, C. S., & McKee, M. G. (2010). Biofeedback in medicine: Who, when, why and how? *Mental Health in Family Medicine, 7*, 85–91.

Fredrickson, B. L. (2001). The role of positive emotions in positive psychology: The broaden-and-build theory of positive emotions. *American Psychologist, 56*, 218–226.

Fredrickson, B. L. (2005). Positive emotions. In C. R. Snyder & S. J. Lopez (Eds.), *Handbook of positive psychology* (pp. 120–134). New York: Oxford University Press.

Fredrickson, B. L., & Branigan, C. (2005). Positive emotions broaden the scope of attention and thought-action repertoires. *Cognition and Emotion, 19*, 313–332.

Fredrickson, B. L., & Losada, M. F. (2005). Positive affect and the complex dynamics of human flourishing. *American Psychologist, 60*, 678–686.

Frijda, N. H., Kuipers, P., & ter Schure, E. (1989). Relations among emotion, appraisal, and emotional action readiness. *Journal of Personality and Social Psychology, 57*, 212–228.

Gabbett, T. J. (2006). Skill-based conditioning games as an alternative to traditional conditioning for rugby league players. *The Journal of Strength and Conditioning Research, 20*, 309–315.

Galli, N., & Gonzalez, S. P. (2015). Psychological resilience in sport: A review of the literature and implications for research and practice. *International Journal of Sport and Exercise Psychology, 13*, 243–257.

Galli, N., & Vealey, R. (2008). Bouncing back from adversity: Athletes' experiences of resilience. *The Sport Psychologist, 22*, 316–335.

Gamble, P. (2004). A skill-based conditioning games approach to metabolic conditioning for elite rugby football players. *Journal of Strength and Conditioning Research, 18*, 491–497.

Ganguly, K., & Poo, M. M. (2013). Activity-dependent neural plasticity from bench to bedside. *Neuron, 80*, 729–741.

Ganio, M. S., Armstrong, L. E., Casa, D. J., McDermott, B. P., Lee, E. C., Yamamoto, L. M., Marzano, S., Lopez, R. M., Jimenez, L., Le Bellego, L., Chevillotte, E., & Lieberman, H. R. (2011). Mild dehydration impairs cognitive performance and mood of men. *British Journal of Nutrition, 106*, 1535–1543.

García, A., & Díaz, F. (2010). Relación entre optimismo/pesimismo disposicional, rendimiento y edad en jugadores de fútbol de competición. *Revista Iberoamericana de psicología del ejercicio y el deporte, 5*, 45–60.

Garza, D., & Feltz, D. (1998). Effects of selected mental practice on performance, self-efficacy, and competition confidence of figure skaters. *The Sport Psychologist, 12*, 1–15.

Gentile, A. M. (1972). A working model of skill acquisition with applications to teaching. *Quest, 17*, 3–23.

Gerin, W., Davidson, K. W., Christenfeld, N. J., Goyal, T., & Schwartz, J. E. (2006). The role of angry rumination and distraction in blood pressure recovery from emotional arousal. *Psychosomatic Medicine, 68*, 64–72.

Giacobbi, P. R., Foore, B., & Weinberg, R. S. (2004). Broken clubs and expletives: The sources of stress and coping responses of skilled and moderately skilled golfers. *Journal of Applied Sport Psychology, 16*, 166–182.

Giacobbi Jr., P. R., & Weinberg, R. S. (2000). An examination of coping in sport: Individual trait anxiety differences and situational consistency. *Sport Psychologist, 14*, 42–62.

Gibson, E. L., & Green, M. W. (2002). Nutritional influences on cognitive function: Mechanisms of susceptibility. *Nutrition Research Reviews, 15*, 169–206.

Gibson, J. J. (1986). *The ecological approach to visual perception.* Hillsdale, NJ: Erlbaum.

Gigerenzer, G. (2007). *Gut feelings: The intelligence of the unconscious.* New York: Viking Press.

Gilovich, T., Griffin, D., & Kahneman, D. (Eds.). (2002). *Heuristics and biases: The psychology of intuitive judgment.* New York: Cambridge University Press.

Giske, R., Rodahl, S. E., & Høigaard, R. (2014). Shared mental task models in elite ice hockey and handball teams: Does it exist and how does the coach intervene to make an impact? *Journal of Applied Sport Psychology, 27*, 20–34.

Gist, M. E. (1989). The influence of training method on self-efficacy and idea generating among managers. *Personnel Psychology, 42*, 787–805.

Gladwell, M. (2008). *Outliers: The story of success.* New York: Little, Brown, and Co.

Gobet, F., & Campitelli, G. (2007). The role of domain-specific practice, handedness, and starting age in chess. *Developmental Psychology, 43*, 159–172.

Golby, J., & Sheard, M. (2004). Mental toughness and hardiness at different levels of rugby league. *Personality and Individual Differences, 37*, 933–942.

Goldstein, E. B. (2015). *Cognitive psychology: Connecting mind, research, and everyday experience* (4th edn). Belmont, CA: Wadsworth/Cengage.

Gollwitzer, P. M. (1999). Implementation intentions: Strong effects of simple plans. *American Psychologist, 54*, 493–503.

Gomez-Pinilla, F. (2008). Brain foods: The effects of nutrients on brain function. *Nature Reviews in Neuroscience, 9*, 568–578.

Goss, S., Hall, C., Buckolz, E., & Fishburne, G. (1986). Imagery ability and the acquisition and retention of movements. *Memory & Cognition, 14*, 469–477.

Gould, D. (2001). Goal setting for peak performance. In J. M. Williams (Ed.), *Applied sport psychology: Personal growth to peak performance* (4th edn, pp. 190–205). Mountain View, CA: Mayfield.

Gould, D., Dieffenbach, K., & Moffett, A. (2002). Psychological characteristics and their development in Olympic champions. *Journal of Applied Sport Psychology, 14*, 172–204.

Gould, D., Ekland, S. A., & Jackson, R. C. (1992). 1988 U.S. Olympic wrestling excellence I: Mental preparation, pre-competition cognition and affect. *The Sport Psychologist, 6*, 358–382.

Gould, D., Guinan, D., Greenleaf, C., Medbery, R., & Peterson, K. (1999). Factors affecting Olympic performance: Perceptions of athletes and coaches from more and less successful teams. *The Sport Psychologist, 13*, 371–394.

Gould, D., Petlichkoff, L., Simons, J., & Vevera, M. (1987). Relationship between competitive state anxiety inventory-2 subscale scores and pistol shooting performance. *Journal of Sport Psychology, 9*, 33–42.

Gould, D., & Udry, E. (1994). Psychological skills for enhancing performance: Arousal regulation strategies. *Medicine and Science in Sport and Exercise, 26*, 478–485.

Grantham-McGregor, S. M., Chang, S., & Walker, S. P. (1998). Evaluation of school feeding programs: Some Jamaican examples. *American Journal of Clinical Nutrition, 67 (Suppl.)*, S785–S789.

Gray, R. (2004). Attending to the execution of a complex sensorimotor skill: Expertise differences, choking and slumps. *Journal of Experimental Psychology: Applied, 10*, 42–54.

Greenlees, I. A., Bradley, R., Holder, T., & Thelwell, R. C. (2005). The impact of opponents' non-verbal behaviour on the first impressions and outcome expectations of table tennis players. *Psychology of Sport and Exercise, 6*, 103–115.

Gregory, R. L. (1980). Perceptions as hypotheses. *Philosophical Transactions of the Royal Society of London, Series B, 290*, 181–197.

Gréhaigne, J.-F., Godbout, P., & Bouthier, D. (1999). The foundations of tactics and strategy in team sports. *Journal of Teaching in Physical Education, 18*, 159–174.

Gréhaigne, J.-F., & Wallian, N. (2007). Response to "Think SMART": Some elements of perception/decision/action in team sports. *Physical Education and Sport Pedagogy, 12*, 16–22.

Griffin, J., & Tyrell, I. (2004). *Dreaming reality: How dreams keep us sane, or can drive us mad.* Chalvington: HG Publishing.

Grinblatt, M., & Keloharju, M. (2009). Sensation seeking, overconfidence, and trading activity. *The Journal of Finance, 64*, 549–578.

Gross, J. J. (1998). Antecedent- and response-focused emotion regulation: Divergent consequences for experience, expression, and physiology. *Journal of Personality and Social Psychology, 74*, 224–237.

Gross, J. J. (2002). Emotion regulation: Affective, cognitive, and social consequences. *Psychophysiology, 39*, 281–291.

Gross, J. J., & Levenson, R. W. (1997). Hiding feelings: The acute effects of inhibiting negative and positive emotion. *Journal of Abnormal Psychology, 106*, 95–103.

Gross, J. J., & Thompson, R. A. (2007). Emotion regulation: Conceptual foundations. In J. J. Gross (Ed.), *Handbook of emotion regulation* (pp. 3–24). New York: Guilford Press.

Grove, J. R., & Heard, N. P. (1997). Optimism and sport-confidence as correlates of slump-related coping among athletes. *The Sport Psychologist, 11*, 400–410.

Gucciardi, D. F., & Dimmock, J. A. (2008). Choking under pressure in sensorimotor skills: Conscious processing or depleted attentional resources? *Psychology of Sport and Exercise, 9*, 45–59.

Gucciardi, D. F., & Gordon, S. (2009). Development and preliminary validation of the cricket mental toughness inventory (CMTI). *Journal of Sports Sciences, 27*, 1293–1310.

Gucciardi, D. F., & Gordon, S. (2011). *Mental toughness in sport: Developments in research and theory.* Abingdon: Routledge.

Gucciardi, D. F., Gordon, S., & Dimmock, J. A. (2009). Development and preliminary validation of a mental toughness inventory for Australian football. *Psychology of Sport and Exercise, 10*, 201–209.

Gucciardi, D. F., & Jones, M. J. (2012). Beyond optimal performance: Mental toughness profiles and developmental success in adolescent cricketers. *Journal of Sport & Exercise Psychology, 34*, 16–36.

Gucciardi, D. F., Longbottom, J., Jackson, B., & Dimmock, J. A. (2010). Experienced golfers' perspectives on choking under pressure. *Journal of Sport and Exercise Psychology, 32*, 61–83.

Guilford, J. P. (1956). The structure of intellect. *Psychology Bulletin, 53*, 267–293.

Guilford, J. P. (1967). *The nature of human intelligence.* New York: McGraw-Hill.

Guillot, A., Collet, C., Nguyen, V. A., Malouin, F., Richards, C., & Doyon, J. (2009). Brain activity during visual versus kinesthetic imagery: An fMRI study. *Human Brain Mapping, 30*, 2157–2172.

Gutierrez Diaz del Campo, D., Gonzalez Villora, S., & Garcia Lopez, L. M. (2011). Differences in decision making development between expert and novice invasion game players. *Perceptual & Motor Skills, 112*, 871–888.

Gwyn, R. G., & Patch, C. E. (1993). Comparing two putting styles for putting accuracy. *Perceptual and Motor Skills, 76*, 387–390.

Hall, C. R. (1998). Measuring imagery abilities and imagery use. In J. L. Duda (Ed.), *Advances in sport and exercise psychology measurement* (pp. 165–172). Morgantown, WV: Fitness Information Technology.

Hambrick, D. Z., & Engle, R. W. (2002). Effects of domain knowledge, working memory capacity and age on cognitive performance: An investigation of the knowledge-is-power hypothesis. *Cognitive Psychology, 44*, 339–387.

Hambrick, D. Z., Oswald, F. L., Altmann, E. M., Meinz, E. J., Gobet, F., & Campitelli, G. (2014). Deliberate practice: Is that all it takes to become an expert? *Intelligence, 45*, 34–45.

Hamilton, R. A., Scott, D., & MacDougall, M. P. (2007). Assessing the effectiveness of self-talk interventions on endurance performance. *Journal of Applied Sport Psychology, 19*, 226–239.

Hammermeister, J., Pickering, M., & Lennox, A. (2010). Military applications of performance psychology methods and techniques: An overview of practice and research. *The Journal of Performance Psychology, 3*, 1–12.

Hammermeister, J., Pickering, M. A., McGraw, L., & Ohlson, C. (2012). The relationship between sport related psychological skills and indicators of PTSD among stryker brigade soldiers: The mediating effects of perceived psychological resilience. *Journal of Sport Behavior, 35*, 40–60.

Hammond, D. C. (2007). What is neurofeedback? *Journal of Neurotherapy, 10*, 25–26.

Hardy, J., Oliver, E., & Tod, D. (2009). A framework for the study and application of self-talk within sport. In S. D. Mellalieu & S. Hanton (Eds.), *Advances in applied sport psychology: A review* (pp. 37–74). London: Routledge.

Hardy, L., Bell, J., & Beattie, S. (2013). A neuropsychological model of mentally tough behavior. *Journal of Personality, 82*, 69–81.

Hardy, L., & Fazey, J. A. (1987). The inverted-U hypothesis: A catastrophe for sport psychology? Paper presented at the Annual Conference of the North American Society for the Psychology of Sport and Physical Activity, Vancouver, BC, Canada.

Hardy, L., Jones, G., & Gould, D. (1996). *Understanding psychological preparation for sport: Theory and practice of elite performers.* Chichester: Wiley.

Hardy, L., Parfitt, G., & Pates, J. (1994). Performance catastrophes in sport: A test of the hysteresis hypothesis. *Journal of Sport Sciences, 12*, 327–334.

Hardy, L., Woodman, T., & Carrington, S. (2004). Is self-confidence a bias factor in higher order catastrophe models? An exploratory analysis. *Journal of Sport & Exercise Psychology, 26*, 359–368.

Harju, B. L., & Bolen, L. M. (1998). The effects of optimism on coping and perceived quality of life of college students. *Journal of Social Behavior and Personality, 13*, 185–200.

Hartel, C. E. J., Gough, H., & Hartel, G. F. (2008). Work-group emotional climate, emotion management skills, and service attitudes and performance. *Asia Pacific Journal of Human Resources, 46*, 21–37.

Hassmén, P., Koivula, N., (2001). Cardiac deceleration in elite golfers as modified by noise and anxiety during putting. *Perceptual Motor Skills, 92*, 947–957.

Hatchett, G. T., & Park, H. L. (2004). Relationships among optimism, coping styles, psychopathology, and counseling outcomes. *Personality & Individual Differences, 36*, 1755–1769.

Hatfield, B. D., Landers, D. M., & Ray, W. J. (1984). Cognitive processes during self-paced motor performance: An electroencephalographic profile of skilled marksmen. *Journal of Sport Psychology, 6*, 42–59.

Hatfield, B. D., Landers, D. M., & Ray, W. J. (1987). Cardiovascular–CNS interactions during a self-paced, intentional attentive state. *Psychophysiology, 24*, 542–549.

Hatzigeorgiadis, A., Theodorakis, Y., & Zourbanos, N. (2004). Self-talk in the swimming pool: The effects of self-talk on thought content and performance on water-polo tasks. *Journal of Applied Sport Psychology, 16*, 138–150.

Hatzigeorgiadis, A., Zourbanos, N., Galanis, E., & Theodorakis, Y. (2011). Self-talk and sport performance: A meta-analysis. *Perspectives on Psychological Science, 6*, 348–356.

Hatzigeorgiadis, A., Zourbanos, N., Mpoumpaki, S., & Theodorakis, Y. (2009). Mechanisms underlying the self-talk-performance relationship: The effects of motivational self talk on self-confidence and anxiety. *Psychology of Sport and Exercise, 10*, 185–192.

Haufler, A. J., Spalding, T. W., Santa Maria, D. L., & Hatfield, B. D. (2000). Neurocognitive activity during a self-paced visuospatial task: Comparative EEG profiles in marksmen and novice shooters. *Biological Psychology, 53*, 131–160.

Hauri, P. (1991). *The sleep disorders: Current concepts.* Kalamazoo, MI: Scope Publications.

Haworth, J. (1993). Skills-challenge relationships and psychological well-being in everyday life. *Society & Leisure, 16*, 115–128.

Hays, K., Maynard, I., Thomas, O., & Bawden, M. (2007). Sources and types of confidence identified by world class sports performers. *Journal of Applied Sport Psychology, 19*, 434–456.

Hays, K., Thomas, O., Maynard, I., & Bawden, M. (2009). The role of confidence in worldclass sport performance. *Journal of Sports Sciences, 27*, 1185–1199.

Hays, K. F. (2012). The psychology of performance in sport and other domains. In S. Murphy (Ed.), *The Oxford handbook of sport and performance psychology* (pp. 24–45). New York: Oxford University Press.

Hazell, J., Cotterill, S. T., & Hill, D. M. (2014). An exploration of pre-performance routines, self-efficacy, and performance in semi-professional soccer. *European Journal of Sport Science, 14*, 603–610.

He, F., Cao, R., Feng, Z., Guan, H., & Peng, J. (2013). The impacts of dispositional optimism and psychological resilience on the subjective well-being of burn patients: A structural equation modelling analysis. *PLoS ONE, 8*.

Headrick, J., Renshaw, I., Davids, K., Pinder, R., & Araújo, D. (2015). The dynamics of expertise acquisition in sport: The role of affective learning design. *Psychology of Sport and Exercise, 16*, 83–90.

Heilman, R. M., Crişan, L. G., Houser, D., Miclea, M., & Miu, A. C. (2010). Emotion regulation and decision making under risk and uncertainty. *Emotion, 10*, 257–265.

Heitz, R. P., & Engle, R. W. (2007). Focusing the spotlight: Individual differences in visual attention control. *Journal of Experimental Psychology: General, 136*, 217–240.

Hikosaka, O., Nakamura, K., Sakai, K., & Nakahara, H. (2002). Central mechanisms of motor skill learning. *Current Opinion in Neurobiology, 12*, 217–222.

Hill, D. M., Hanton, S., Fleming, S., & Matthews, N. (2009). A re-examination of choking in sport. *European Journal of Sport Science, 9*(4), 203–212.

Hill, D. M., Hanton, S., Matthews, N., & Fleming, S. (2011). Alleviation of choking under pressure in elite golf: An action research study. *The Sport Psychologist, 25*, 465–488.

Hill, T., Smith, N. D., & Mann, M. F. (1987). Role of efficacy expectations in predicting the decision to use advanced technologies. *Journal of Applied Psychology, 72*, 307–314.

Hodges, N. J., Starkes, J. L., & MacMahon, C. (2006). Expert performance in sport: A cognitive perspective. In K. A. Ericsson, N. Charness, P. J. Feltovich, & R. R. Hoffman (Eds.), *The Cambridge handbook of expertise and expert performance* (pp. 471–488). New York: Cambridge University Press.

Hogarth, R. M. (2001). *Educating intuition.* Chicago: University of Chicago Press.

Hoge, E. A., Austin, E. D., & Pollack, M. H. (2007). Resilience: Research evidence and conceptual considerations for post traumatic stress disorder. *Depression and Anxiety, 24*, 139–152.

Hofman, M. A. (1983). Energy metabolism, brain size, and longevity in mammals. *Quarterly Review of Biology, 58*, 495–512.

Hofmann, S. G., Heering, S., Sawyer, A. T., & Asnaani, A. (2009). How to handle anxiety: The effects of reappraisal, acceptance, and suppression strategies on anxious arousal. *Behaviour Research and Therapy, 47*, 389–394.

Hollon, D. S., & Dimidjian, S. (2009). Cognitive and behavioral treatment of depression. In I. H. Gotlib & C. L. Hammen (Eds.), *Handbook of depression* (2nd edn, pp. 586–603). New York: Guilford Press.

Holmes, P., & Calmels, C. (2008). A neuroscientific review of imagery and observation use in sport. *Journal of Motor Behavior, 40*, 433–445.

Holmqvist, K., Nyström, M., Andersson, R., Dewhurst, R., Jarodzka, H., & Van de Weijer, J. (2011). *Eye tracking: A comprehensive guide to methods and measures.* New York: Oxford University Press.

Holt, N. L., & Hogg, J. M. (2002). Perceptions of stress and coping during preparations for the 1999 women's soccer World Cup Finals. *The Sport Psychologist, 16*, 251–271.

Horton, S., Baker, J., & Schorer, J. (2008). Expertise and aging: Maintaining skills through the lifespan. *European Review of Aging and Physical Activity, 5*, 89–96.

Horton, S., Baker, J., & Wier, P. (2015). Career length, aging, and expertise. In J. Baker & D. Farrow (Eds.), *Routledge handbook of sport expertise*. Oxford: Routledge.

Howe, A., Smajdor, A., & Stokl, A. (2012). Towards an understanding of resilience and its relevance to medical training. *Medical Education, 46*, 349–356.

Howe, J. E., Warm, S. R., & Dember, J. S. (1995). Meta analysis of the sensitivity decrement of vigilance. *Psychological Bulletin, 117*, 230–249.

Howe, M. J. A., Davidson, J. W., & Sloboda, J. (1998). Innate talents: Reality or myth? *Behavior and Brain Sciences, 21*, 399–442.

Howells, N., & Fletcher, D. (2015). Sink or swim: Adversity – and growth – related experiences in Olympic swimming champions. *Psychology of Sport and Exercise, 16*, 37–48.

Hoyland, A., Lawton, C. L., & Dye, L. (2008). Acute effects of macronutrient manipulations on cognitive test performance in healthy young adults: A systematic review. *Neuroscience and Biobehavioral Reviews, 32*, 72–85.

Hristovski, R., Davids, K., & Araújo, D. (2006). Affordance-controlled bifurcations of action patterns in martial arts. *Nonlinear Dynamics, Psychology, and Life Sciences, 19*, 409–444.

Hsu, J. L., Leemans, A., Bai, C. H., Lee, C. H., Tsai, Y. F., Chiu, H. C., & Chen, W. H. (2008). Gender differences and age-related white matter changes of the human brain: A diffusion tensor imaging study. *NeuroImage, 39*, 566–577.

Hu, S., & Stern, R. M. (1999). The retention of adaptation to motion sickness eliciting stimulation. *Aviation, Space & Environment Medicine, 70*, 766–768.

Hubbard, T. L. (1995). Environmental invariants in the representation of motion: Implied dynamics and representational momentum, gravity, friction, and centripetal force. *Psychonomic Bulletin & Review, 2*, 322–338.

Hubbard, T. L. (2005). Representational momentum and related displacements: A review of the findings. *Psychonomic Bulletin & Review, 12*, 822–851.

Hugdahl, K. (1995). *Psychophysiology: The mind-body perspective*. Cambridge, MA: Harvard University Press.

Humphrey, J. H., Yow, D. A., & Bowden, W. W. (2000). *Stress in college athletics: Causes, consequences, coping*. Binghamton, NY: The Haworth Half-Court Press.

Hunt, C. A., Rietschel, J. C., Hatfield, B. D., & Iso-Ahola, S. E. (2013). A psychophysiological profile of winners and losers in competitive sport competition. *Sport, Exercise and Performance Psychology, 2*, 220–231.

Isaacowitz, D. M. (2005). Correlates of well-being in adulthood and old age: A tale of two optimisms. *Journal of Research in Personality, 39*, 224–244.

Jackson, R. C., Ashford, K. J., & Norsworthy, G. (2006). Attentional focus, dispositional reinvestment, and skilled motor performance under pressure. *Journal of Sport & Exercise Psychology, 28*, 49–68.

Jackson, S., & Csikszentmihalyi, M. (1999). *Flow in sports: The keys to optimal experiences and performances*. Champaign, IL: Human Kinetics.

Jackson, S., & Roberts, G. (1992). Positive performance state of athletes: Towards a conceptual understanding of peak performance. *The Sport Psychologist, 6*, 156–171.

Jackson, S. A., Thomas, P. R., Marsh, H. W., & Smethurst, C. J. (2001). Relationship between flow, self-concept, psychological skill, and performance. *Journal of Applied Sport Psychology, 13*, 129–135.

Jacobs, D. M., & Michaels, C. F. (2002). On the apparent paradox of learning and realism. *Ecological Psychology, 14*, 127–140.

Janelle, C. M., & Hillman, C. H. (2003). Expert performance in sport: Current perspective and critical issues. In J. L. Starkes & K. A. Ericsson (Eds.), *Expert Performance in sports: Advances in research on sport expertise*. Champaign, IL: Human Kinetics.

Janelle, C. M., Hillman, C. H., Apparies, R. J., Murray, N. P., Meili, L., Fallon, E. A., & Hatfield, B. D. (2000). Expertise differences in cortical activation and gaze behavior during rifle shooting. *Journal of Sport and Exercise Psychology, 22*, 167–182.

Jasper, H. H. (1958). The ten-twenty electrode system of the International Federation. *Electroencephalography and Clinical Neurophysiology, 10*, 371–375.

Jeneson, A., & Squire, L. R. (2012). Working memory, long-term memory, and medial temporal lobe function. *Learning and Memory, 19*, 15–25.

Johnsen, B. H., Eid, J., Pallesen, S., Bartone, P. T., & Nissestad, A. O. (2009). Predicting transformational in naval cadets: Effects of personality hardiness and training. *Journal of Applied Social Psychology, 39*, 2213–2235.

Johnson, J., & Raab, M. (2003). Take the first: option generation and resulting choices. *Organizational Behavior and Human Decision Processes, 91*, 215–229.

Johnson, J. G. (2006). Cognitive modelling of decision making in sports. *Psychology of Sport and Exercise, 7*, 631–652.

Johnson, J. J. M., Hrycaiko, D. W., Johnson, G. V., & Hallas, J. M. (2004). Self-talk and female youth soccer performance. *The Sport Psychologist, 18*, 44–59.

Johnson, W. A., & Dark, V. J. (1986). Selective attention. *Annual Review of Psychology, 37*, 43–75.

Jones, G. (1995). More than just a game: Research developments and issues in competitive anxiety in sport. *British Journal of Psychology, 86*, 449–478.

Jones, G., Hanton, S., & Connaughton, D. (2002). What is this thing called mental toughness? An investigation of elite sport performers. *Journal of Applied Sport Psychology, 14*, 205–218.

Jones, G., Hanton, S., & Connaughton, D. (2007). A framework of mental toughness in the world's best performers. *The Sport Psychologist, 21*, 243–264.

Jones, G., Swain, A., & Hardy, L. (1993). Intensity and direction dimensions of competitive state anxiety and relationships with performance. *Journal of Sports Sciences, 11*, 525–532.

Jones, M. V. (2003). Controlling emotions in sport. *The Sport Psychologist, 17*, 471–486.

Jones, M. V. (2012). Emotion regulation and performance. In S. M. Murphy (Ed.), *The Oxford handbook of sport and performance psychology*. Oxford: Oxford University Press.

Jones, M. V., Meijen, C., McCarthy, P. J., & Sheffield, D. (2009). A theory of challenge and threat states in athletes. *International Review of Sport and Exercise Psychology, 2*, 161–180.

Joslyn, S., & Hunt, E. (1998). Evaluating individual differences in response to time-pressure situations. *Journal of Experimental Psychology: Applied, 4*, 16–43.

Kadota, T., Horinouchi, T., & Kuroda, C. (2001). Development and aging of the cerebrum: Assessment with proton MR spectroscopy. *American Journal of Neuroradiology, 22*, 128–135.

Kahneman, D. (2011). *Thinking, fast and slow*. New York: Farrar, Straus, and Giroux.

Kao, S.-C., Huang, C.-J., & Hung, T.-M. (2013). Frontal midline theta is a specific indicator of optimal attentional engagement during skilled putting performance. *Journal of Sport & Exercise Psychology, 35*, 470–478.

Kaplan, R. J., Greenwood, C. E., Winocur, G., & Wolever, T. M. (2001). Dietary protein, carbohydrate, and fat enhance memory performance in the healthy elderly. *American Journal of Clinical Nutrition, 74*, 687–693.

Kaufman, J. C., & Beghetto, R. A. (2009). Beyond big and little: The four C model of creativity. *Review of General Psychology, 13*, 1–12.

Kavussanu, M., Crews, D. J., & Gill, D. L. (1998). The effects of single versus multiple measures of biofeedback on basketball free throw shooting performance. *International Journal of Sport Psychology, 29*, 132–144.

Kazemi, R. M., Khaberi, M., & Farokhi, A. (2003, November). The effect of mental training on the performance of elite gymnasts. In Y. L. Hanin (Chair), Oral presentations. Symposium conducted at the meeting of the 2nd International Congress on Psychology Applied to Sport, Madrid, Spain.

Kennedy, D., & Scholey, A. (2000). Glucose administration, heart rate and cognitive performance: Effects of increasing mental effort. *Psychopharmacology, 149*, 63–71.

Kéri, S. (2011). Solitary minds and social capital: Latent inhibition, general intellectual functions and social network size predict creative achievements. *Psychology of Aesthetics, Creativity, and the Arts, 5*, 215–221.

Kerick, S. E., Douglass, L. W., & Hatfield, B. (2004). Cerebral cortical adaptations associated with visuomotor practice. *Medicine in Science in Sports and Exercise, 36*, 118–129.

Kerr, R. (1982). *Perceptual motor learning.* Philadelphia: Saunders College Publications.

Kibele, A. (2006). Non-consciously controlled decision-making for fast motor reactions in sports: A priming approach for motor responses to non-consciously perceived movement features. *Psychology of Sport and Exercise, 7*, 591–610.

Kimiecik, J. C., & Jackson, S. A. (2002). Optimal experience in sport: A flow perspective. In T. S. Horn (Ed.), *Advances in sport psychology* (2nd edn, pp. 501–527). Champaign, IL: Human Kinetics.

Kingston, K., & Hardy, L. (1997). Effects of different types of goals on processes that support performance. *The Sport Psychologist, 11*, 277–293.

Klein, G. (1992). *Decision making in complex military environments.* Fairborn, OH: Klein Associates.

Klein, G. (1997). An overview of naturalistic decision making applications. In G. Klein & C. E. Zsambok (Eds.), *Naturalistic decision making* (pp. 49–59). Mahwah, NJ: Lawrence Erlbaum Associates Inc.

Klein, G. (2008). *Naturalistic decision making.* Fairborn, OH: Klein Associates, Division of ARA.

Klein, G., & Calderwood, R. (1991). Decision model: Lessons from the field. IEEE transactions on systems. *Man & Cybernetics, 21*, 1018–1026.

Klein, G., Calderwood, R., & Clinton-Cirocco, A. (1986). Rapid decision making of the fireground. *Proceedings of the Human Factors and Ergonomics Society 30th Annual Meeting, 1*, 576–580.

Klimesch, W. (1999). EEG alpha and theta oscillations reflect cognitive and memory performance: A review and analysis. *Brain Research Reviews, 29*, 169–195.

Kobasa, S. C. (1979). Stressful life events, personality, and health: An inquiry into hardiness. *Journal of Personality and Social Psychology, 37*, 1–11.

Kobasa, S. C., Maddi, S. R., & Kahn, S. (1982). Hardiness and health: A prospective study. *Journal of Personality and Social Psychology, 42*, 168–177.

Koch, C. (1999). *Biophysics of computation: Information processing in single neurons.* New York: Oxford University Press.

Koehler, D. J., & Harvey, N. (2004). *Blackwell handbook of judgment and decision making.* Malden, MA: Blackwell.

Koehn, S., & Morris, T. (2012). The relationship between flow state and performance in tennis competition. *Journal of Sports Medicine and Physical Fitness, 52*, 437–447.

Koehn, S., Morris, T., & Watt, A. P. (2013). Correlates of dispositional and state flow in tennis competition. *Journal of Applied Sport Psychology, 25*, 354–369.

Kornspan, A. S. (2012). History of sport and performance psychology. In S. M. Murphy (Ed.), *The Oxford handbook of sport and performance psychology.* Oxford: Oxford University Press.

Kowler, E. (2011). Eye movements: The past 25 years. *Vision Research, 51*, 1457–1483.

Krampe, R. T. (2002). Aging, expertise and fine motor movement. *Neuroscience and Behavioral Reviews, 26*, 769–776.

Krampe, R. T., & Baltes, P. B. (2002). Intelligence as adaptive resource development and resource allocation: A new look through the lense of SOC and expertise. In R. J. Sternberg & E. L. Grigorenko (Eds.), *Perspectives on the psychology of abilities, competencies, and expertise* (pp. 31–69). New York: Cambridge University Press.

Krampe, R. T., & Charness, N. (2006). Aging and expertise. In K. A. Ericsson, N. Charness, P. J. Feltovich, & R. Hoffman (Eds.), The *Cambridge handbook of expertise and expert performance* (pp. 723–742). New York: Cambridge University Press.

Krampe, R. T., & Ericsson, K. A. (1996). Maintaining excellence: Deliberate practice and elite performance in young and older pianists. *Journal of Experimental Psychology: General, 125*, 331–359.

Krane, V., & Williams, J. M. (2006). Psychological characteristics of peak performance. In J. M. Williams (Ed.), *Applied sport psychology: Personal growth to peak performance* (pp. 207–227). New York: McGraw-Hill.

Kreibig, S.vD. (2010). Autonomic nervous system activity in emotion: A review. *Biological Psychology, 84*, 394–421.

Kremer, J., & Moran, A. (2008). *Pure sport: Practical sport psychology*. Hove: Routledge.

Krohne, H. W., & Hindel, C. (1988). Trait-anxiety, state anxiety, and coping behaviors as predictors of athletic performance. *Anxiety Research, 1*, 225–234.

Kuhl, B. A., & Chun, M. (2014). Memory and attention. In A. C. Nobre & S. Kastner (Eds.), *The Oxford handbook of attention*. Oxford: Oxford University Press.

Kyllo, L. B., & Landers, D. M. (1995). Goal setting in sport and exercise: A research synthesis to resolve the controversy. *Journal of Sport & Exercise Psychology, 17*, 117–137.

Kyllonen, P. C., & Christal, R. E. (1990). Reasoning ability (is little more than) working memory capacity?! *Intelligence, 14*, 389–433.

Lacey, B. C., & Lacey, J. I. (1974). Studies of heart rate and other bodily processes in sensorimotor behaviour. In P. A. Obrist, A. H. Black, J. Brener, & L. V. DiCara (Eds.), *Cardiovascular psychophysiology* (pp. 538–564). Chicago: Aldine.

Lacey, B. C., & Lacey, J. I. (1978). Two-way communication between the heart and the brain, significance of time within the cardiac cycle. *American Psychologist, 33*, 99–113.

Lacey, B. C., & Lacey, J. I. (1980). Cognitive modulation of time-dependent primary bradycardia. *Psychophysiology, 17*, 209–221.

Land, M. F., & McLeod, P. (2000). From eye movements to actions: How batsmen hit the ball. *Nature: Neuroscience, 3*, 1340–1345.

Land, W., & Tenenbaum, G. (2012). An outcome- and process-oriented examination of a golf-specific secondary task strategy to prevent choking under pressure. *Journal of Applied Sport Psychology, 24*, 1–20.

Land, W. M., Frank, C., & Schach, T. (2014). The influence of attentional focus on the development of skill representation in a complex action. *Psychology of Sport and Exercise, 15*, 30–38.

Landers, D. M., Han, M. W., Salazer, W., Petruzzello, S. J., Kubitz, K. A., & Gannon, T. L. (1994). Effects of learning on electroencephalographic and electrocardiographic patterns in novice archers. *International Journal of Sport Psychology, 25*, 313–330.

Landers, D. M., Petruzzello, S. J., Salazar, W., Crews, D. J., Kubitz, K. A., Gannon, T. L., et al. (1991). The influence of electrocortical biofeedback on performance in pre-elite archers. *Medicine & Science in Sport & Exercise, 23*, 123–129.

Landin, D., & Hebert, E. P. (1999). The influence of ST on the performance of skilled female tennis players. *Journal of Applied Sport Psychology, 11*, 263–282.

Larkin, P., O'Connor, D., & Williams, A. M. (2016). Does grit influence sport-specific engagement and perceptual-cognitive expertise in elite youth soccer? *Journal of Applied Sport Psychology, 28*, 129–138.

Laughlin, S. B., & Sejnowski, T. J. (2003). Communication in neural networks. *Science, 301*, 1870–1874.

Lavie, N. (2010). Attention, distraction and cognitive control under load. *Current Directions in Psychological Science, 19*, 143–148.

Lazarus, R. S. (1991). *Emotion and adaptation.* New York: Oxford University Press.

Lazarus, R. S. (1999). Hope: An emotion and a vital coping resource against despair. *Social Research, 66*, 653–678.

Lazarus, R. S. (2000). How emotions influence performance in competitive sports. *The Sport Psychologist, 14*, 229–252.

Lazarus, R. S., & Folkman, S. (1984). *Stress, appraisal, and coping.* New York: Springer.

LeCoutre, J., & Schmitt, J. A. J. (2008). Food ingredients and cognitive functions. *Current Opinion in Clinical Nutrition and Metabolic Care, 11*, 706–710.

Lee, B., Lee, M., Yoh, M. S., You, H., Park, H., Jung, K., Lee, B. H., Na, D. L., & Kim, G. H. (2015). The effects of age, gender, and hand on force control capabilities of healthy adults. *Human Factors and Ergonomics Society, 57*, 1348–1358.

Lehrer, P., Vaschillo, B., Zucker, T., Graves, J., Katsamanis, M., Aviles, M., & Wamboldt, F. (2013). Protocol for heart-rate variability biofeedback training. *Biofeedback, 41*, 98–109.

Leipold, B., & Greve, W. (2009). Resilience: A conceptual bridge between coping and development. *European Psychologist, 14*, 40–50.

Leocani, L., Toro, C., Manganotti, P., Zhuang, P., & Hallett, M. (1997). Event-related coherence and event-related desynchronization/synchronization in the 10 Hz and 20 Hz EEG during self-paced movements. *Electroencephalography and Clinical Neurophysiology, 104*, 199–206.

Lerner, J. S., Small, D. A., & Loewenstein, G. (2004). Heart strings and purse strings: Carryover effects of emotions on economic decisions. *Psychological Science, 15*, 337–341.

Lerner, J. S., & Tiedens, L. Z. (2006). Portrait of the angry decision maker: How appraisal tendencies shape anger's influence on cognition. *Journal of Behavioral Decision Making, 19*(2), 115–137.

Lewis, B. R, & Linder, D. E. (1997). Thinking about choking? Attentional processes and paradoxical performance. *Personality and Social Psychology Bulletin, 23*, 937–944.

Lewis, M. D. (2004). The emergence of mind in the emotional brain. In A. Demetriou & A. Raftopoulos (Eds.), *Cognitive developmental change.* New York: Cambridge University Press.

Lidor, R., & Singer, R. N. (2000). Teaching pre-performance routines to beginners. *Journal of Physical Education, Recreation and Dance, 71*, 34–36.

Linley, A. (2008). *Average to A+: Realising strengths in yourself and others.* Coventry: CAPP Press.

Lipshitz, R., Klein, G., Orasanu, J., & Salas, E. (2001). Taking stock of naturalistic decision making. *Journal of Behavioral Decision Making, 14*, 331–352.

Lipshitz, R., & Strauss, O. (1997). Coping with uncertainty: A naturalistic decision-making analysis. *Organizational Behavior and Human Decision Processes, 69*, 149–163.

Lloyd, H. M., Green, M. W., & Rogers, P. J. (1994). Mood and cognitive performance effects of isocaloric lunches differing in fat and carbohydrate content. *Physiology and Behavior 56*, 51–57.

Lobinger, B. H. (2016). Bridging the gap between action and cognition: An overview. In M. Raab, B. Lobinger, S. Hoffmann, A. Pizzera, & S. Laborde (Eds.), *Performance psychology: Perception, action, cognition, and emotion.* London: Elsevier.

Lonsdale, C., & Tam, J. T. M. (2008). On the temporal and behavioral consistency of pre-performance routines: An intra-individual analysis of elite basketball players' free throw shooting accuracy. *Journal of Sport Sciences, 26*, 259–266.

Lorains, M., Ball, K., & MacMahon, C. (2013). Expertise differences in a video decision-making task: Speed influences on performance. *Psychology of Sport and Exercise, 14*, 293–297.

Lotze, M., & Halsband, U. (2006). Motor imagery. *Journal of Physiology (Paris), 99*, 386–395.

Loze, G. M., Collins, D., & Holmes, P. (2001). Pre-shot EEG alpha power reactivity during expert air-pistol shooting: A comparison of best and worst shots. *Journal of Sport Science, 19*, 727–733.

Lubart, T. I. (2001). Models of the creative process: Past, present, and future. *Creativity Research Journal, 13*, 295–308.

Luthar, S. S., & Cicchetti, D. (2000). The construct of resilience: Implications for interventions and social policies. *Development and Psychopathology, 12*, 857–885.

MacIntyre, T. E., Igou, E. R., Campbell, M. J., Moran, A. P., & Matthews, J. (2014). Metacognition and action: A new pathway to understanding social and cognitive aspects of expertise in sport. *Frontiers in Psychology, 5*, 1–12.

Macnamara, B. N., Hambrick, D. Z., & Oswald, F. L. (2014). Deliberate practice and performance in music, games, sports, education, and professions: A meta-analysis. *Psychological Science, 25*, 1608–1618.

Macquet, A. C. (2009). Recognition within the decision-making process: A case study of expert volleyball. *Journal of Applied Sport Psychology, 21*, 64–79.

Maddi, S. R. (2006). Hardiness: the courage to grow from stresses. *Journal of Positive Psychology, 1*, 160–168.

Maddi, S. R., Harvey, R. H., Khoshaba, D. M., Lu, J. L., Persico, M., & Brow, M. (2006). The personality construct of hardiness, III: Relationships with repression, innovativeness, authoritarianism, and performance. *Journal of Personality, 74*, 575–598.

Maddi, S. R., & Hess, M. J. (1992). Personality hardiness and success in basketball. *International Journal of Sport Psychology, 23*, 360–368.

Maddux, J. E., & Gosselin, J. T. (2003). Self-efficacy. In M. R. Leary & J. P. Tangney (Eds.), *Handbook of self and identity* (pp. 218–238). New York: Guilford Press.

Maddux, J. E., & Lewis, J. (1995). Self-efficacy and adjustment: Basic principles and issues. In J. E. Maddux (Ed.), *Self-efficacy, adaptation and adjustment: Theory, research, and application* (pp. 37–68). New York: Plenum Press.

Magill, R. A. (2011). *Motor learning and control: Concepts and applications* (9th edn). New York: McGraw-Hill.

Magnotta, V. A., Andreasen, N. C., Schultz, S. K., Harris, G., Cizadlo, T., Heckel, D., Nopoulos, P., & Flaum, M. (1999). Quantitative in vivo measurement of gyrification in the human brain: Changes associated with aging. *Cerebral Cortex, 9*, 151–160.

Malmendier, U., & Tate, G. (2005). CEO overconfidence and corporate investment. *Journal of Finance, 60*, 2661–2700.

Marcotte, D. (1997). Treating depression in adolescence: A review of the effectiveness of cognitive-behavioral treatments. *Journal of Youth and Adolescence, 26*, 273–283.

Marlow, C., Bull, S., Heath, B., & Shambrook, C. (1998). The use of a single case design to investigate the effect of a pre-performance routine on the water polo penalty shot. *Journal of Science and Medicine in Sport, 1*, 143–155.

Marteniuk, R. G. (1976). *Information processing in motor skills.* New York: Holt, Rinehart, and Winston.

Martens, R., Burton, D., Vealey, R. S., Bump, L. A., & Smith, D. E. (1990). Development and validation of the Competitive State Anxiety Inventory-2. In R. Martens, R. S. Vealey, & D. Burton (Eds.), *Competitive anxiety in sport* (pp. 117–190). Champaign, IL: Human Kinetics.

Martens, R., Vealey, R. S., & Burton, D. (1990). *Competitive anxiety in sport*. Champaign, IL: Human Kinetics.

Martin, K. A., Moritz, S. E., & Hall, C. R. (1999). Imagery use in sport: A literature review and applied model. *The Sport Psychologist, 13*, 245–268.

Martin-Krumm, C. P., Sarrazin, P. G., Peterson, C., & Famose, J. (2003). Explanatory style and resilience after sports failure. *Personality and Individual Differences, 35*, 1685–1695.

Martinez-Conde, S., Macknik, S. L., & Hubel, D. H. (2004). The role of fixational eye movements in visual perception. *Nature Review Neuroscience, 5*, 229–240.

Mascarenhas, D. R. D., & Smith, N. C. (2011). Developing the performance brain: Decision making under pressure. In D. Collins, A. Button, & H. Richards (Eds.), *Performance psychology: A practitioner's guide*. Edinburgh: Church Livingstone.

Masters, R., & Maxwell, J. (2008). The theory of reinvestment. *International Review of Sport & Exercise Psychology, 1*, 160–184.

Masters, R. S. W., Poolton, J. M., Maxwell, J. P., & Raab, M. (2008). Implicit motor learning and complex decision making in time-constrained environments. *Journal of Motor Behavior, 40*, 71–79.

Matlin, M. (2002). *Cognition* (6th edn). New York: John Wiley.

Matthews, G., Davies, D. R., Westerman, S. J., & Stammers, R. B. (2000). *Human performance: Cognition, stress and individual differences*. Hove: Psychology Press.

Mattlin, J., Wethington, E., & Kessler, R. C. (1990). Situational determinants of coping and coping effectiveness. *Journal of Health and Social Behavior, 31*, 103–122.

Maule, A. J., Hockey, G. R. J., & Bdzola, L. (2000). Effects of time-pressure on decision-making under uncertainty: Changes in affective state and information processing strategy. *Acta Psychologica, 104*, 283–301.

Mayer, R. E. (1992). *Thinking, problem solving, cognition* (2nd edn). New York: Freeman.

Mayer, R. E., & Wittrock, M. C. (2006). Problem solving. In P. A. Alexander & P. H. Winne (Eds.), *Handbook of educational psychology* (2nd edn, pp. 287–304). Mahwah, NJ: Erlbaum.

Maynard, I. W. (1998). *Improving concentration*. Leeds: National Coaching Foundation.

McAuley, E. (1985). Modelling and self-efficacy: A test of Bandura's model. *Journal of Sport Psychology, 7*, 283–295.

McGrath, H., & Noble, T. (2003). *BOUNCE BACK! A classroom resiliency program. (Teacher's handbook. Teacher's resource books, Level 1: K–2; Level 2: Yrs 3–4; Level 3: Yrs 5–8)*. Sydney: Pearson Education.

McKay, J., Niven, A. G., Lavallee, D., & White, A. (2008). Sources of strain among elite UK track athletes. *The Sport Psychologist, 22*, 143–163.

McMenamin, J. J. (1992). *Operational decision making: The impact of time and information*. Newport, RI: Naval War College.

McMorris, T. (1998). Teaching games for understanding: Its contributions to knowledge of skill acquisition from a motor learning perspective. *European Journal of Physical Education, 3*, 65–74.

McNevin, N. H., Shea, C. H., & Wulf, G. (2003). Increasing the distance of an external focus of attention enhances learning. *Psychological Research, 67*, 22–29.

McRobert, A., & Taylor, M. (2005). Perceptual abilities of experienced and inexperienced cricket batsmen in differentiating between left and right hand bowling deliveries. *Journal of Sports Sciences, 23*, 190–191.

McRobert, A. P., Ward, P., Eccles, D. W., & Williams, A. M. (2011). The effect of manipulating context-specific information on perceptual-cognitive processes during a simulated anticipation task. *British Journal of Psychology, 102*, 519–534.

Mele, M. L., & Federici, S. (2012). Gaze and eye-tracking solutions for psychological research. *Cognitive Processes, 13*, S261–S265.

Mellalieu, S. D., Neil, R., Hanton, S., & Fletcher, D. (2009). Competition stress in sport performers: Stressors experienced in the competition environment. *Journal of Sports Sciences, 27*, 729–744.

Memmert, D., Huttermann, S., & Orliczek, J. (2013). Decide like Lionel Messi! The impact of regulatory focus on divergent thinking in sports. *Journal of Applied Social Psychology, 43*, 2163–2167.

Mendes, W. B., Blascovich, J., Hunter, S. B., Lickel, B., & Jost, J. T. (2007). Threatened by the unexpected: Physiological responses during social interactions with expectancy-violating partners. *Journal of Personality and Social Psychology, 92*, 698–716.

Mesagno, C., Harvey, J. T., & Janelle, C. M. (2011). Self presentation origins of choking: Evidence from separate pressure manipulations. *Journal of Sport & Exercise Psychology, 33*, 441–459.

Mesagno, C., Harvey, J., & Janelle, C. (2012). Choking under pressure: The role of fear of negative evaluation. *Psychology of Sport and Exercise, 13*(1), 60–68.

Mesagno, C., & Hill, D. M. (2013). Definition of choking in sport: Reconceptualization and debate. *International Journal of Sport Psychology, 44*, 267–277.

Mesagno, C., Marchant, D., & Morris, T. (2009). Alleviating choking: The sounds of distraction. *Journal of Applied Sport Psychology, 21*, 131–147.

Mesagno, C., & Mullane-Grant, T. (2010). A comparison of different pre-performance routines as possible choking interventions. *Journal of Applied Sport Psychology, 22*, 343–360.

Messier, C. (2004). Glucose improvement of memory: A review. *European Journal of Pharmacology, 490*, 33–57.

Meyers, A. W., Whelan, J. P., & Murphy, S. M. (1996). Cognitive behavioural strategies in athletic performance enhancement. *Progress in Behavior Modification, 30*, 137–164.

Miller, G. A. (1956). The magical number seven, plus or minus two: Some limits of our capacity for processing information. *Psychological Review, 63*, 81–97.

Milner, A. D., & Goodale, M. A. (1998). The visual brain in action. *Psyche, 4*, 1–14.

Mitchell, T. R., Hopper, H., Daniels, D., George-Falvy, J., & James, L. R. (1994). Predicting self-efficacy and performance during skill acquisition. *Journal of Applied Psychology, 79*, 506–517.

Mitsch, J. R., & Hackfort, D. (2016). Theoretical framework of performance psychology: An action theory perspective. In M. Raab, B. Lobinger, S. Hoffmann, A. Pizzera, & S. Laborde (Eds.), *Performance psychology: Perception, action, cognition, and emotion.* London: Academic Press.

Miu, A. C., Heilman, R. M., & Houser, D. (2008). Anxiety impairs decision-making: Psychophysiological evidence from an Iowa Gambling Task. *Biological Psychology, 77*, 353–358.

Montano, N., Porta, A., Cogliati, C., Costantino, G., Tobaldini, E., Casali, K. R., & Iellamo, F. (2009). Heart rate variability explored in the frequency domain: A tool to investigate the link between heart and behavior. *Neuroscience and Biobehavioral Reviews, 33*, 71–80.

Montgomery, H., Lipshitz, R., & Brehmer, B. (2005). Introduction: From the first to the fifth volume of naturalistic decision-making research. In H. Montgomery, R. Lipshitz, & B. Brehmer (Eds.), *How professionals make decisions.* Mahwah, NJ: Lawrence Erlbaum.

Moore, L. J., Vine, S. J., Wilson, M. R., & Freeman, P. (2012). The effect of challenge and threat states on performance: An examination of potential mechanisms. *Psychophysiology, 49*, 1417–1425.

Moran, A. (2012). Concentration: Attention and performance. In S. M. Murphy (Ed.), *The Oxford handbook of sport and performance psychology*. Oxford: Oxford University Press.

Moran, A., Byrne, A., & McGlade, N. (2002). The effects of anxiety and strategic planning on visual search behavior. *Journal of Sports Sciences, 20*, 225–236.

Moran, A. P. (1996). *The psychology of concentration in sports performers: A cognitive analysis*. Hove: Psychology Press.

Morgan, P. B. C., Fletcher, D., & Sarkar, M. (2015). Understanding team resilience in the world's best athletes: A case study of a rugby union world cup winning team. *Psychology of Sport and Exercise, 16*, 91–100.

Morin, C. M., Bootzin, R. R., Buysse, D. J., Edinger, J. D., Espie, C. A., & Lichstein, K. L. (2006). Psychological and behavioral treatment of insomnia: Update of the recent evidence (1998–2004). *Sleep, 29*, 1398–1414.

Moritz, S. E., Feltz, D. L., Fahrbach, K. R., & Mack, D. E. (2000). The relationship of self-efficacy measures to sport performance: A meta-analytical review. *Research Quarterly for Exercise and Sport, 71*, 280–294.

Morris, L. W., Davis, M. A., & Hutchings, C. H. (1981). Cognitive and emotional components of anxiety: Literature review and a revised worry-emotionality scale. *Journal of Educational Psychology, 73*, 541–555.

Morris, T., Spittle, M., & Watt, A. P. (2005). *Imagery in sport*. Leeds: Human Kinetics.

Morris, T., & Thomas, P. (1995). Approaches to applied sport psychology. In T. Morris, & J. Summers (Eds.), *Sport psychology: Theory, applications and issues* (pp. 215–258). Chichester: Wiley.

Mulder, L. J. M. (1992). Measurement and analysis methods of heart rate and respiration for use in applied environments. *Biological Psychology, 34*, 205–236.

Mullen, R., Hardy, L., & Tattersall, A. (2005). The effects of anxiety on motor performance: A test of the conscious processing hypothesis. *Journal of Sport & Exercise Psychology, 27*, 212–225.

Muraven, M., Tice, D. M., & Baumeister, R. F. (1998). Self-control as limited resource: Regulatory depletion patterns. *Journal of Personality and Social Psychology, 74*, 774–789.

Murphy, J. M., Pagano, M., Nachmani, J., Sperling, P., Kane, S., & Kleinman, R. (1998). The relationship of school breakfast to psychosocial and academic functioning: Cross-sectional and longitudinal observations in an inner-city school sample. *Archives of Pediatrics and Adolescent Medicine, 152*, 899–907.

Murphy, S. M. (1994). Imagery interventions in sport. *Medicine & Science in Sports & Exercise, 26*, 486–494.

Neisser, U. (1967). *Cognitive psychology*. New York: Appleton-Century-Crofts.

Neumann, D. L., & Thomas, P. R. (2011). Cardiac and respiratory activity and golf putting performance under attentional focus instructions. *Psychology of Sport and Exercise, 12*, 451–459.

Newell, A., & Simon, H. A. (1972). *Human problem solving*. Englewood Cliffs, NJ: Prentice-Hall.

Nicholls, A. R., Holt, N. L., Polman, R. J. C., & Bloomfield, J. (2006). Stressors, coping, and coping effectiveness among professional rugby union players. *The Sport Psychologist, 20*, 314–329.

Nicholls, A. R., Holt, N. L., Polman, R. J. C., & James, D. W. G. (2005). Stress and coping among international adolescent golfers. *Journal of Applied Sport Psychology, 17*, 333–340.

Nicholls, A. R., Levy, A. R., Polman, R. C. J., & Crust, L. (2011). Mental toughness, coping, self-efficacy, and coping effectiveness among athletes. *International Journal of Sport & Exercise Psychology, 42*, 513–524.

Nicholls, A. R., Polman, R., Morley, D., & Taylor, N. J. (2009). Coping and coping effectiveness in relation to a competitive sport event: Pubertal status, chronological age, and gender among adolescent athletes. *Journal of Sport & Exercise Psychology, 31*, 299–317.

Nieuwenhuys, A., & Oudejans, R. R. D. (2011). Training with anxiety: Short- and long-term effects on police officers' shooting behavior under pressure. *Cognitive Processing, 12*, 227–288.

Noblet, A. J., & Gifford, S. M. (2002). The sources of stress experienced by professional Australian footballers. *Journal of Applied Sport Psychology, 14*, 1–13.

Nolen-Hoeksema, S. (1991). Responses to depression and their effects on the duration of depressive episodes. *Journal of Abnormal Psychology, 100*, 569–582.

Nunez, P. L., & Srinivasan, R. (2006). *Electric fields of the brain: The neurophysics of EEG*. New York: Oxford University Press.

O'Doherty, J. P., & Bossaerts, P. (2008). Toward a mechanistic understanding of human decision making: Contributions of functional neuroimaging. *Current Directions in Psychological Science, 17*, 119–123.

Okamoto-Mizuno, K., Tsuzuki, K., & Mizuno, K. (2005). Effects of humid heat exposure in later sleep segments on sleep stages and body temperature in humans. *International Journal of Biometeorology, 49*, 232–237.

Olszewski-Kubilius, P., Subotnik, R. F., & Worrell, F. C. (2015). Antecedent and concurrent psychosocial skills that support high levels of achievement within talent domains. *High Ability Studies, 26*, 195–210.

Otten, M. (2009). Choking vs. clutch: A study of sport performance under pressure. *Journal of Sport & Exercise Psychology, 31*, 583–601.

Oudejans, R., & Pijpers, J. R. (2010). Training with mild anxiety may prevent choking under higher levels of anxiety. *Psychology of Sport & Exercise, 11*, 44–50.

Oudejans, R. R. D., Kuijpers, W., Kooijman, C., & Bakker, F. C. (2011). Thoughts and attention of athletes under pressure: Skill-focus or performance worries? *Anxiety, Stress & Coping, 24*, 59–73.

Owens, D. S., Macdonald, I., Tucker, P., Sytnik, N., Totterdell, P., Minors, D., Waterhouse, J., & Folkard, S. (2000). Diurnal variations in the mood and performance of highly practised young women living under strictly controlled conditions. *British Journal of Psychology, 91*, 41–60.

Paivio, A. (1985). Cognitive and motivational functions of imagery in human performance. *Canadian Journal of Applied Sport Sciences, 10*, 22–28.

Parkinson, B. (1994). Emotion. In A. M. Coleman (Ed.), *Companion encyclopaedia of psychology* (Vol. 2). London: Routledge.

Pasquier, P., Dubost, C., Boutonnet, M., & Chrisment, A., et al. (2014). Predeployment training for forward medicalization in a combat zone: The specific policy of the French military health service. *Injury, 45*, 1307–1311.

Pates, J., Karageorghis, C. I., Fryer, R., & Maynard, I. (2003). Effects of asynchronous music on flow states and shooting performance among netball players. *Psychology of Sport and Exercise, 4*, 415–427.

Payne, J. W., Bettman, J. R., & Johnson, E. J. (1993). *The adaptive decision maker*. New York: Cambridge University Press.

Penrose, J. M. T., & Roach, N. K. (1995). Decision making and advanced cue utilisation by cricket batsmen. *Journal of Human Movement Studies, 29*, 199–218.

Perkos, S., Theodorakis, Y., & Chroni, S. (2002). Enhancing performance and skill acquisition in novice basketball players with instructional self-talk. *The Sport Psychologist, 16*, 368–383.

Perrig, W. J., & Wippich, W. (1995). *Intuition in the context of perception, memory and judgement.* In B. Boothe, R. Hirsig, A. Helminger, B. Meier, & R. Volkart (Eds.), *Perception–evaluation–interpretation. Swiss monographs in psychology* (pp. 21–31). Bern: Huber.

Perry, P. (2011). Concept analysis: Confidence/self-confidence. *Nursing Forum, 46*(4), 218–230.

Pervin, L. A., & John, O. P. (2001). *Personality, theory and research* (8th edn). Hoboken, NJ: John Wiley & Sons, Inc.

Petersen, C. J., Pyne, D. B., Dawson, B. T., Kellett, A. D., & Portus, M. R. (2011). Comparison of training and game demands of national level cricketers. *Journal of Strength and Conditioning Research, 25*, 1306–1311.

Peterson, C. (2000). The future of optimism. *American Psychologist, 55*(1), 44–55.

Petrie, T. A., & Stoever, S. (1997). Academic and nonacademic predictors of female student athletes' academic performances. *Journal of College Student Development, 38*, 599–608.

Pieperhoff, P., Homke, L., Schneider, F., Habel, U., Shah, N. J., Zilles, K., & Amunts, K. (2008). Deformation field morphometry reveals age-related structural differences between the brains of adults up to 51 years. *Journal of Neuroscience, 28*, 828–842.

Pfurtscheller, G., & Aranibar, A. (1979). Evaluation of event-related desynchronization (ERD) preceding and following voluntary self-paced movement. *Electroencephalography and Clinical Neurophysiology, 46*, 138–146.

Pfurtscheller, G., & Lopes da Silva, F. H. (1999). Event-related EEG/MEG synchronization and desynchronization: Basic principles. *Clinical Neurophysiology, 110*, 1842–1857.

Pfurtscheller, G., Stancak, A., & Neuper, C. (1996). Event-related synchronization (ERS) in the alpha band – An electrophysiological correlate of cortical idling: A review. *International Journal of Psychophysiology, 24*, 39–46.

Pinder, R. A., Davids, K., Renshaw, I., & Araújo, D. (2011). Representative design and functionality of research and practice in sport. *Journal of Sport and Exercise Psychology, 33*, 146–155.

Pinder, R. A., Renshaw, I., & Davids, K. (2009). Information-movement coupling in developing cricketers under changing ecological practice constraints. *Human Movement Science, 28*, 468–479.

Polivy, C. P., & Herman, J. (2002). If at first you don't succeed: False hopes of self-change. *American Psychologist, 57*, 677–689.

Poolton, J. M., Masters, R. S. W., & Maxwell, J. P. (2006). The influence of analogy learning on decision-making in table tennis: Evidence from behavioural data. *Psychology of Sport and Exercise, 7*, 677–688.

Preston, S. D., Buchanan, T. W., Stansfield, R. B., & Bechara, A. (2007). Effects of anticipatory stress on decision making in a gambling task. *Behavioral Neuroscience, 121*, 257–263.

Pusenjak, N., Grad, A., Tusak, M., Leskovsek, M., & Schwarlin, R. (2015). Can biofeedback training of psychophysiological responses enhance athletes' sport performance? A practitioner's perspective. *The Physician and Sportsmedicine, 43*, 287–299.

Quick, J. C., Wright, T. A., Adkins, J. A., Nelson, D. L., & Quick, J. D. (2013). *Preventative stress management in organizations* (2nd edn). Washington, DC: American Psychological Association.

Raab, M. (2003). Implicit and explicit learning of decision making in sport is affected by complexity of situation. *International Journal of Sport Psychology, 34*, 273–288.

Raab, M. (2016). The building blocks of performance: An overview. In M. Raab, B. Lobinger, S. Hoffmann, A. Pizzera, & S. Laborde (Eds.), *Performance psychology: Perception, action, cognition, and emotion.* London: Elsevier.

Raab, M., & Laborde, S. (2011). When to blink and when to think: Preference for intuitive decisions results in faster and better tactical choices. *Research Quarterly for Exercise and Sport, 82,* 89–98.

Raab, M., Lobinger, B., Hoffmann, S., Pizzera, A., & Laborde, S. (2016). *Performance psychology: Perception, action, cognition, and emotion.* London: Academic Press.

Raab, M., Masters, R., & Maxwell, J. (2005). Improving the how and what decisions of table tennis elite players. *Human Movement Science, 24,* 326–344.

Radlo, S. J., Steinberg, G. M., Singer, R. N., Barba, D. A., & Melnikov, A. (2002). The influence of an attentional focus strategy on alpha brain wave activity, heart rate, and dartthrowing performance. *International Journal of Sport Psychology, 33,* 205–217.

Raedeke, T. D., & Smith, A. L. (2004). Coping resources and athlete burnout: An examination of stress mediated and moderation hypotheses. *Journal of Sport and Exercise Psychology, 26*(1), 1–17.

Raickle, M. E., & Gusuard, D. A. (2002). Appraising the brain's energy budget. *Proceedings of the National Academy of Sciences of the United States of America, 99,* 10237–10239.

Rangel, A., Camerer, C., & Montague, P. R. (2008). A framework for studying the neurobiology of value-based decision making. *Nature Reviews Neuroscience, 9,* 545–556.

Rees, T., & Hardy, L. (2004). Matching social support with stressors. Effects on factors underlying performance in tennis. *Psychology of Sport and Exercise, 5,* 319–337.

Rees, T., Hardy, L., & Freeman, P. (2007). Stressors, social support, and effects upon performance in golf. *Journal of Sport Science, 25,* 33–42.

Reeve, J. (2005). *Understanding motivation and emotion* (4th edn). Hoboken, NJ: Wiley.

Reeves, J., Tenebaum, G., & Lidor, R. (2007). Choking in front of the goal: The effects of self-consciousness training. *International Journal of Sport and Exercise Psychology, 5,* 240–254.

Reich, J. W., Zautra, A. J., & Hall, J. S. (Eds.). (2010). *Handbook of adult resilience.* New York: Guilford Press.

Reilly, T., Morris, T., & Whyte, G. (2009). The specificity of training prescription and physiological assessment: A review. *Journal of Sports Sciences, 27,* 575–589.

Reinecke, K., Cordes, M., Lerch, C., Koutsandréou, F., Schubert, M., Weiss, M., & Baumeister, J. (2011). From lab to field conditions: A pilot study on EEG methodology in applied sports sciences. *Applied Psychophysiology and Biofeedback, 36,* 265–271.

Reisberg, D. (2013). *The Oxford handbook of cognitive psychology.* Oxford: Oxford University Press.

Reivich, K. J., Seligman, M. E. P., & McBride, S. (2011). Master resilience training in the US Army. *American Psychologist, 66,* 25–34.

Renshaw, I., Chappell, G., Fitzgerald, D., Davison, J., & McFadyen, B. (2010). The battle zone: Constraint-led coaching in action. In M. Portus (Ed.), *Conference of science, medicine and coaching in cricket* (pp. 181–184). Sheraton Mirage, Gold Coast, Queensland, Australia, 1–3 June.

Renshaw, I., & Fairweather, M. M. (2000). Cricket bowling deliveries and the discrimination ability of professional and amateur batters. *Journal of Sports Sciences, 18,* 951–957.

Riley, P. O., Dicharry, J., Franz, J., Croce, U. D., Wilder, R. P., & Kerrigan, D. C. (2008). A kinematics and kinetic comparison of overground and treadmill running. *Medicine and Science in Sports and Exercise, 40,* 1093–1100.

Roberts, R., Callow, N., Hardy, L., Markland, D., & Bringer, J. (2008). Movement imagery ability: Development and assessment of a revised version of the vividness of movement imagery questionnaire. *Journal of Sport & Exercise Psychology, 30,* 200–221.

Roca, A., Williams, A. M., & Ford, P. R. (2012). Developmental activities and the acquisition of superior anticipation and decision making in soccer players. *Journal of Sports Sciences, 30,* 1643–1652.

Roseman, I., Spindel, M. S., & Jose, P. E. (1990). Appraisals of emotion-eliciting events: Testing a theory of discrete emotions. *Journal of Personality and Social Psychology, 59,* 899–915.

Rosenfeld, L. B., & Richman, J. M. (1997). Developing effective social support: Team building and the social support process. *Journal of Applied Sport Psychology, 9,* 133–153.

Rostami, R., Sadeghi, H., Karami, K. A., Abadi, M. N., & Salamati, P. (2012). The effect of neurofeedback on the improvement of rifle shooters' performance. *Journal of Neurotherapy, 16,* 264–269.

Roth, T. (2007). Insomnia: Definition, prevalence, etiology, and consequences. *Journal of Clinical Sleep Medicine, 3,* S7–S10.

Rothenberg, A. (1983). Psychopathology and creative cognition: A comparison of hospitalized patients, Nobel laureates, and controls. *Archives of General Psychiatry, 40,* 937–942.

Runco, M. A. (2007). Achievement sometimes requires creativity. *High Ability Studies, 18,* 75–77.

Runco, M., & Jaeger, G. J. (2012). The standard definition of creativity. *Creativity Research Journal, 24,* 92–96.

Rutter, M. (2012). Resilience: Causal pathways and social ecology. In M. Ungar (Ed.), *The social ecology of resilience: A handbook of theory and practice* (pp. 33–42). New York: Springer.

Saks, A. M. (1995). Longitudinal field investigation of the moderating and mediating effects of self-efficacy on the relationship between training and newcomer adjustment. *Journal of Applied Psychology, 80,* 211–225.

Salat, D. H., Buckner, R. K., Snyder, A. Z., Greve, D. N., Desikan, R. S. R., Busa, E., Morris, J. C., Dale, A. M., & Fischl, A. (2004). Thinning of the cerebral cortex in aging. *Cerebral Cortex, 14,* 721–730.

Salazar, W., Landers, D., Petruzzello, S., Han, M., Crews, D., & Kubitz, K. (1990). Hemispheric asymmetry, cardiac response and performance in elite archers. *Research Quarterly in Exercise and Sport, 61,* 351–359.

Salim, J., Wadey, R., & Diss, C. (2016). Examining hardiness, coping and stress-related growth following sport injury. *Journal of Applied Sport Psychology, 28,* 154–169.

Salo, I., & Allwood, C. M. (2011). Decision-making styles, stress, and gender among investigators. *Policing: An International Journal of Police Strategies & Management, 34,* 97–119.

Salthouse, T. A. (1984). Effects of aging and skill in typing. *Journal of Experimental Psychology: General, 113,* 345–371.

Salthouse, T. A. (2009). When does age-related cognitive decline begin? *Neurobiology Aging, 30,* 507–514.

Samuels, C. (2008). Sleep, recovery, and performance: The new frontier in high-performance athletics. *Neurologic Clinics, 26,* 169–180.

Sandman, C. A., Walker, B. B., & Berka, C. (1982). Influence of afferent cardiovascular feedback on behaviour and the cortical evolved potential. In J. T. Cacioppi & R. E. Petty (Eds.), *Perspectives in cardiovascular psychophysiology* (pp. 189–222). New York: Guilford.

Sarason, I. G., Sarason, B. R., Potter, E. H., & Antoni, M. H. (1985). Life events, social support, and illness. *Psychosomatic Medicine, 47,* 156–163.

Sarkar, M., & Fletcher, D. (2013). How should we measure psychological resilience in sport performers? *Measurement in Physical Education & Exercise Science, 17,* 264–280.

Savis, J. C. (1994). Sleep and athletic performance: Overview and implications for sport psychology. *The Sport Psychologist, 8,* 111–125.

Schack, T. (1997). *Ängstliche Schüler im Sport – interventionsverfahren zur Entwicklung der Handlungskontrolle.* Schorndorf. Germany: Hofmann.

Schacter, D. L., & Tulving, E. (1994). What are the memory systems of 1994? In D. L. Schacter & E. Tulving (Eds.), *Memory systems* (pp. 1–38). Cambridge, MA: MIT Press.

Schaefer, C., Coyne, J. C., & Lazarus, R. S. (1982). The health related functions of social support. *Journal of Behavioural Medicine, 4*, 381–406.

Scheier, M. F., & Carver, C. S. (1985). Optimism, coping and health: Assessment and implications of generalized outcome expectancies. *Health Psychology, 4*, 219–247.

Scheier, M. F., & Carver, C. S. (1987). Dispositional optimism and physical well-being: The influence of generalized outcome expectancies on health. *Journal of Personality, 55*, 169–210.

Scheier, M. F., & Carver, C. S. (1992). Effects of optimism on psychological and physical well-being: Theoretical overview and empirical update. *Cognitive Therapy and Research, 16*, 201–228.

Scheier, M. F., Carver, C. S., & Bridges, M. W. (2001). Optimism, pessimism, and psychological well-being. In E. C. Chang (Ed.), *Optimism and pessimism: Implications for theory, research and practice* (pp. 189–216). Washington, DC: American Psychological Association.

Scherer, K. R., & Wallbott, H. G. (1994). Evidence for universality and cultural variation of differential emotion response patterning. *Journal of Personality and Social Psychology, 66*, 310–328.

Schilder, K. K. (2002). 'Thinking for success': A cognitive restructuring intervention for female adolescent athletes. Retrospective Theses and Dissertations. Paper 1027.

Schinke, R. J., & Jerome, W. C. (2002). Understanding and refining the resilience of elite athletes: An intervention strategy. *Athletic Insight, 4*, 1–13.

Schläppi-Lienhard, O., & Hossner, E.-J. (2015). Decision making in beach volleyball defense: Crucial factors derived from interviews with top-level experts. *Psychology of Sport and Exercise, 16*, 60–73.

Schmitt, J. A. J. (2010). Nutrition and cognition: Meeting the challenge to obtain credible and evidence-based facts. *Nutrition Reviews, 68*, S2–S5.

Schmitt, J. A. J., & LeCoutre, J. (2009). Nutrition for cognition. *Frontiers in Neuroscience, 3*, 88–89.

Schorer, J., & Baker, J. (2009). Aging and perceptual-motor expertise in handball goalkeepers. *Experimental Aging Research, 35*, 1–19.

Schultz, R., & Short, S. E. (2006). Who do athletes compare to? How the standard comparison affects confidence ratings. Association for the Advancement of Applied Sport Psychology – 2006 *Conference Proceedings*, pp. 82–83. Madison, WI: AAASP.

Seery, M. D. (2011). Challenge or threat? Cardiovascular indexes of resilience and vulnerability to potential stress in humans. *Neuroscience & Biobehavioural Reviews, 35*, 1603–1610.

Seery, M. D., Weisbuch, M., Hetenyi, M. A., & Blascovich, J. (2010). Cardiovascular measures independently predict performance in a university course. *Psychophysiology, 47*, 535–539.

Seifert, L., Button, C., & Davids, K. (2013). Key properties of expert movement systems in sport. *Sports Medicine, 43*, 167–178.

Seiler, R., & Stock, A. (1994). *Handbuch psychotraining im sport.* Reinbek: Rowohlt.

Seitsonen, E., Yli-Hankala, A., & Korttila, K. (2000). Are electrocardiogram electrodes acceptable for electroencephalogram bispectral index monitoring. *Acta Anaesthesiologica Scandinavica, 44*, 1266–1270.

Seligman, M. E. P. (1991). *Learned optimism.* New York: Knopf.

Seligman, M. E. P. (2004). *Aprenda optimismo.* Madrid: Debolsillo.

Seligman, M. E. P., Nolen-Hoeksema, S., Thornton, N., & Thornton, K. M. (1990). Explanatory style as a mechanism of disappointing athletic performance. *Psychological Science, 1*, 143–146.

Seymour, B., & Dolan, R. (2008). Emotion, decision making, and the amygdala. *Neuron, 58*, 662–671.

Shapcott, J. B., Bloom, G. A., Johnston, K. M., Loughead, T. M., & Delaney, J. S. (2007). The effects of explanatory style on concussion outcomes in sport. *Neuro Rehabilitation, 22*, 161–167.

Shaw, D. (2002). Confidence and the pre-shot routine in golf: A case study. In I. Cockerill (Ed.), *Solutions in sport psychology* (pp. 108–119). London: Thomson.

Sheard, M., & Golby, J. (2006). Effect of a psychological skills training program on swimming performance and positive psychological development. *International Journal of Sport and Exercise Psychology, 2*, 7–24.

Sheeran, P. (2002). Intention-behavior relations: A conceptual and empirical review. In W. Stroebe & M. Hewstone (Eds.), *European review of social psychology* (Vol. 12, pp. 1–30). New York: Wiley.

Sheline, Y. I., Mintun, M. A., Moerlein, S. M., & Snyder, A. Z. (2002). Greater loss of 5-HT2A receptors in midlife than in late life. *American Journal of Psychiatry, 159*, 430–435.

Shiota, M. N., & Levenson, R. W. (2009). Effects of aging on experimentally instructed detached reappraisal, positive reappraisal, and emotional behavior suppression. *Psychology and Aging, 24*, 890–900.

Short, S., & Ross-Stewart, L. (2009). A review of self-efficacy based interventions. In S. D. Mellalieu & S. Hanton (Eds.), *Advances in applied sport psychology*. Abingdon: Routledge.

Simonton, D. K. (1997). Creative productivity: A predictive and explanatory model of career trajectories and landmarks. *Psychological Review, 104*, 66–89.

Simonton, D. K. (1999). *Origins of genius: Darwinian perspectives on creativity*. Oxford: Oxford University Press.

Simonton, D. K. (2012). Teaching creativity: Current findings, trends, and controversies in the psychology of creativity. *Teaching of Psychology, 39*, 217–222.

Simonson, E., Brozek, J., & Keys, A. (1948). Effects of meals on visual performance and fatigue. *Journal of Applied Physiology, 1*, 270.

Singer, R. N. (2002). Pre-performance state, routines, and automaticity: What does it take to realize expertise in self-paced events? *Journal of Sport and Exercise Psychology, 24*, 359–375.

Sitzmann, T., & Ely, K. (2010). Sometimes you need a reminder: The effects of prompting self-regulation on regulatory processes, learning, and attrition. *Journal of Applied Psychology, 95*, 132–144.

Sitzmann, T., & Yeo, G. (2013). A meta-analytic investigation of the within-person self efficacy domain: Is self efficacy a product of past performance or a driver of future performance? *Personnel Psychology, 66*, 531–568.

Skinner, B. F. (1963). Operant behavior. *American Psychologist, 18*, 503–515.

Skinner, N., & Brewer, N. (2004). Adaptive approaches to competition: Challenge appraisals and positive emotion. *Journal of Sport and Exercise Psychology, 26*, 283–305.

Smith, A. P., Clark, R., & Gallagher, J. (1999). Breakfast cereal and caffeinated coffee: Effects on working memory, attention, mood, and cardiovascular function. *Physiology and Behavior, 67*, 9–17.

Smith, A. P., & Kendrick, A. M. (1992). Meals and performance. In A. P. Smith & D. M. Jones (Eds.), *Handbook of human performance, Vol. 2, Health and performance* (pp. 1–23). London: Academic Press.

Smith, A. P., Kendrick, A., Maben, A., & Salmon, J. (1994). Effects of fat content, weight, and acceptability of the meal on postlunch changes in mood, performance, and cardio-vascular function. *Physiology and Behavior, 55*, 417–422.

Smith, A. P., & Miles, C. (1986a). Acute effects of meals, noise and nightwork. *British Journal of Psychology, 77*, 377–387.

Smith, A. P., & Miles, C. (1986b). Effects of lunch on selective and sustained attention. *Neuropsychobiology, 16*, 117–120.

Solso, R. L. (1998). *Cognitive psychology*. Boston, MA: Allyn & Bacon.

Spittle, M., & Morris, T. (1997). Concentration skills for cricket bowlers. *Sports Coach, 20*, 32.

Spring, B., Maller, O., Wurtman, J., Digman, L., & Gozolino, L. (1983). Effects of protein and carbohydrate meals on mood and performance: Interactions with sex and age. *Journal of Psychiatric Research, 17*, 155.

Stajkovic, A. D., & Lee, D. S. (2001). A meta-analysis of the relationship between collective efficacy and group performance. Paper presented at the 61st Annual Meeting of the Academy of Management, Washington, DC.

Stajkovic, A. D., & Luthans, F. (1998). Self-efficacy and work-related performance: A meta analysis. *Psychological Bulletin, 124*, 240–261.

Starkes, J. L. (1993). Motor experts: Opening thoughts. In J. L. Starkes & F. Allard (Eds.), *Cognitive issues in motor expertise* (pp. 3–16). Amsterdam: Elsevier Science.

Starkes, J. L. (2000). The road to expertise: Is practice the only determinant? *International Journal of Sport Psychology, 31*, 431–451.

Starkes, J. L., Weir, P. L., Singh, P., Hodges, N. J., & Kerr, T. (1999). Aging and the reten-tion of sport expertise. *International Journal of Sport Psychology, 30*, 283–301.

Starkes, J. L., Weir, P. L., & Young, B. W. (2003). What does it take for older athletes to continue to excel? In J. L. Starkes & K. A. Ericsson (Eds.), *Expert performance in sports: Advances in research on sport expertise* (pp. 251–272). Champaign, IL: Human Kinetics.

Stefano, G., Fricchione, G. L., Slingsby, B. T., & Benson, H. (2001). The placebo effect and relaxation response: Neural processes and their coupling to constitutive nitric oxide. *Brain Research Brain Research Reviews, 35*, 1–19.

Sternberg, R. J. (2006). Creativity is a habit. *Education Week, 25*, 47–64.

Sternberg, R. J. (2012). The assessment of creativity: An investment-based approach. *Crea-tivity Research Journal, 24*, 3–12.

Stevens, J. A., & Stoykov, M. E. (2003). Using motor imagery in the rehabilitation of hemi-paresis. *Archives of Physical Medicine and Rehabilitation, 84*, 1090–1092.

Stoffregen, T. A., Bardy, B. G., Smart, L. J., & Pagulayan, R. (2003). On the nature and evaluation of fidelity in virtual environments. In L. J. Hettinger & M. W. Haas (Eds.), *Virtual and adaptive environments: Applications, implications and human performance issues* (pp. 111–128). Mahwah, NJ: Lawrence Erlbaum Associates.

Strack, F., Martin, L. L., & Stepper, S. (1988). Inhibiting and facilitating conditions of facial expressions: A non-obtrusive test of the facial feedback hypothesis. *Journal of Personality and Social Psychology, 54*, 768–776.

Stumpf, S. A., Brief, A. P., & Hartman, K. (1987). Self-efficacy expectations and coping with career related events. *Journal of Vocational Behavior, 31*, 91–108.

Sud, A. (1993). Efficacy of two short term cognitive therapies for test anxiety. *Journal of Personality and Clinical Studies, 9*, 39–46.

Sullivan, E. V., & Pfefferbaum, A. (2006). Diffusion tensor imaging and aging. *Neuroscience and Biobehavior Reviews, 30*, 749–761.

Swann, C., Keegan, R. J., Piggott, D. J. S., & Crust, L. (2012). A systematic review of the experience, occurrence, and controllability of flow states in elite sport. *Psychology of Sport and Exercise, 13*, 807–819.

Syed, M. (2010). *Bounce: Mozart, Federer, Picasso, Beckham, and the science of success*. New York: HarperCollins.

Szinnai, G., Schachinger, H., Arnaud, M. J., et al. (2005). Effect of water deprivation on cognitive-motor performance in healthy men and women. *American Journal of Physiology Regulatory Integrative and Comparative Physiology, 289*, R275–R280.

Tamminen, K. A., Holt, N. L., & Neely, K. C. (2013). Exploring adversity and the potential for growth among elite female athletes. *Psychology of Sport and Exercise, 14*, 28–36.

Tanaka, H., & Seals, D. R. (2003). Dynamic exercise performance in masters athletes: Insight into the effects of primary human aging on physiological functional capacity. *Journal of Applied Physiology, 95*, 2152–2162.

Tanaka, H., & Seals, D. R. (2008). Endurance exercise performance in Masters athletes: Age-associated changes and underlying physiological mechanisms. *Journal of Physiology, 586*, 55–63.

Tellegen, A. (1985). Structure of mood and personality and their relevance to assessing anxiety, with an emphasis on self-report. In A. H. Tuma & J. D. Maser (Eds.), *Anxiety and the anxiety disorders* (pp. 681–706). Hillsdale, NJ: Erlbaum.

Terry, P. C. (2004). Mood and emotions in sport. In T. Morris & J. Summers (Eds.), *Sport psychology: Theory, applications and issues* (2nd edn, pp. 48–73). Milton, Australia: Wiley.

Tharp, T. (2005). *The creative habit: Learn it and use it for life*. New York: Simon & Schuster.

Thiruchselvam, R., Blechert, J., Sheppes, G., Rydstrom, A., & Gross, J. J. (2011). The temporal dynamics of emotion regulation: An EEG study of distraction and reappraisal. *Biological Psychology, 87*, 84–92.

Thomas, D. R., Cote, T. R., Lawhorne, L., & Levenson, S., et al. (2008). Understanding clinical dehydration and its treatment. *Journal of the American Medical Directors Association, 9*, 292–301.

Thomas, J. R., French, K. E., & Humphries, C. A. (1986). Knowledge development and sport skill performance: Directions for motor behaviour research. *Journal of Sport Psychology, 8*, 259–272.

Thomas, M., Sing, H., Belenky, G., Holcomb, H., Mayberg, H., Dannals, R., Wagner, H., Thorne, D., Popp, K., Rowland, L., Welsh, A., Balwinski, S., & Redmond, D. (2000). Neural basis of alertness and cognitive performance impairments during sleeping. Effects of 24h of sleep deprivation on waking human regional brain activity. *Journal of Sleep Research, 9*, 335–352.

Thomas, O., Lane, A., & Kingston, K. (2011). Defining and contextualizing robust sport-confidence. *Journal of Applied Sport Psychology, 23*, 189–208.

Thompson, R. A. (1990). Emotion and self-regulation. In R. A. Thompson (Ed.), *Socio-emotional development. Nebraska Symposium on Motivation, Vol. 36* (pp. 367–467). Lincoln, NE: University of Nebraska Press.

Thompson, T., Steffert, T., Ros, T., Leach, J., & Gruzelier, J. (2008). EEG applications for sport and performance. *Methods, 45*, 279–288.

Torrance, E. P. (1966). *The Torrance tests of creative thinking: Norms technical manual research edition – verbal tests, forms A and B figural tests, forms A and B*. Princeton, NJ: Personnel Press.

Travassos, B., Araújo, D., Duarte, R., & McGarry, T. (2012). Spatiotemporal coordination behaviors in futsal (indoor football) are guided by informational game constraints. *Human Movement Science, 31*, 932–945.

Tremayne, P., & Barry, R. J. (2001). Elite pistol shooters: Physiological patterning of best vs. worst shots. *International Journal of Psychophysiology, 41*, 19–29.

Triandis, H. C. (1980). Values, attitudes, and interpersonal behavior. In H. E. Howe Jr. & M. M. Page (Eds.), *Nebraska symposium on motivation*. Lincoln, NE: University of Nebraska Press.

Tucker, R., & Collins, M. (2012). What makes champions? A review of the relative contribution of genes and training to sporting success. *British Journal of Sports Medicine, 46,* 555–561.

Tuomilehto, H., Vuorinen, V.-P., Penttila, E., Kivimaki, M., Vuorenmaa, M., Venojarvi, M., Airaksinen, O., & Pihlajamaki, J. (2016). Sleep of professional athletes: Underexploited potential to improve health and performance. *Journal of Sports Sciences* [Online first 13 May].

Turner, M. J., & Jones, M. V. (2014). Stress, emotions and athletes' positive adaptation to sport: Contributes from a transactional perspective. In R. Gomes, R. Resende, & A. Albuquerque (Eds.), *Positive human functioning from a multidimensional perspective.* New York: Nova Science.

Turner, M. J., Jones, M. V., Sheffield, D., & Cross, S. L. (2012). Cardiovascular indices of challenge and threat states predict competitive performance. *International Journal of Psychophysiology, 86,* 48–57.

Turner, M. J., Jones, M. V., Sheffield, D., Slater, M., Barker, J. B., & Bell, J. (2013). Who thrives under pressure? Predicting the performance of elite academy cricketers using the cardiovascular indicators of challenge and threat states. *Journal of Sport and Exercise Psychology, 35,* 387–397.

Turvey, M. T., & Shaw, R. E. (1999). Ecological foundations of cognition: I. Symmetry and specificity of animal–environment systems. *Journal of Consciousness Studies, 6,* 95–110.

Turvey, M. T., Shaw, R. E., Reed, E. S., & Mace, W. M. (1981). Ecological laws of perceiving and acting: In reply to Fodor and Pylyshyn (1981). *Cognition, 9,* 237–304.

Uehara, L., Button, C., Falcous, M., & Davids, K. (2016). Contextualised skill acquisition research: A new framework to study the development of expertise. *Physical Education and Sport Pedagogy, 21,* 153–168.

Uphill, M., Groom, R., & Jones, M. (2014). The influence of in-game emotions on basketball performance. *European Journal of Sport Science, 14,* 76–83.

Vallerand, R. J. (1983). On emotion in sport: Theoretical and social psychological perspectives. *Journal of Sport Psychology, 5,* 197–215.

Vallerand, R. J., & Blanchard, C. M. (2000). The study of emotion in sport and exercise: Historical, definitional, and conceptual perspectives. In Y. L. Hanin (Ed.), *Emotions in sport* (pp. 3–37). Champaign, IL: Human Kinetics.

Vandekerckhove, M., & Cluydts, R. (2010). The emotional brain and sleep: An intimate relationship. *Sleep Medicine Reviews, 14,* 219–226.

van Orden, G., Holden, J., & Turvey, M. (2003). Selforganization of cognitive performance. *Journal of Experimental Psychology: General, 132,* 331–350.

Van Raalte, J. L., Brewer, B. W., Lewis, B. P., Linder, G. E., Wildman, G., & Kozimor, J. (1995). Cork! The effects of positive and negative self-talk on dart throwing performance. *Journal of Sport Behavior, 18,* 50–57.

Vealey, R., & Chase, M. (2008). Self-confidence in sport. In T. S. Horn (Ed.), *Advances in sport psychology* (3rd edn, pp. 65–98). Champaign, IL: Human Kinetics.

Vealey, R., Hayashi, S. W., Garner-Holman, M., & Giacobbi, P. (1998). Sources of sport confidence: Conceptualization and instrument development. *Journal of Sport and Exercise Psychology, 21,* 54–80.

Vealey, R. S. (1986). Conceptualization of sport-confidence and competitive orientation: Preliminary investigation and instrument development. *Journal of Sport Psychology, 8,* 221–246.

Vealey, R. S. (2001). Understanding and enhancing self-confidence in athletes. In R. N. Singer, H. A. Hausenblas, & C. M. Janelle (Eds.), *Handbook of sport psychology* (2nd edn, pp. 290–318). Chichester: John Wiley & Sons, Inc.

Vealey, R. S. (2007). Mental skills training in sport. In G. Tenenbaum & R. C. Eklund (Eds.), *Handbook of sport psychology* (3rd edn, pp. 287–309). Hoboken, NJ: John Wiley & Sons.

Vealey, R. S., Low, W., Pierce, S., & Quinones-Paredes, D. (2014). Choking in sport: ACT on it! *Journal of Sport Psychology in Action, 5*, 156–169.

Vealey, R. S., & Vernau, D. (2010). Confidence. In S. J. Hanrahan & M. B. Andersen (Eds.), *Routledge handbook of applied sport psychology: A comprehensive guide for students and practitioners* (pp. 518–527). Abingdon: Routledge.

Veenman, M. V. J. (2005). The assessment of metacognitive skills: What can be learned from multi-method designs? In C. Arlett & B. Moschner (Eds.), *Lernstralegien und Metakognition: Implikationen fur Forschung und Praxis* (pp. 75–97). Berlin: Waxmann.

Veenman, M. V. J., Van Hout-Wolters, B. H. A. M., & Afflerbach, P. (2006). Metacognition and learning: Conceptual and methodological considerations. *Metacognition Learning, 1*, 3–14.

Vergeer, I., & Hanrahan, C. (1998). What modern dancers do to prepare: Content and objectives of preperformance routines. *AVANTE, 4*, 49–71.

Vernon, D. J. (2005). Can neurofeedback training enhance performance? An evaluation of the evidence with implications for future research. *Applied Psychophysiology and Biofeedback, 30*, 347–363.

Verplanken, B. (2006). Beyond frequency: Habit as a mental construct. *British Journal of Social Psychology, 45*, 639–656.

Vickers, J. N. (1996). Visual control when aiming at a far target. *Journal of Experimental Psychology: Human Perception and Performance, 22*, 342–354.

Vickers, J. N. (2009). Advances in coupling perception and action: The quiet eye as a bidirectional link between gaze, attention, and action. *Progress in Brain Research, 174*, 279–288.

Vickers, J. N., & Lewinski, W. (2012). Performing under pressure: Gaze control, decision making and shooting performance of elite and rookie police officers. *Human Movement Science, 31*, 101–117.

Vickery, W., Dascombe, B., & Duffield, R. (2014). Physiological, movement and technical demands of centre-wicket Battlezone, traditional net based training and one-day cricket matches: A comparative study of sub-elite cricket players. *Journal of Sport Sciences, 32*(8), 722–737.

Vickery, W., Dascombe, B., Duffeld, R., Kellett, A., & Portus, M. (2013). The influence of field size, player number and rule changes on the physiological responses and movement demands of small-sided games for cricket training. *Journal of Sports Sciences, 31*, 629–638.

Vilar, L., Araújo, D., Davids, K., & Travassos, B. (2012). Constraints on competitive performance of attacker-defender dyads in team sports. *Journal of Sports Science, 30*, 459–469.

Vine, S. J., Freeman, P., Moore, L. J., Chandra-Ramanan, R., & Wilson, M. R. (2013). Evaluating stress as a challenge is associated with superior attentional control and motor skill performance: Testing the predictions of the biopsychosocial model of challenge and threat. *Journal of Experimental Psychology: Applied, 19*, 185–194.

Vinson, N. G., & Reed, C. L. (2002). Sources of object-specific effects in representational momentum. *Visual Cognition, 9*, 41–65.

Volkow, N. D., Logan, J., Fowler, J. S., Wang, G. J., Gur, R. C., Wong, C., Felder, C., Gatley, S. J., Ding, Y. S., Hitzemann, R., & Pappas, N. (2000). Association between age-related decline in brain dopamine activity and impairment in frontal and cingulate metabolism. *American Journal of Psychiatry, 157*, 75–80.

Wadey, R., Evans, L., Hanton, S., & Neil, R. (2012). An examination of hardiness throughout the sport injury process. *British Journal of Health Psychology, 17,* 103–128.

Wallace, H. M., Baumeister, R. F., & Vohs, K. D. (2005). Audience support and choking under pressure: A home disadvantage? *Journal of Sports Science, 23,* 429–438.

Ward, P., Ericsson, K. A., & Williams, A. M. (2013). Complex perceptual-cognitive expertise in a simulated task environment. *Journal of Cognitive Engineering and Decision Making, 7,* 231–254.

Ward, P., & Williams, A. M. (2003). Perceptual and cognitive skill development in soccer: The multidimensional nature of expert performance. *Journal of Sport and Exercise Psychology, 25,* 93–111.

Watts, F. (2007). Emotion regulation and religion. In J. J. Gross (Ed.), *Handbook of emotion regulation* (pp. 504–520). New York: Guilford Press.

Webb, T. L., Sheeran, P., & Luszczynska, A. (2009). Planning to break unwanted habits: Habit strength moderates implementation intention effects on behaviour change. *British Journal of Social Psychology, 48,* 507–523.

Weber, R. B., & Daroff, R. B. (1972). Corrective movements following refixation saccades: Type and control system analysis. *Vision Research, 12*(3), 467–475.

Wedell-Wedellsborg, M. (2015). *Battle mind: How to navigate in chaos and perform under pressure.* Berlin: Lindhardt og Ringhof.

Weinberg, R. (2010a). Activation/arousal control. In S. J. Hanrahan & M. B. Andersen (Eds.), *Routledge handbook of applied sport psychology: A comprehensive guide for students and practitioners* (pp. 471–480). New York: Routledge.

Weinberg, R. (2010b). Making goals effective: A primer for coaches. *Journal of Sport Psychology in Action, 1,* 57–65.

Weinberg, R., Butt, J., & Knight, B. (2001). High school coaches' perceptions of the process of goal-setting. *The Sport Psychologist, 15,* 20–47.

Weinberg, R. S., & Gould, D. (2007). *Foundations of sport & exercise psychology* (4th edn). Champaign, IL: Human Kinetics.

Weinberg, R. S., & Williams, J. M. (2001). Integrating and implementing a psychological skills training program. In J. M. Williams (Ed.), *Applied sport psychology: Personal growth to peak performance* (4th edn, pp. 347–377). Mountain View, CA: Mayfield.

Weiner, B. (1985). An attributional theory of achievement motivation and emotion. *Psychological Review, 92,* 548–573.

Weiner, B., Frieze, I. H., Kukla, A., Reed, L., Rest, S., & Rosenbaum, R. M. (1971). *Perceiving the causes of success and failure.* Morristown, NJ: General Learning Press.

Weir, P. L., Kerr, T., Hodges, N. J., McKay, S. M., & Starkes, J. L. (2002). Master swimmers: How are they different from younger elite swimmers? An examination of practice and performance patterns. *Journal of Aging and Physical Activity, 10,* 41–63.

Weiss, M. R., & Friedrichs, W. D. (1986). The influence of leader behaviors, coach attributes, and institutional variables on performance and satisfaction of collegiate basketball teams. *Journal of Sport Psychology, 8,* 332–346.

Weller, J. A., Levin, I. P., Shiv, B., & Bechara, A. (2007). Neural correlates of adaptive decision making for risky gains and losses. *Psychological Science, 18,* 958–964.

Werner, E. E., & Smith, R. S. (1992). *Overcoming the odds: High-risk children from birth to adulthood.* Ithaca, NY: Cornell University Press.

Werner, K. (2016). Performing under pressure: High-level cognition in high-pressure environments. In M. Raab, B. Lobinger, S. Hoffmann, A. Pizzera, & S. Laborde (Eds.), *Performance psychology: Perception, action, cognition, and emotion.* London: Academic Press.

Weston, M., Castagna, C., Impellizzeri, F. M., Rampinini, E., & Breivik, S. (2010). Ageing and physical match performance in English premier league soccer referees. *Journal of Science and Medicine in Sport, 13*, 96–100.

Westphal, M., & Bonanno, G. A. (2007). Posttraumatic growth and resilience to trauma: Different sides of the same coin or different coins? *Applied Psychology: An International Review, 56*, 417–427.

White, A., & Hardy, L. (1998). An in-depth analysis of the uses of imagery by high-level slalom canoeists and artistic gymnasts. *The Sport Psychologist, 12*, 387–403.

White, B. (2009). Dietary fatty acids. *American Family Physician, 80*(4), 345–350.

Whitehouse, P. J., Juengst, E., Mehlman, M., & Murray, T. H. (2012). Enhancing cognition in the intellectually intact. *Haastings Center Report, 27*, 14–22.

Williams, A. M., Davids, K., & Williams, J. K. (1999). *Perception and action in sport*. London: E and FN Spon.

Williams, A. M., Hodges, N. J., North, J., & Barton, G. (2006). Perceiving patterns of play in dynamic sport tasks: Investigating the essential information underlying skilled performance. *Perception, 35*, 317–332.

Williams, A. M., Ward, P., & Chapman, C. (2003). Training perceptual skill in field hockey: Is there transfer from the laboratory to the field? *Research Quarterly for Exercise and Sport, 74*, 98–103.

Williams, A. M., Ward, P., Smeeton, N. J., & Allen, D. (2004). Developing anticipation skills in tennis using on-court instruction: Perception versus perception and action. *Journal of Applied Sport Psychology, 16*, 350–360.

Williams, J. M. (2001). Psychology of injury risk and prevention. In R. N. Singer, H. A. Hausenblas, & C. M. Janelle (Eds.), *Handbook of sport psychology* (2nd edn, pp. 766–786). New York: John Wiley & Sons.

Williams, J. M., & Krane, V. (1993). Psychological characteristics of peak performance. In J. Williams (Ed.), *Applied sport psychology: Personal growth to peak performance* (pp. 137–147). Mountain View, CA: Mayfield.

Williams, J. M., & Krane, V. (2001). Psychological characteristics of peak performance. In J. M. Williams (Ed.), *Applied sport psychology: Personal growth to peak performance* (4th edn, pp. 162–178). Mountain View, CA: Mayfield.

Williams, S. E., Cumming, J., Ntoumanis, N., Nordin-Bates, S. M., Ramsey, R., & Hall, C. (2012). Further validation and development of the Movement Imagery Questionnaire. *Journal of Sport & Exercise Psychology, 34*, 621–646.

Willingham, D. B. (1998). A neuropsychological theory of motor skill learning. *Psychological Review, 105*, 558–584.

Wilson, M. R., Wood, G., & Vine, S. J. (2009). Anxiety, attentional control, and performance impairment in penalty kicks. *Journal of Sport & Exercise Psychology, 31*, 761–775.

Wilson, R., Sullivan, P., Myers, N., & Feltz, D. (2004). Sources of sport confidence of master athletes. *Journal of Sport and Exercise Psychology, 26*, 369–384.

Windle, G. (2011). What is resilience? A review and concept analysis. *Reviews in Clinical Gerontology, 21*, 152–169.

Wise, S. P., & Shadmehr, R. (2002). *Motor control*. New York: Academic Press.

Wolpaw, J. R. (2007). Spinal cord plasticity in acquisition and maintenance of motor skills. *Acta Physiol, 189*, 155–169.

Wood, R., Bandura, A., & Bailey, T. (1990). Mechanisms governing organizational performance in complex decision-making environments. *Organizational Behavior and Human Decision Processes, 46*, 181–201.

Wood, W., & Neal, D. T. (2007). A new look at habits and the habit-goal interface. *Psychological Review, 114*, 843–863.

Woodman, T., Akehurst, S., Hardy, L., & Beattie, S. (2010). Self-confidence and performance: A little self-doubt helps. *Psychology of Sport and Exercise, 10*, 467–470.

Woodman, T., & Hardy, L. (2001). Stress and anxiety. In R. N. Singer, H. A. Hausenblas, & C. M. Janelle (Eds.), *Handbook of research on sport psychology* (pp. 290–318). New York: John Wiley and Sons.

Woodman, T., & Hardy, L. (2003). The relative impact of cognitive anxiety and self confidence upon sport performance: A meta-analysis. *Journal of Sports Sciences, 21*, 443–457.

Woodman, T., & Hardy, L. (2005). Tenenbaum and Becker's critique: Much ado about nothing. *Journal of Sport & Exercise Psychology, 27*, 382–392.

Worthy, D. A., Gorlick, M. A., Pacheco, J. L., Schnyer, D. M., & Maddox, W. T. (2011). With age comes wisdom: Decision-making in younger and older adults. *Psychological Science, 22*, 1375–1380.

Wright, E. F., & Jackson, W. (1991). The home-course disadvantage in golf championships: Further evidence for the undermining effect of supportive audiences on performance under pressure. *Journal of Sport Behavior, 14*, 51–60.

Wright, E. F., & Voyer, D. (1995). Supporting audiences and performance under pressure: The home-ice disadvantage in hockey championships. *Journal of Sport Behavior, 18*, 21–28.

Wulf, G. (2007). *Attention and motor skill learning*. Champaign, IL: Human Kinetics.

Wulf, G., & Su, J. (2007). An external focus of attention enhances golf shot accuracy in beginners and experts. *Research Quarterly for Exercise and Sport, 78*, 384–389.

Wulf, G., & McNevin, N. (2003). Simply distracting learners is not enough: More evidence for the learning benefits of an external focus of attention. *European Journal of Sport Sciences, 3*, 1–13.

Wulf, G., McNevin, N., & Shea, C. H. (2001). The automaticity of complex motor skill learning as a function of attentional focus. *Quarterly Journal of Experimental Psychology, 54*, 1143–1154.

Wulf, G., Shea, C., & Lewthwaite, R. (2010). Motor skill learning and performance: A review of influential factors. *Medical Education, 44*, 75–84.

Young, D. L., Goodie, A. S., Hall, D. B., & Wu, E. (2012). Decision-making under time pressure, modelled in a prospect theory framework. *Organizational Behavior and Human Decision Processes, 118*, 179–188.

Zachry, T., Wulf, G., Mercer, J., & Bezodis, N. (2004). Increased movement accuracy and reduced EMG activity as the result of adopting an external focus of attention. *Brain Research Bulletin, 67*, 304–309.

Zakay, D. (1985). Post-decision confidence and conflict experienced in a choice process. *Acta Psychologica, 58*, 75–80.

Zelaznik, H. (2014). The past and future of motor learning and control: What is the proper level of description and analysis? *Kinesiological Reviews, 3*, 38–43.

Zhao, X., Huang, C., Li, X., Zhao, X., & Peng, J. (2015). Dispositional optimism, self-framing and medical decision-making. *International Journal of Psychology, 50*, 121–127.

Zhu, F. F., Poolton, J. M., Wilson, M. R., Maxwell, J. P., & Masters, R. S. W. (2011). Neural coactivation as a yardstick of implicit motor learning and the propensity for conscious control of movement. *Biological Psychology, 87*, 66–73.

Zinsser, N., Bunker, L., & Williams, J. M. (2006). Cognitive techniques for building confidence and enhancing performance. In J. M. Williams (Ed.), *Applied sport psychology: Personal growth to peak performance* (5th edn, pp. 284–311). Boston, MA: McGraw-Hill.

INDEX